Practical Cryptography

Practical Cryptography

Jamie White

MURPHY & MOORE
www.murphy-moorepublishing.com

Practical Cryptography
Jamie White
ISBN: 978-1-63987-444-6 (Hardback)

(M) MURPHY & MOORE

Published by Murphy & Moore Publishing,
1 Rockefeller Plaza,
New York City, NY 10020, USA

Cataloging-in-Publication Data

Practical cryptography / Jamie White.
      p. cm.
Includes bibliographical references and index.
ISBN 978-1-63987-444-6
1. Data encryption (Computer science). 2. Cryptography. 3. Ciphers.
4. Computer security. I. White, Jamie.
QA76.9.A25 P73 2022
005.8--dc23

For more information regarding Murphy & Moore Publishing and its products, please visit the publisher's website www.murphy-moorepublishing.com

Table of Contents

Preface   **VII**

Chapter 1 **An Introduction to Cryptography**   **1**
    a. Cryptanalysis   5
    b. Cryptographic Algorithms   7
    c. Cryptographic Attack   10
    d. Cryptographic Key Management   43
    e. Cryptographic Hardware and Software   52
    f. Cryptographic Hash Function   71
    g. Cryptographic Applications   79

Chapter 2 **Branches of Cryptography**   **85**
    a. Classical Cryptography   85
    b. Symmetric Key Cryptography   90
    c. Public-Key Cryptography   96
    d. Multivariate Cryptography   102
    e. Post-Quantum Cryptography   111
    f. Lattice-Based Cryptography   111
    g. Quantum Cryptography   115
    h. Steganography   121
    i. Visual Cryptography   123

Chapter 3 **Elliptic Curves**   **134**
    a. Elliptic Curve Discrete Logarithm Problem   139
    b. Elliptic Curve Cryptography   155

Chapter 4 **Digital Signature and Ciphering**   **164**
    a. Digital Signature   164
    b. Cipher   182

Chapter 5 **Cryptographic Technologies**   **189**
    a. Rotor Machine   189
    b. Cryptographically Secure Pseudorandom Number Generator   195
    c. Disk Encryption   200
    d. Cryptosystem   204
    e. Hybrid Cryptosystem   205
    f. Onion Routing   206
    g. Secure Multi-Party Computation   208

Chapter 6 **Diverse Aspects of Cryptography**   **218**
    a. Encryption   218
    b. Plaintext   220
    c. RSA Problem   222

d. Key Schedule   222
e. Block Size   224
f. Avalanche Effect   224
g. Optimal Asymmetric Encryption Padding   225
h. Message Authentication Code   227
i. Secure Channel   230

Permissions

Index

Preface

The discipline of cryptography studies the techniques and practices which can be used for secure communication in the presence of hostile parties. Its primary objective is to construct and analyze protocols which can be used to stop unauthorized parties from reading private messages. Cryptography is a multidisciplinary field which draws on the principles of computer science, mathematics, electrical engineering, physics and communication science. The guiding principles of this subject are data integrity, data confidentiality, non-repudiation and authentication. Modern cryptography can be categorized into various sub fields such as symmetric key cryptography, public key cryptography, cryptanalysis and cryptosystems. It finds application across various domains such as electronic commerce, digital currencies, computer passwords, military communications and payment systems. This book presents the complex subject of cryptography in the most comprehensible and easy to understand language. The topics included herein on cryptography are of utmost significance and bound to provide incredible insights to readers. This book is an essential guide for both academicians and those who wish to pursue this discipline further.

A short introduction to every chapter is written below to provide an overview of the

content of the book:

Chapter 1 - Cryptography is the use of codes for protecting information and communications, so that only the intended person can read and process the information. Analyzing information systems to study hidden aspects of the system is known as cryptanalysis. This chapter will serve as an introduction for a more in-depth look at cryptography; **Chapter 2 -** There are many branches of cryptography such as classical cryptography, symmetric-key cryptography, public-key cryptography, multivariate cryptography, post-quantum cryptography, quantum cryptography, etc. This chapter deals with each branch and its specific subject matter in a clear and concise manner for the benefit of the reader; **Chapter 3 -** The algebraic curve whose solutions are restricted to a region of space that is topologically equivalent to a torus is known as the elliptic curve. Elliptic curve cryptography is a key-based technique used for the encryption of the data. This chapter discusses in detail the theories and methodologies related to elliptic curves; **Chapter 4 -** Digital signature is a mathematical programme to verify the authenticity of documents or digital messages. Cipher is a series of well-defined steps that are followed for performing the encryption and decryption. In order to completely understand digital signatures and ciphering it is necessary to understand the processes related to it. The following chapter elucidates the varied processes and mechanisms associated with this area of study; **Chapter 5 -** There are various technologies related to cryptography like rotor machine which is a stream cipher device used for the encryption and decryption of messages. Disk encryption is another technology which is used for the protection of information by converting the information in an unreadable code. Other technologies like cryptosystem, hybrid cryptosystem, onion routing, secure multi-party communication, etc. are also carefully analyzed in this chapter; **Chapter 6 -** Encryption is the process in which the original representation of the information is converted into an alternative form known as ciphertext. There is a desirable property of any encryption algorithm and a slight change in key or plain-text results in a significant change in the ciphertext.

This property is known as avalanche effect. This chapter closely examines the various aspects of cryptography.

Finally, I would like to thank my fellow scholars who gave constructive feedback and my family members who supported me at every step.

Jamie White

An Introduction to Cryptography

Cryptography is the use of codes for protecting information and communications, so that only the intended person can read and process the information. Analyzing information systems to study hidden aspects of the system is known as cryptanalysis. This chapter will serve as an introduction for a more in-depth look at cryptography.

In simple terms, the process of altering messages in a way that their meaning is hidden from an enemy or opponent who might seize them, is known as Cryptography. Cryptography is the science of secret writing that brings numerous techniques to safeguard information that is present in an unreadable format. Only the designated recipients can be converted this unreadable format into the readable format.

In secure electronic transactions, cryptographic techniques are adopted to secure E-mail messages, credit card details, audio/video broadcasting, storage media and other sensitive information. By using cryptographic systems, the sender can first encrypt a message and then pass on it through the network. The receiver on the other hand can decrypt the message and restore its original content.

Components of Cryptography

- Plaintext: Plaintext can be text, binary code, or an image that needs to be converted into a format that is unreadable by anybody except those who carry the secret to unlocking it. It refers to the original unencrypted or unadulterated message that the sender wishes to send.

- Ciphertext: During the process of encryption *plaintext* get converted into a rushed format, the resulting format is called the ciphertext. It relates to the encrypted message, the receiver receives that. However, ciphertext is like the plaintext that has been operated on by the encryption process to reproduce a final output. This final output contains the original message though in a format, that is not retrievable unless official knows the correct means or can crack the code.

- Encryption: Encryption receives information and transforms it to an unreadable format that can be reversed. It is the process of encrypting the plaintext so it can provide the ciphertext. Encryption needs an algorithm called a cipher and a secret key. No one can decrypt the vital information on the encrypted message without knowing the secret key. Plaintext gets transformed into ciphertext using the encryption cipher.

- Decryption: This is the reverse of the encryption process, in which it transforms the ciphertext back into the plaintext using a decryption algorithm and a secret key. In symmetric encryption, the key used to decrypt is the same as the key used to encrypt. On other hand, in asymmetric encryption or public-key encryption the key used to decrypt differs from the key used to encrypt.

- Ciphers: The encryption and decryption algorithms are together known as ciphers. Perhaps the trickiest, interesting and most curious part in the encryption process is the algorithm or cipher. The algorithm or cipher is nothing more than a formula that comprises various steps that illustrate how the encryption/decryption process is being implemented on information. A basic cipher takes bits and returns bits and it doesn't care whether bits represent textual information, an image, or a video.

- Key: A key is generally a number or a set of numbers on which the cipher operates. In technical terms, a key is a discrete piece of information that is used to control the output (ciphertext and plaintext) of a given cryptographic algorithm. An encryption and decryption algorithm needs this key to encrypt or decrypt messages, respectively. Sender uses the encryption algorithm and the secret key to convert the plaintext into the ciphertext. On other hand receiver uses same decryption algorithm and the secret key to convert ciphertext back into the plaintext. The longer the secret key is, the harder it is for an attacker to decrypt the message.

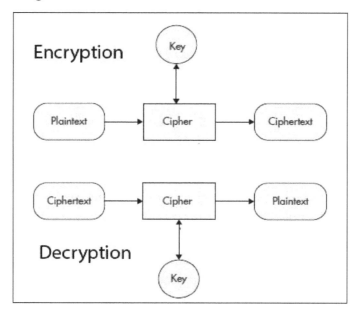

Example of Cryptography (Classical Cipher)

Below is very basic example, we have created a simple cipher to encrypt and decrypt a plaintext into ciphertext and vice versa. The algorithm cipherAlgorithm() is same for encryption and decryption. The key, we have used is 01, 10 and 15 to encrypt and decrypt the message. The output of encryption is different each time when the key is different. This cipher shifts the letter based on key value, key plays an important role in cryptography.

```
package main

import (

    "fmt"

    "unicode"

)
```

```go
// Cipher encrypts and decrypts a string.
type Cipher interface {
    Encryption(string) string
    Decryption(string) string
}
// Cipher holds the key used to encrypts and decrypts messages.
type cipher []int
// cipherAlgorithm encodes a letter based on some function.
func (c cipher) cipherAlgorithm(letters string, shift func(int, int) int) string
{
    shiftedText := ""
    for _, letter := range letters {
        if !unicode.IsLetter(letter) {
            continue
        }
        shiftDist := c[len(shiftedText)%len(c)]
        s := shift(int(unicode.ToLower(letter)), shiftDist)
        switch {
        case s < 'a':
            s += 'z' - 'a' + 1
        case 'z' < s:
            s -= 'z' - 'a' + 1
        }
        shiftedText += string(s)
    }
    return shiftedText
}
// Encryption encrypts a message.
func (c *cipher) Encryption(plainText string) string {
    return c.cipherAlgorithm(plainText, func(a, b int) int { return a + b })
}
// Decryption decrypts a message.
func (c *cipher) Decryption(cipherText string) string {
    return c.cipherAlgorithm(cipherText, func(a, b int) int { return a - b })
```

```
}

// NewCaesar creates a new Caesar shift cipher.

func NewCaesar(key int) Cipher {

    return NewShift(key)

}

// NewShift creates a new Shift cipher.

func NewShift(shift int) Cipher {

    if shift < -25 || 25 < shift || shift == 0 {

        return nil

    }

    c := cipher([]int{shift})

    return &c

}

func main() {

    c := NewCaesar(1)

    fmt.Println("Encrypt Key(01) abcd =>", c.Encryption("abcd"))

    fmt.Println("Decrypt Key(01) bcde =>", c.Decryption("bcde"))

    fmt.Println()

    c = NewCaesar(10)

    fmt.Println("Encrypt Key(10) abcd =>", c.Encryption("abcd"))

    fmt.Println("Decrypt Key(10) klmn =>", c.Decryption("klmn"))

    fmt.Println()

    c = NewCaesar(15)

    fmt.Println("Encrypt Key(15) abcd =>", c.Encryption("abcd"))

    fmt.Println("Decrypt Key(15) pqrs =>", c.Decryption("pqrs"))

}
```

Encryption

In a simplest form, encryption is to convert the data in some unreadable form. This helps in protecting the privacy while sending the data from sender to receiver. On the receiver side, the data can be decrypted and can be brought back to its original form. The reverse of encryption is called as decryption. The concept of encryption and decryption requires some extra information for encrypting and decrypting the data. This information is known as key. There may be cases when same key can be used for both encryption and decryption while in certain cases, encryption and decryption may require different keys.

Authentication

This is another important principle of cryptography. In a layman's term, authentication ensures that the message was originated from the originator claimed in the message. Now, one may think how to make it possible? Suppose, Alice sends a message to Bob and now Bob wants proof that the message has been indeed sent by Alice. This can be made possible if Alice performs some action on message that Bob knows only Alice can do. Well, this forms the basic fundamental of Authentication.

Integrity

Now, one problem that a communication system can face is the loss of integrity of messages being sent from sender to receiver. This means that Cryptography should ensure that the messages that are received by the receiver are not altered anywhere on the communication path. This can be achieved by using the concept of cryptographic hash.

Non Repudiation

What happens if Alice sends a message to Bob but denies that she has actually sent the message? Cases like these may happen and cryptography should prevent the originator or sender to act this way. One popular way to achieve this is through the use of digital signatures.

Cryptanalysis

Cryptanalysis is an important component of the process of creating strong cryptosystems. A reliance on "security via obscurity" (violating Kerckhoff's Law) can result in the use of weak cryptosystems if the creators did not consider all possible attack vectors.

Instead, the cryptographic algorithms in common use today have been published for cryptanalytic review. The ones currently considered "trusted" and in common use are the ones for which an effective attack has not yet been discovered.

Simple Cryptanalytic Techniques

Modern cryptographic algorithms are designed to be resistant against all known cryptanalytic techniques. However, a few simple techniques can be useful for evaluating the security (and potentially breaking) older or amateur cryptosystems.

Entropy Calculations

Entropy is the measure of the amount of randomness that exists within a system. A strong cryptographic algorithm should produce a ciphertext with very high randomness, indicating that there is little or no useful information linking the ciphertext to the original plaintext or secret key.

This makes entropy testing a useful tool for identification of encrypted data. While entropy can be calculated manually, tools like Binwalk and radare2 have built-in entropy testers that can be used to identify encrypted data within a file.

After encrypted data has been identified, other features can be used to help identify the encryption algorithms used. Some examples of useful information include:

- Ciphertext and block length.

- Function names.

If the encryption algorithm can be identified, it is possible to determine if it is a broken algorithm. Alternatively, knowledge of the algorithm can help in the search for an encryption key within a file.

Character Frequency Analysis

Unlike a good ciphertext, modern languages are anything but random. With sufficient knowledge of a language, it is often possible to guess which letter comes next after a given series. For example, in the English language, which letter almost always comes after the letter Q?

The lack of randomness in language is useful for cryptanalysis because it can make it easy to break weak ciphers. Character frequency analysis can easily break substitution and rotational ciphers. The graph above shows the relative frequencies of letters in the English language. As shown, some letters (such as E, T and A) are much more common than others (such as Z, Q and J).

This is useful for analysis of substitution and rotation ciphers since the most common letter in the ciphertext is likely to map to E, the second most common is likely to map to T, etcetera, as long as the ciphertext is long enough. With a rotational cipher, a single correct match is enough to determine the step size and decrypt the message. With a substitution cipher, every pairing must be determined; however, knowledge of a few letters within a word makes it possible to guess the remainder.

Encoding Vs. Encryption

Encoding and encryption are both techniques for data obfuscation. However, their implementation and effects are very different. Encryption requires a secret key for encryption and decryption. Without knowledge of this secret key, the plaintext cannot be retrieved from the ciphertext.

Encoding algorithms apply a reversible operation to data without using a secret key. This means that anyone with knowledge of the encoding algorithm can reverse it. Encoding algorithms are commonly used in malware as a simple replacement for encryption. However, they are easily reversed if the encoding algorithm can be identified.

Base64 Encoding

Base64 encoding is an encoding technique designed to make it possible to send any type of data over protocols limited to alphanumeric characters and symbols. This is accomplished by mapping sequences of three bytes to sets of four characters.

This mapping makes it possible to assign a sequence of six bits (four sets of six characters is twenty-four bits, which is the length of three bytes) to one of sixty-four printable characters. The base64 system uses padding so that an input that is not exactly a multiple of three bytes in length will result in an encoded version with one or two equal signs (=) at the end. The combination of the base64 character set and these option equal signs make this encoding style relatively easy to identify.

Base64 encoding is used to make unprintable data printable, so a common use is to encode encrypted data. However, in some cases, encoding is used instead of encryption, making it easily reversible.

URL Encoding

URL encoding is another example of an encoding style designed to allow data to be passed in a protocol with a constrained character set. In this case, URL encoding is intended to allow characters that are reserved in URLs, such as ? and /, to be included in a domain name or other parts of the URL.

As shown above, URL encoding uses a percent sign (%) followed by the ASCII representation of a value to replace that value. This eliminates the reserved character from the URL but enables it to be easily retrieved when needed. URL encoding is intended to enable the use of reserved characters in URLs. However, it is commonly abused in injection attacks or as a simple layer of obfuscation since it defeats simple string matching.

Cryptographic Algorithms

Cryptographic algorithms that are either FIPS-approved or NIST-recommended must be used if cryptographic services are needed. These algorithms have undergone extensive security analysis and are continually tested to ensure that they provide adequate security. Cryptographic algorithms will usually use cryptographic keys and when these algorithms need to be strengthened, it can often be done by using larger keys.

Classes of Cryptographic Algorithms

There are three general classes of NIST-approved cryptographic algorithms, which are defined by the number or types of cryptographic keys that are used with each.

Hash Functions

A cryptographic hash function does not use keys for its basic operation. This function creates a small digest or "hash value" from often large amounts of data through a one-way process. Hash functions are generally used to create the building blocks that are used in key management and provide security services such as:

- Providing source and integrity authentication services by generating message authentication codes (MACs).

- Compressing messages for generating and verifying digital signatures.

- Deriving keys in key-establishment algorithms.

- Generating deterministic random numbers.

Symmetric-Key Algorithms

Also referred to as a secret-key algorithm, a symmetric-key algorithm transforms data to make it extremely difficult to view without possessing a secret key. The key is considered symmetric because it is used for both encrypting and decrypting. These keys are usually known by one or more authorized entities. Symmetric key algorithms are used for:

- Providing data confidentiality by using the same key for encrypting and decrypting data.

- Providing Message Authentication Codes (MACs) for source and integrity authentication services. The key is used to create the MAC and then to validate it.

- Establishing keys during key-establishment processes.

- Generating deterministic random numbers.

Asymmetric-Key Algorithms

Also referred to as public-key algorithms, asymmetric-key algorithms use paired keys (a public and a private key) in performing their function. The public key is known to all, but the private key is controlled solely by the owner of that key pair. The private key cannot be mathematically calculated through the use of the public key even though they are cryptographically related. Asymmetric algorithms are used for:

- Computing digital signatures.

- Establishing cryptographic keying material.

- Identity Management.

Security Services Provided by Cryptographic Algorithms

Specific security services can be achieved by using different cryptographic algorithms. Often, a single algorithm can be used for multiple services.

Hash Functions

A hash function is often a component of many cryptographic algorithms and schemes, including digital signature algorithms, Keyed-Hash Message Authentication Codes (HMAC), key-derivation functions/methods and random number generators. A hash function operates by taking an arbitrary, but bounded length input and generating an output of fixed length. This output is often referred to as hash, hash value, message digest or digital fingerprint. FIPS180 (Secure Hash Standard) and FIPS202 (Secure Hash Algorithm-3) define the approved hash functions.

Symmetric-Key Algorithms for Encryption and Decryption

Encryption provides confidentiality of data by transforming the "plaintext" into "ciphertext." Decryption transforms ciphertext back to plaintext. AES and 3DES are the approved symmetric-key algorithms used for encryption/decryption services. 3DES is likely to be retired in the near future.

Advanced Encryption Standard (AES)

The AES is based on the Rijndael algorithm. AES encrypts and decrypts data using 128/192/256-bit keys into 128-bit blocks.

3DES/Triple DEA (TDEA)

3DES is a symmetric-key block cipher which applies the DES cipher algorithm three times to each data block. The official name as used by NIST is the Triple Data Encryption Algorithm (TDEA). TDEA encrypts and decrypts data using three 56-bit keys into 64-bit blocks. TDEA has two additional variations:

- Two-key TDEA (2TDEA) using 3 keys, however key 1 and key 3 are identical. This leads to 112 effective bits.

- Three-key TDEA uses 3 different keys, leading to 168 bits. 2TDEA is widely used in the payment card industry as it provided a good trade-off of security and compute time.

However, evolving technology made it inappropriate to withstand attacks. A comparative study, pointed out that even 3DES (also referred to as 3TDEA) is vulnerable to differential cryptanalysis. The Advanced Encryption Standard (AES) proved itself to be much safer, being strong against differential cryptanalysis, but also against truncated differential or linear cryptanalysis as well as against interpolation and square attacks.

Modes of Operation for the Application of AES and TDEA

Cryptographic modes of operation are algorithms which cryptographically transform data that features symmetric key block cipher algorithms, in this case AES and TDEA. The modes of operation solve the problems that occur with block-cipher encryption: when multiple blocks are encrypted separately within a message, that could allow an adversary to substitute individual blocks, often without detection. To alleviate this, NIST prescribes the combination of the applied algorithm with:

- Variable initialization vectors (special data blocks used in an initial step of the encryption and in the subsequent and corresponding decryption of the message).

- Feedback of the information that has been derived from the cryptographic operation.

Message Authentication Codes (MACs)

MACs can be used in providing authentication for the origin/source and integrity of messages. This cryptographic mechanism resolves the problem of adversaries altering messages by creating a MAC key that is shared by both the message originator and the recipient.

- MACs using block cipher algorithms: This algorithm uses an approved block cipher algorithm, for example, AES or TDEA to further secure a MAC.

- MACs using hash functions: an approved hash function may also be used for computing a mac.

Digital Signature Algorithms

Digital signatures are used with hash functions to provide source authentication, integrity authentication, and support for non-repudiation. The Digital Signature Algorithm (DSA), RSA algorithm and ECDSA algorithm are approved by FIPS 186 for use in generating digital signatures.

Key Establishment Schemes

Key transport and key agreement are two types of automated key establishment schemes that are used to create keys that will be used between communicating entities. The sending entity encrypts the keying material, which is then decrypted by the receiving entity.

- Discrete logarithm based key-agreement schemes: Discrete logarithm based public-key algorithms rely on schemes that use finite field math or elliptic curve math. Ephemeral, static or both keys may be used in a single key-agreement transaction.

- Key establishment using integer-factorization schemes: integer factorization based public-key algorithms are used for key establishment schemes where one party always has and uses a static key pair, while the other party may or may not use a key pair.

- Security properties of the key-establishment schemes: It is not always practical for both parties to use both static and ephemeral keys with certain applications, even though using both types of keys in key-establishment schemes provides more security than schemes that use fewer keys.

Key Encryption and Key Wrapping

Key encryption further enhances the confidentiality and protection of a key by encrypting the said key. The process of key unwrapping then decrypts the ciphertext key and provides integrity verification.

Key Confirmation

Key confirmation provides assurance between two parties in a key-establishment process that common keying materials have been established.

Key Establishment Protocols

Protocols for key establishment specify the processing that is needed to establish a key along with its message flow and format.

RNGs (Random Number Generators)

RNGs are needed to generate keying material and are classified into two categories: deterministic and non-deterministic.

Cryptographic Attack

In the present era, not only business but almost all the aspects of human life are driven by information. Hence, it has become imperative to protect useful information from malicious activities such as attacks. Let us consider the types of attacks to which information is typically subjected to.

Attacks are typically categorized based on the action performed by the attacker. An attack, thus, can be passive or active.

Passive Attacks

The main goal of a passive attack is to obtain unauthorized access to the information. For example, actions such as intercepting and eavesdropping on the communication channel can be regarded as passive attack. These actions are passive in nature, as they neither affect information nor disrupt the communication channel. A passive attack is often seen as *stealing* information. The only difference in stealing physical goods and stealing information is that theft of data still leaves the owner in possession of that data. Passive information attack is thus more dangerous than stealing of goods, as information theft may go unnoticed by the owner.

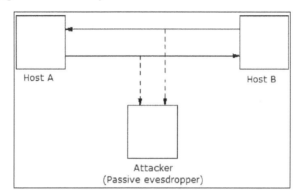

Active Attacks

An active attack involves changing the information in some way by conducting some process on the information. For example:

- Modifying the information in an unauthorized manner.

- Initiating unintended or unauthorized transmission of information.

- Alteration of authentication data such as originator name or timestamp associated with information.

- Unauthorized deletion of data.

- Denial of access to information for legitimate users (denial of service).

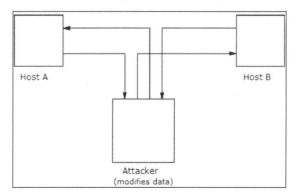

Cryptography provides many tools and techniques for implementing cryptosystems capable of preventing most of the attacks described above.

Assumptions of Attacker

Let us see the prevailing environment around cryptosystems followed by the types of attacks employed to break these systems.

Environment around Cryptosystem

While considering possible attacks on the cryptosystem, it is necessary to know the cryptosystems environment. The attacker's assumptions and knowledge about the environment decides his capabilities. In cryptography, the following three assumptions are made about the security environment and attacker's capabilities.

Encryption Scheme

The design of a cryptosystem is based on the following two cryptography algorithms:

- Public algorithms: With this option, all the details of the algorithm are in the public domain, known to everyone.

- Proprietary algorithms: The details of the algorithm are only known by the system designers and users.

In case of proprietary algorithms, security is ensured through obscurity. Private algorithms may not be the strongest algorithms as they are developed in-house and may not be extensively investigated for weakness.

Secondly, they allow communication among closed group only. Hence they are not suitable for modern communication where people communicate with large number of known or unknown entities. Also, according to Kerckhoff's principle, the algorithm is preferred to be public with strength of encryption lying in the key.

Thus, the first assumption about security environment is that the encryption algorithm is known to the attacker.

Availability of Ciphertext

We know that once the plaintext is encrypted into ciphertext, it is put on unsecure public channel (say email) for transmission. Thus, the attacker can obviously assume that it has access to the ciphertext generated by the cryptosystem.

Availability of Plaintext and Ciphertext

This assumption is not as obvious as other. However, there may be situations where an attacker can have access to plaintext and corresponding ciphertext. Some such possible circumstances are:

- The attacker influences the sender to convert plaintext of his choice and obtains the ciphertext.

- The receiver may divulge the plaintext to the attacker inadvertently. The attacker has access to corresponding ciphertext gathered from open channel.

- In a public-key cryptosystem, the encryption key is in open domain and is known to any potential attacker. Using this key, he can generate pairs of corresponding plaintexts and ciphertexts.

Practicality of Attacks

The attacks on cryptosystems described here are highly academic, as majority of them come from the academic community. In fact, many academic attacks involve quite unrealistic assumptions about environment as well as the capabilities of the attacker. For example, in chosen-ciphertext attack, the attacker requires an impractical number of deliberately chosen plaintext-ciphertext pairs. It may not be practical altogether. Nonetheless, the fact that any attack exists should be a cause of concern, particularly if the attack technique has the potential for improvement.

Birthday Attack

Birthday attack is a type of cryptographic attack that belongs to a class of brute force attacks. It exploits the mathematics behind the birthday problem in probability theory. The success of this attack largely depends upon the higher likelihood of collisions found between random attack attempts and a fixed degree of permutations, as described in the birthday paradox problem.

Birthday Paradox Problem

Let us consider the example of a classroom of 30 students and a teacher. The teacher wishes to find pairs of students that have the same birthday. Hence the teacher asks for everyone's birthday to find such pairs. Intuitively this value may seem small. For example, if the teacher fixes a particular date say October 10, then the probability that at least one student is born on that day is $1 - (364/365)^{30}$ which is about 7.9%. However, the probability that at least one student have same birthday as any other student is around 70% using the following formula:

```
1 - 365!/((365 - n!) * (365ⁿ)) (substituting n = 70 here)
```

Derivation of the above Term

Assumptions:

1. Assuming a non-leap year (hence 365 days).

2. Assuming that a person has equally likely chance of being born on any day of the year.

Let us consider n = 2.

P (Two people have the same birthday) = $1 - $ P(Two people having different birthday),

$= 1 - (365*365)*(364*365)$

$= 1 - 1*(364/365)$

$= 1 - 364/365 = 1/365$.

So for n people the probability that all of them have different birthday is:

P (N people having different birthdays),

= (365/365)*(365-1/365)*(365-2/365)*...(365-n+1)/365.

= 365!/((365-n)! * 365n)

Hash Function

A hash function H is a transformation that takes a variable sized input m and returns a fixed size string called as hash value(h = H(m)). Hash functions chosen in cryptography must satisfy the following requirements:

- The input is of variable length.

- The output has a fixed length.

- H(x) is relatively easy to compute for any given x.

- H(x) is one-way.

- H(x) is collision-free.

A hash function H is said to be one-way if it is hard to invert, where "hard to invert" means that given a hash value h, it is computationally infeasible to find some input x such that H(x) = h. If, given a message x, it is computationally infeasible to find a message y not equal to x such that H(x) = H(y) then H is said to be a weakly collision-free hash function.

A strongly collision-free hash function H is one for which it is computationally infeasible to find any two messages x and y such that H(x) = H(y). Let H: M => $\{0, 1\}^n$ be a hash function ($|M| \gg 2^n$). Following is a generic algorithm to find a collision in time $O(2^{n/2})$ hashes.

Algorithm

- Choose $2^{n/2}$ random messages in M: m_1, m_2, ..., $m_{n/2}$.

- For i = 1, 2, ..., $2^{n/2}$ compute $t_i = H(m_i)$ => $\{0, 1\}^n$.

- Look for a collision ($t_i = t_j$). If not found, go back to step 1.

We consider the following experiment. From a set of H values we choose n values uniformly at random thereby allowing repetitions. Let p(n; H) be the probability that during this experiment at least one value is chosen more than once. This probability can be approximated as:

```
p(n; H) = 1 - ( (365-1)/365) * (365-2)/365) * ...(365-n+1/365))
```

```
p(n; H) = e^{-n(n-1)/(2H)} = e^{-n2}/(2H)
```

Digital Signature Susceptibility

Digital signatures can be susceptible to birthday attack. A message m is typically signed by first computing H(m), where H is cryptographic hash function, and then using some secret key to sign H(m). Suppose Alice want to trick Bob into signing a fraudulent contract. Alice prepares a fair contract m and fraudulent one m'. She then finds a number of positions where m can be changed without changing the meaning, such as inserting commas, empty lines, one versus two spaces after a sentence, replacing synonyms etc. By combining these changes she can create a huge number of variations on m which are all fair contracts.

Similarly, Alice can also make some of these changes on m' to take it even more closer towards m, that is H(m) = H(m'). Hence, Alice can now present the fair version m to Bob for signing. After Bob has signed, Alice takes the signature and attaches to it the fraudulent contract. This signature proves that Bob has signed the fraudulent contract.

To avoid such an attack the output of hash function should be a very long sequence of bits such that birthday attack now becomes computationally infeasible.

Brute Force Attack

A brute force attack uses trial-and-error to guess login info, encryption keys, or find a hidden web page. Hackers work through all possible combinations hoping to guess correctly. These attacks are done by 'brute force' meaning they use excessive forceful attempts to try and 'force' their way into your private account(s).

This is an old attack method, but it's still effective and popular with hackers. Because depending on the length and complexity of the password, cracking it can take anywhere from a few seconds to many years.

What do Hackers Gain from Brute Force Attacks?

Brute force attackers have to put in a bit of effort to make these schemes pay off. While technology does make it easier, you might still question: why would someone do this? Here's how hackers benefit from brute force attacks:

- Profiting from ads or collecting activity data.
- Stealing personal data and valuables.
- Spreading malware to cause disruptions.
- Hijacking your system for malicious activity.
- Ruining a website's reputation.

Profiting from Ads or Collecting Activity Data

Hackers can exploit a website alongside others to earn advertising commissions. Popular ways to do this include:

- Putting spam ads on a well-travelled site to make money each time an ad is clicked or viewed by visitors.
- Rerouting a website's traffic to commissioned ad sites.

- Infecting a site or its visitors with activity-tracking malware — commonly spyware. Data is sold to advertisers without your consent to help them improve their marketing.

Stealing Personal Data and Valuables

Breaking into online accounts can be like cracking open a bank vault: everything from bank accounts to tax information can be found online. All it takes is the right break-in for a criminal to steal your identity, money, or sell your private credentials for profit. Sometimes, sensitive databases from entire organizations can be exposed in corporate-level data breaches.

Spreading Malware to Cause Disruptions

If a hacker wants to cause trouble or practice their skills, they might redirect a website's traffic to malicious sites. Alternatively, they may directly infect a site with concealed malware to be installed on visitor's computers.

Hijacking your System for Malicious Activity

When one machine isn't enough, hackers enlist an army of unsuspecting devices called a botnet to speed up their efforts. Malware can infiltrate your computer, mobile device, or online accounts for spam phishing, enhanced brute force attacks and more. If you don't have an antivirus system, you may be more at risk of infection.

Ruining a Website's Reputation

If you run a website and become a target of vandalism, a cybercriminal might decide to infest your site with obscene content. This might include text, images, and audio of a violent, pornographic, or racially offensive nature.

Types of Brute Force Attacks

Each brute force attack can use different methods to uncover your sensitive data. You might be exposed to any of the following popular brute force methods:

- Simple brute force attacks: Hackers attempt to logically guess your credentials — completely unassisted from software tools or other means. These can reveal extremely simple passwords and PINs. For example, a password that is set as *"guest12345"*.

- Dictionary attacks: In a standard attack, a hacker chooses a target and runs possible passwords against that username. These are known as dictionary attacks. Dictionary attacks are the most basic tool in brute force attacks. While not necessarily being brute force attacks in themselves, these are often used as an important component for password cracking. Some hackers run through unabridged dictionaries and augment words with special characters and numerals or use special dictionaries of words, but this type of sequential attack is cumbersome.

- Hybrid brute force attacks: These hackers blend outside means with their logical guesses to attempt a break-in. A hybrid attack usually mixes dictionary and brute force attacks. These attacks are used to figure out combo passwords that mix common words with random characters. A brute force attack example of this nature would include passwords such as *NewYork1993* or *Spike1234*.

- Reverse brute force attacks: Just as the name implies, a reverse brute force attack reverses the attack strategy by starting with a known password. Then hackers search millions of usernames until they find a match. Many of these criminals start with leaked passwords that are available online from existing data breaches.

- Credential stuffing: If a hacker has a username-password combo that works for one website, they'll try it in tons of others as well. Since users have been known to reuse login info across many websites, they are the exclusive targets of an attack like this.

Tools Aid Brute Force Attempts

Guessing a password for a particular user or site can take a long time, so hackers have developed tools to do the job faster.

Automated tools help with brute force attacks. These use rapid-fire guessing that is built to create every possible password and attempt to use them. Brute force hacking software can find a single dictionary word password within one second. Tools like these have workarounds programmed in them to:

- Work against many computer protocols (like FTP, MySQL, SMPT, and Telnet).

- Allow hackers to crack wireless modems.

- Identify weak passwords.

- Decrypt passwords in encrypted storage.

- Translate words into leetspeak — for example "don'thackme" becomes "d0n7H4cKm3".

- Run all possible combinations of characters.

- Operate dictionary attacks.

Some tools scan pre-compute rainbow tables for the inputs and outputs of known hash functions. These "hash functions" are the algorithm-based encryption methods used to translate passwords into long, fixed-length series of letters and numerals. In other words, rainbow tables remove the hardest part of brute force attacking to speed up the process.

GPU Speeds Brute Force Attempts

Tons of computer brainpower is needed to run brute force password software. Unfortunately, hackers have worked out hardware solutions to make this part of the job a lot easier.

Combining the CPU and graphics processing unit (GPU) accelerates computing power. By adding the thousands of computing cores in the GPU for processing, this enables the system to handle multiple tasks at once. GPU processing is used for analytics, engineering, and other computing-intensive applications. Hackers using this method can crack passwords about 250 times faster than a CPU alone.

So, how long would it take to crack a password? To put it in perspective, a six-character password that includes numbers has approximately 2 billion possible combinations. Cracking it with a powerful CPU that tries 30 passwords per second takes more than two years. Adding a single, powerful GPU card lets the same computer test 7,100 passwords per second and cracks the password in 3.5 days.

Steps to Protect Passwords for Professionals

To keep yourself and your network safe, you'll want to take your precautions and help others do so as well. User behavior and network security systems will both need reinforcement. For IT specialists and users alike, you'll want to take a few general pieces of advice to heart:

- Use an advanced username and password. Protect yourself with credentials that are stronger than *admin* and *password1234* to keep out these attackers. The stronger this combination is, the harder it will be for anyone to penetrate it.

- Remove any unused accounts with high-level permissions. These are the cyber equivalent of doors with weak locks that make breaking in easy. Unmaintained accounts are a vulnerability you can't risk. Throw them away as soon as possible.

Once you've got the basics down, you'll want to bolster your security and get users on board.

Passive Backend Protections for Passwords

- High encryption rates: To make it harder for brute force attacks to succeed, system administrators should ensure that passwords for their systems are encrypted with the highest encryption rates possible, such as 256-bit encryption. The more bits in the encryption scheme, the harder the password is to crack.

- Salt the hash: Administrators should also randomize password hashes by adding a random string of letters and numbers (called salt) to the password itself. This string should be stored in a separate database and retrieved and added to the password before it's hashed. By salting the hash, users with the same password have different hashes.

- Two-factor authentication (2FA): Additionally, administrators can require two-step authentication and install an intrusion detection system that detects brute force attacks. This requires users to follow-up a login attempt with a second factor, like a physical USB key or fingerprint biometrics scan.

- Limit number of login re-tries: Limiting the number of attempts also reduces susceptibility to brute-force attacks. For example, allowing three attempts to enter the correct password before locking out the user for several minutes can cause significant delays and cause hackers to move on to easier targets.

- Account lockdown after excessive login attempts: If a hacker can endlessly keep retrying passwords even after a temporary lockout, they can return to try again. Locking the account and requiring the user to contact IT for an unlock will deter this activity. Short lockout timers are more convenient for users, but convenience can be a vulnerability. To balance this, you might consider using the long-term lockdown if there are excessive failed logins after the short one.

- Throttle rate of repeated logins: You can further slow an attacker's efforts by creating space between each single login attempt. Once a login fails, a timer can deny login until a short amount of time has passed. This will leave lag-time for your real-time monitoring team to spot and work on stopping this threat. Some hackers might stop trying if the wait is not worth it.

- Required Captcha after repeated login attempts: Manual verification does stop robots from brute-forcing their way into your data. Captcha comes in many types, including retyping the text in an image, checking a checkbox, or identifying objects in pictures. Regardless of what you use, you can use this before the first login and after each failed attempt to protect further.

- Use an IP denylist to block known attackers. Be sure that this list is constantly updated by those who manage it.

Active IT Support Protections for Passwords

- Password education: User behavior is essential to password security. Educate users on safe practices and tools to help them keep track of their passwords. Services allow users to save their complex, hard-to-remember passwords in an encrypted "vault" instead of unsafely writing them down on sticky notes. Since users tend to compromise their safety for the sake of convenience, be sure to help them put convenient tools in their hands that will keep them safe.

- Watch accounts in real-time for strange activity: Odd login locations, excessive login attempts etc. Work to find trends in unusual activity and take measures to block any potential attackers in real-time. Look out for IP address blocks, account lockdown, and contact users to determine if account activity is legitimate (if it looks suspicious).

How Users can Strengthen Passwords Against Brute Force Attacks

As a user, you can do a lot to support your protection in the digital world. The best defense against password attacks is ensuring that your passwords are as strong as they can be.

Brute force attacks rely on time to crack your password. So, your goal is to make sure your password slows down these attacks as much as possible, because if it takes too long for the breach to be worthwhile most hackers will give up and move on.

- Longer passwords with varied character types: When possible, users should choose 10-character passwords that include symbols or numerals. Doing so creates 171.3 quintillion (1.71×10^{20}) possibilities. Using a GPU processor that tries 10.3 billion hashes per second, cracking the password would take approximately 526 years. Although, a supercomputer could crack it within a few weeks. By this logic, including more characters makes your password even harder to solve.

- Elaborate passphrases: Not all sites accept such long passwords, which means you should choose complex passphrases rather than single words. Dictionary attacks are built specifically for single word phrases and make a breach nearly effortless. Passphrases — passwords composed of multiple words or segments — should be sprinkled with extra characters and special character types.

- Create rules for building your passwords: The best passwords are those you can remember but won't make sense to anyone else reading them. When taking the passphrase route, consider using truncated words, like replacing "wood" with "wd" to create a string that makes sense only to you. Other examples might include dropping vowels or using only the first two letters of each word.

- Stay away from frequently used passwords: It's important to avoid the most common passwords and to change them frequently.

- Use unique passwords for every site you use: To avoid being a victim of credential stuffing, you should never reuse a password. If you want to take your security up a notch, use a different username for every site as well. You can keep other accounts from getting compromised if one of yours is breached.

- Use a password manager: Installing a password manager automates creating and keeping track of your online login info. These allow you to access all your accounts by first logging into the password manager. You can then create extremely long and complex passwords for all the sites you visit, store them safely, and you only have to remember the one primary password.

Boomerang Attack

A means of improving the flexibility of differential cryptanalysis was discovered by David A. Wagner. Called the boomerang attack, it allows the use of two unrelated characteristics for attacking two halves of a block cipher.

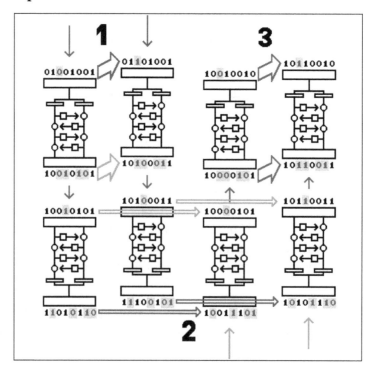

This diagram shows how the attack might work if everything goes perfectly for a particular initial block. The numbered points in the diagram show the steps involved in the attack:

- Start with a random block of plaintext. Based on the characteristic known for the first half of the cipher, if we XOR a certain vector with it, called d1 (equal to 00100000 in the diagram), the result after half-enciphering the two plaintext blocks, before and after the XOR, will differ by c1 (equal to 00110110 in the diagram), *if* what we wish to learn about the key happens to be true.

- Since the characteristic applies only to the first half of the cipher, the results after the whole block cipher won't be related. Take those two results, and XOR each one with d2 (equal to 01001011 in the diagram), which is the vector corresponding to the characteristic for the second half of the cipher. In each case, XORing d2 with a ciphertext block is expected to change the result after deciphering halfway by c2 (equal to 00010000 in the diagram), again, *if* something is true of the key.

- With two intermediate results that differ by c1, if each one has c2 XORed to it, the two results of the XOR will still differ by c1. Since this difference now relates to the *first* half characteristic, it can be seen in the final output, thus indicating the truth or otherwise of two hypotheses about the key.

This increases the potential effectiveness of differential cryptanalysis, because one can make use of characteristics that do not propagate through the complete cipher. Also, certain kinds of added complexities, such as a bit transpose in the middle of the cipher, do not serve as a barrier to this method, since two values differing by an XOR with some value merely differ by an XOR with some other value after a bit transpose.

However, it has its limitations. It only produces a result if both characteristics are present; it does not allow testing for each characteristic independently. Even so, it seems to double the number of rounds a cipher needs to be considered secure.

Since at one end of a sequence of rounds, the precise difference between blocks that is required for the characteristic must be input, it isn't possible directly to cascade this method to break a block cipher into four or more pieces.

Note that any single Feistel round has a large family of "characteristics" that is 100% probable, but which tells nothing about the key, since any pattern that involves leaving the half that is input to the F-function unchanged, but involves an XOR to the half that is XORed with the output of the F-function applies, so one of the things this method can do is allow the use of attacks against the first or last 15 rounds of DES against 16-round DES. Hence, if by some other trick a block cipher with 16 rounds could be broken into 16 pieces like this, one could test for an informative characteristic which applied to any single round.

The Boomerang Amplifier Attack

A technique called the *boomerang amplifier* attack works like this: instead of considering the pairs of inputs, differing by the XOR required for the characteristic of the first few rounds, as completely independent, one could note that it would be quite likely that somehow, taking two such pairs at a

time, one could obtain any desired XOR difference between two such pairs by the birthday paradox. This allows a boomerang attack to be mounted with only chosen plaintext, instead of adaptive
chosen ciphertext as well. We wondered if one could use the boomerang amplifier technique noted
above to allow breaking a block cipher up into *three* pieces instead of two.

First, you start by enciphering a large number of chosen plaintext pairs, differing by the XOR
amount required for the characteristic of the first piece. By the birthday paradox, there will be a
good chance of some pair of two of those pairs, somewhere among that number, which differ by the
right amount to engage the differential characteristic of the middle piece.

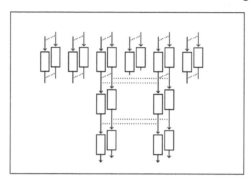

We then take all the outputs of this process, and XOR them by the quantity required to engage,
upon decipherment, the characteristic of the third piece.

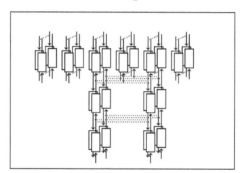

Doing so ensures that the corresponding two pairs of blocks also has the XOR amount for the characteristic of the middle piece, this time in the reverse direction, as can be seen more clearly when
we look at the following diagram of the upwards journey by itself.

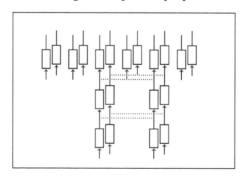

Unfortunately, though, the thing about a differential characteristic is that it only refers to the XOR
between two blocks, and not the values of the blocks.

If a characteristic implies that A xor B equals X xor Y, and equals the characteristic, then it is true that A xor X and B xor Y are equal, but the value to which both of them are equal could have any value. Hence, we have not preserved any structure that implies that we will have the correct differential for the first piece, during decipherment.

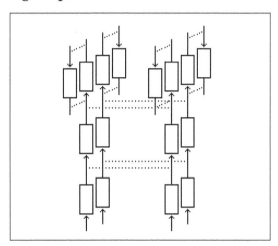

Well, we can still apply the differential for the first piece, and then continue in the reverse order again.

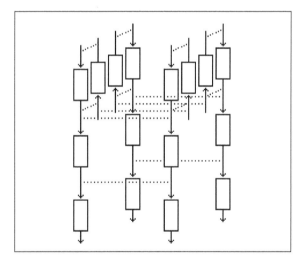

But we run into the same problem; we have no characteristic preserved on output. So it appears that breaking a block cipher into three parts is hopeless. But then we notice that, by iterating in this fashion over our large number of input pairs, we can indefinitely preserve the characteristic in the middle.

This would only work if the characteristics involved had probability one, or very nearly one. Assuming that somehow this could be overcome, though, since one has produced a large number of pairs, in the same spot within our large number of pairs, that have the middle differential activated, if one of the elements of each of two pairs differs from the same element in another cycle by the right amount for the top differential, then the one connected with it by the middle differential will also match, not the other member of the same pair, and this is how the two pairs involved with the middle differential can finally be distinguished.

But because the birthday paradox just says that, to find two matching values for a block having N values, you only need a number of blocks proportional to the square root of N. Using the birthday paradox twice means that the complexity of this attack is proportional to the square root of N times itself, in other words, to N, and so this attack, even if it were possible, has a complexity equivalent to that of the codebook attack: just use as chosen plaintext every possible input block, and record the result.

Man-in-the-Middle

Man-in-the-middle attacks (MITM) are a common type of cybersecurity attack that allows attackers to eavesdrop on the communication between two targets. The attack takes place in between two legitimately communicating hosts, allowing the attacker to "listen" to a conversation they should normally not be able to listen to, hence the name "man-in-the-middle."

Here's an analogy: Alice and Bob are having a conversation; Eve wants to eavesdrop on the conversation but also remain transparent. Eve could tell Alice that she was Bob and tell Bob that she was Alice. This would lead Alice to believe she's speaking to Bob, while actually revealing her part of the conversation to Eve. Eve could then gather information from this, alter the response, and pass the message along to Bob (who thinks he's talking to Alice). As a result, Eve is able to transparently hijack their conversation.

Types of Man-in-the-Middle Attacks

Rogue Access Point

Devices equipped with wireless cards will often try to auto connect to the access point that is emitting the strongest signal. Attackers can set up their own wireless access point and trick nearby devices to join its domain. All of the victim's network traffic can now be manipulated by the attacker. This is dangerous because the attacker does not even have to be on a trusted network to do this—the attacker simply needs a close enough physical proximity.

ARP Spoofing

ARP is the Address Resolution Protocol. It is used to resolve IP addresses to physical MAC (media access control) addresses in a local area network. When a host needs to talk to a host with a given IP address, it references the ARP cache to resolve the IP address to a MAC address. If the address is not known, a request is made asking for the MAC address of the device with the IP address.

An attacker wishing to pose as another host could respond to requests it should not be responding to with its own MAC address. With some precisely placed packets, an attacker can sniff the private traffic between two hosts. Valuable information can be extracted from the traffic, such as exchange of session tokens, yielding full access to application accounts that the attacker should not be able to access.

mDNS Spoofing

Multicast DNS is similar to DNS, but it's done on a local area network (LAN) using broadcast like ARP. This makes it a perfect target for spoofing attacks. The local name resolution system is supposed to make the configuration of network devices extremely simple. Users don't have to know exactly which addresses their devices should be communicating with; they let the system resolve it for them. Devices such as TVs, printers, and entertainment systems make use of this protocol since they are typically on trusted networks. When an app needs to know the address of a certain device, such as tv. local, an attacker can easily respond to that request with fake data, instructing it to resolve to an address it has control over. Since devices keep a local cache of addresses, the victim will now see the attacker's device as trusted for duration of time.

DNS Spoofing

Similar to the way ARP resolves IP addresses to MAC addresses on a LAN, DNS resolves domain names to IP addresses. When using a DNS spoofing attack, the attacker attempts to introduce corrupt DNS cache information to a host in an attempt to access another host using their domain name, such as www.onlinebanking.com. This leads to the victim sending sensitive information to a malicious host, with the belief they are sending information to a trusted source. An attacker who has already spoofed an IP address could have a much easier time spoofing DNS simply by resolving the address of a DNS server to the attacker's address.

Man-in-the-Middle Attack Techniques

Sniffing

Attackers use packet capture tools to inspect packets at a low level. Using specific wireless devices that are allowed to be put into monitoring or promiscuous mode can allow an attacker to see packets that are not intended for it to see, such as packets addressed to other hosts.

Packet Injection

An attacker can also leverage their device's monitoring mode to inject malicious packets into data communication streams. The packets can blend in with valid data communication streams, appearing to be part of the communication, but malicious in nature. Packet injection usually involves first sniffing to determine how and when to craft and send packets.

Session Hijacking

Most web applications use a login mechanism that generates a temporary session token to use for future requests to avoid requiring the user to type a password at every page. An attacker can sniff sensitive traffic to identify the session token for a user and use it to make requests as the user. The attacker does not need to spoof once he has a session token.

SSL Stripping

Since using HTTPS is a common safeguard against ARP or DNS spoofing, attackers use SSL stripping to intercept packets and alter their HTTPS-based address requests to go to their HTTP equivalent endpoint, forcing the host to make requests to the server unencrypted. Sensitive information can be leaked in plain text.

How to Detect a Man-in-the-Middle-Attack

Detecting a Man-in-the-middle attack can be difficult without taking the proper steps. If you aren't actively searching to determine if your communications have been intercepted, a Man-in-the-middle attack can potentially go unnoticed until it's too late. Checking for proper page authentication and implementing some sort of tamper detection are typically the key methods to detect a possible attack, but these procedures might require extra forensic analysis after-the-fact.

It's important to take precautionary measures to prevent MITM attacks before they occur, rather than attempting to detect them while they are actively occuring. Being aware of your browsing practices and recognizing potentially harmful areas can be essential to maintaining a secure network.

Best Practices to Prevent Man-in-the-Middle Attacks

Strong WEP/WAP Encryption on Access Points

Having a strong encryption mechanism on wireless access points prevents unwanted users from joining your network just by being nearby. A weak encryption mechanism can allow an attacker to brute-force his way into a network and begin man-in-the-middle attacking. The stronger the encryption implementation, the safer.

Strong Router Login Credentials

It's essential to make sure your default router login is changed. Not just your Wi-Fi password, but your router login credentials. If an attacker finds your router login credentials, they can change your DNS servers to their malicious servers. Or even worse, infect your router with malicious software.

Virtual Private Network

VPNs can be used to create a secure environment for sensitive information within a local area network. They use key-based encryption to create a subnet for secure communication. This way, even if an attacker happens to get on a network that is shared, he will not be able to decipher the traffic in the VPN.

Force HTTPS

HTTPS can be used to securely communicate over HTTP using public-private key exchange. This prevents an attacker from having any use of the data he may be sniffing. Websites should only use HTTPS and not provide HTTP alternatives. Users can install browser plugins to enforce always using HTTPS on requests.

Public Key Pair based Authentication

Man-in-the-middle attacks typically involve spoofing something or another. Public key pair based authentication like RSA can be used in various layers of the stack to help ensure whether the things you are communicating with are actually the things you want to be communicating with.

Dictionary Attack

A dictionary attack is a systematic method of guessing a password by trying many common words and their simple variations. Attackers use extensive lists of the most commonly used passwords, popular pet names, fictional characters, or literally just words from a dictionary – hence the name of the attack. They also change some letters to numbers or special characters, like "p@ssword".

Hackers use this attack to gain access to online accounts, but also for file decryption – and that's an even bigger problem. Most people put at least some effort into securing their email or social media accounts. However, they choose simple, easy-to-remember everyday words to protect the files they share with other people. If sent over an unsafe connection, those files would be very easy to intercept, and guessing the password by using a dictionary attack wouldn't be a challenge either.

How does a Dictionary Attack Work?

During a dictionary attack, a program systematically enters words from a list as passwords to gain access to a system, account, or encrypted file. A dictionary attack can be performed both online and offline. In an online attack, the attacker repeatedly tries to log in or gain access like any other user. This type of attack works better if the hacker has a list of likely passwords. If the attack takes too long, it might get noticed by a system administrator or the original user. During an offline attack, however, there are no network limitations to how many times you can guess the password. To do it, hackers need to get their hands on the password storage file from the system they want to access, so it's more complicated than an online attack. But once they have the correct password, they will be able to log in without anyone noticing.

What is the Difference between a Brute Force Attack and a Dictionary Attack?

Brute force attacks are also used to guess passwords. They mostly rely on the computing power of the attacker's computer. During a brute force attack, a program also automatically enters combinations of letters, symbols, and numbers, but in this case, they are entirely random. Brute force attacks can also be performed online and offline.

However, there are 1,022,000 words in the English language. By using the alphabet and numbers 0-9, you can make 218,340,105,584,896 eight-character passwords. In this case, a dictionary attack is much more likely to succeed, given that the password will be a simple English word. And it will most likely be a simple English word. A basic brute force attack would take much more time and is less likely to be successful. Dictionary attacks are brute force attacks in nature. The only difference is that dictionary attacks are more efficient – they usually don't need to try as many combinations to succeed. However, if the password is a truly unique one, a dictionary attack won't work. In that case, using brute force is the only option.

How to Avoid a Password Dictionary Attack?

The IT department in any organization should take some precautions to protect their systems from dictionary attacks. Online attacks are rather easy to stop. You can use captchas, implement mandatory two-factor authentication, and limit how many times one user can attempt to log in before their account is locked.

It's a bit more complicated when it comes to offline attacks, though. But you can also use two-factor authentication and set up strict rules concerning passwords: no popular passwords, no common words or phrases, 12 character minimum, etc. And most importantly, make sure that you don't store passwords in plaintext.

But what can you do as a user to prevent your accounts from getting hacked? First and foremost – don't be predictable. The best passwords are words that have no meaning to the general public. Keep in mind that the length of the password is not what makes it strong. It doesn't matter whether you choose "pachycephalosaurus" or "cat" as your password; a computer takes the same amount of time to try either of them. So create new words, use special characters originally, or, best of all, use random strings of upper- and lower-case letters, symbols, and numbers.

Known Plaintext Attack

In cryptography, the known plaintext attack, or KPA, is an attack based on having samples of both the plaintext and corresponding encrypted or ciphertext for that information available. This information is used to conduct an analysis of the data in order to determine the secret key used to encrypt and decrypt the information. Historical ciphers are very susceptible to the attack, while modern-day ciphers are less prone to being cracked using the method.

The history of the known plaintext attack dates to earlier in the 20th century when the cryptologists referred to the action using the term "crib." The term crib was based on the slang for using a "crib sheet" or "cheat sheet" on an exam. The general idea behind the original "cribs" was that if a cryptologist was able to obtain information regarding a word or phrase contained within ciphertext, that he or she would be able to have an advantage when creating a test to break into the cipher.

Without any intelligence advantage to develop the "crib," cryptologists were left to conduct random tests or attacks on the cipher to attempt to obtain common phrases within the ciphertext. Once the cribbed words would start to appear when conducting tests, the cryptologist(s) would know they were on the right track for breaking the cipher.

Breaking the Enigma Code

During WW II, the German military used the Enigma Machine for the encryption of military and other related messages. During this timeframe, the commanders were aware of the potential threat of cribs to the code; however, the German operators in the field were not as conscious about maintaining OPSEC during the war. As a result, British cryptologists were able to make a number of accurate guesses for establishing cribs due to the rigidity of the regimented German military report system. These cribs would typically be created based off of the German weather reports and other recurring information sent from the field to German high command. For example, the German world for weather, "Wetter," occurred in the same location in the same messages every day. Combined with knowing the actual weather conditions, the British cryptologists were able to make significant headway with cracking the Enigma code.

Another example of focusing on likely "known" transmissions by the German military to help crack the Enigma Code was in Africa during WW2. The German Afrika Corps would commonly send reports that stated "Nothing to Report," during the war. These transmissions along with other standard greetings allowed cryptographers working at Bletchley Park in the U.K. to make progress on breaking Enigma messages. Another tactic that the Allies would take to help obtain additional information for crib sheet development was to bomb or mine well-known areas. Once accomplished, the resulting Enigma messages transmitted by the Germans would contain references to set geographic positions. This act became to be known as "seeding" a given area.

Further helping the Allies develop crib sheets to aid in breaking the Enigma code was intelligence gleaned from the interrogation of a German intelligence operative. During this interview, it was ascertained that the German High Command had directed their message operators to spell out numbers to help to encode them. As a result, the now famous cryptology pioneer and computer scientist, Alan Turing, was able to conduct an analysis of decrypted Enigma messages. During this work, he was able to discover that the number "one" was the most common string of characters in the plaintext. He was then able to automate the crib process for the Allies creating the Eins catalog. This work assumed that "enis" (the German word for "one") was the most common string in any given plaintext. The work included all possible positions of the Enigma machine and keysettings.

Prior to World War 2, the Polish Cipher Bureau was able to exploit cribs when attempting to crack Enigma-encoded messages. During these pre-way exploits, the Polish engineers were able to take advantage of the Germans using the characters "ANX" throughout messages (AN is the German word for "to" and the character X was used as a spacer in the message), to develop cribs to decrypt messages.

How Good are Classic Ciphers?

Although classic ciphers worked wonders in their day, they are extremely vulnerable to the known plaintext attack with the technology of today. The Caesar cipher is able to be solved with the attack using only a single letter of plaintext that is corroborated to ciphertext. For general monoalphabetic substitution ciphers, the known plaintext attack only needs several character pairs to quickly crack the cipher.

Modern Day Plaintext Attacks

One of the better known, modern-day plaintext attacks has been against the PKZIP stream cipher against older versions of the zip specification. If an attacker has a zip file encrypted under the older versions of PKZIP, he or she only needs to have part of one of the unencrypted files of the archive to conduct the attack. Freeware is published supporting the attack that is capable of calculating the private or secret key required to decrypt the full archive of information. In order to obtain the unencrypted file, an attacker simply has to search the website of the originating zip file to locate one that is suitable, manually construct a plaintext file using a filename from the archive, or locate the example file from another, related archive. This attack does not work against PKZIP files that have been encrypted using AES.

The Chosen Plaintext Attack

In the chosen plaintext attack, or CPA, the attacker has the ability or access to select random plaintexts and see the corresponding ciphertext. The ultimate goal of this attack is to obtain additional data or information that will reduce or eliminate the security of the cipher being employed. In the best case for the attacker (or worst case for the organization using the cipher), the secret key can be obtained which eliminates the overhead of cracking the cipher. In some instances of the chosen plaintext attack, only a small amount of plaintext must be known by the attacker. In these circumstances, the attack is known as a plaintext injection attack.

Although the chosen plaintext attack may at first appear to be an unrealistic model to leverage when trying to crack a cipher, it is primarily focused on leveraging software or computer hardware to obtain the data or information used in the attack. These attacks are more commonly used against public key cryptography where the attacker can obtain the public key easily and then generate ciphertext at will from a variety of plaintext source.

What are the Two Types of Chosen Plaintext Attack?

There are two types of chosen plaintext attack at the time of this writing: batch chosen plaintext attack and the adaptive chosen plaintext attack. In the batch chosen variant, the analyst is able to select all plaintexts before they are encrypted. This version of the attack is often referred to by the generic chosen plaintext attack label. In the adaptive chosen plaintext attack, the attacker is able to conduct interactive queries of the cipher. Subsequent plaintext queries are able to be made based on the results of previous attempts. Through this progressive attack, the cryptanalyst is able to make more advanced headway on breaking the cipher. A related technique is the Allied "gardening" technique used during WW2. In this technique, the analysts were able to have the military take specific action that would be transmitted in encoded Enigma messages. Knowing the topic to expect in the resulting messages allowed the code breakers to make additional headway in cracking the Enigma code. Today, this variant of the attack is also known as the plaintext injection attack.

Chosen Ciphertext Attack

The chosen ciphertext attack, or CCA, is an attack based on the cryptanalyst obtaining information by selecting ciphertext and then obtaining the plaintext or decryption without knowing the key. To accomplish this attack, the cryptanalyst must be able to enter one to many ciphertexts into the cipher system and then obtain the resulting plain or clear text. From this information, the secret key can be recovered for use in decryption.

The chosen ciphertext attack is able to defeat a number of secure cipher or security algorithms due to the ability of the attacker to be able to obtain plaintext on demand from the ciphertext. For example, the El Gamal cryptosystem is very secure against the chosen plaintext attack. Against the chosen ciphertext attack; however, the system is very unsecure. Additionally, early versions of RSA padding that were used in SSL were vulnerable to this attack and would reveal the SSL session keys. The attack has also been used to successfully target "tamper-resistant" smart cards. Since the card can come under the control of an attacker, a large number of chosen ciphertexts can be issued in an attempt to obtain the secret key used by the smart card.

If a cipher is susceptible to attack by the chosen ciphertext attack, the person or organization that implements the cipher has to be cautious and make sure situations are avoided that an attacker might be able to decrypt selected ciphertexts. Although this action seems simple to implement, even allowing partially chosen ciphertexts can allow various attacks to occur. Additionally, in cryptosystems that use the same cipher to encrypt and decrypt text are particularly susceptible to attack. In the cases where messages are not hashed as part of the encryption process, a better approach to use of the cipher is required for safe employment.

What are the Types of Chosen Ciphertext Attacks?

Similar to other types of cipher attack, chosen ciphertext attacks are either non-adaptive or adaptive. In the adaptive variants of the attack, the attacker selects the ciphertext based on results of previous plaintext to ciphertext decryptions. In non-adaptive attacks, the ciphertexts that will be decrypted are selected in advance. The resulting plaintext does not change the additional ciphertext look ups.

Lunchtime Attack

The lunchtime attack is a special variant of the chosen ciphertext attack. It is also referred to as the midnight, lunchtime, or indifferent attack. In this attack, the individual(s) are able to make adaptive queries on a crypto system up to a certain point that is very system dependent. On reaching this threshold, the attacker must be able to demonstrate an ability to attack the system.

The attack gets its name from the notion that an end-user's computer is open to attack while he or she is away from the desk at lunch time. If the attacker is able to make adaptive chosen ciphertext queries without limitation, no encrypted message is safe that uses the system until the access to make the attacks is removed. Once the ability to adapt queries is removed, the attack becomes known as being "non-adaptive."

Adaptive Chosen Ciphertext Attack

In the adaptive chosen chiphertext attack, ciphertext are able to be selected before and after a challenge ciphertext is provided to the attacker. The only limitation in the attack is that the challenge ciphertext is not able to be queried. This attack is considered to be stronger than a lunchtime attack and is also referred to as a CCA2 attack. There are very few non-academic attacks that take this format. Instead, the adaptive chosen cipherattack is used to test the security of a cipher against chosen ciphertext attacks. Some crypto systems that have been proved to be resistant to this type of attack include RSA-OAEP and the Cramer-Shoup system.

Side Channel Attack

"Side channel attacks" are attacks that are based on "Side Channel Information". Side channel information is information that can be retrieved from the encryption device that is neither the plaintext to be encrypted nor the ciphertext resulting from the encryption process.

In the past, an encryption device was perceived as a unit that receives plaintext input and produces ciphertext output and vice-versa. Attacks were therefore based on either knowing the ciphertext (such as ciphertext-only attacks), or knowing both (such as known plaintext attacks) or on the ability to define what plaintext is to be encrypted and then seeing the results of the encryption (known as chosen plaintext attacks). Today, it is known that encryption devices have additional output and often additional inputs which are not the plaintext or the ciphertext. Encryption devices produce timing information (information about the time that operations take) that is easily measurable, radiation of various sorts, power consumption statistics (that can be easily measured as well), and more. Often the encryption device also has additional "unintentional" inputs such as voltage that can be modified to cause predictable outcomes. Side channel attacks make use of some or all of this information, along with other (known) cryptanalytic techniques, to recover the key the device is using.

Side channel analysis techniques are of concern because the attacks can be mounted quickly and can sometimes be implemented using readily available hardware costing from only a few hundred dollars to thousands of dollars. The amount of time required for the attack and analysis depends on the type of attack (Differential Power Analysis, Simple Power Analysis, Timing, etc.) According to, SPA attacks on smartcards typically take a few seconds per card, while DPA attacks can take several hours.

In a general, we may consider the entire internal state of the block cipher to be all the intermediate results and values that are never included in the output in normal operations. For example, DES has 16 rounds; we can consider the intermediate states, state after each round except the last as a secret internal state. Side channels typically give information about these internal states, or about the operations used in the transition of this internal state from one round to another. The type of side-channel will, of course, determine what information is available to the attacker about these states. The attacks typically work by finding some information about the internal state of the cipher, which can be learned both by guessing part of the key and checking the value directly, and additionally by some statistical property of the cipher that makes that checkable value slightly non-random.

Power Consumption Attacks

These attacks are based on analyzing the power consumption of the unit while it performs the encryption operation. By either simple or differential analysis of the power the unit consumes, an attacker can learn about the processes that are occurring inside the unit and gain some information that, when combined with other cryptanalysis techniques, can assist in the recovery of the secret key.

Integrated circuits are built out of individual transistors, which act as voltage-controlled switches. Current flows across the transistor substrate when charge is applied to (or removed from) the gate. This current then delivers charge to the gates of other transistors, interconnect wires, and other circuit loads. The motion of electric charge consumes power and produces electromagnetic radiation, both of which are externally detectable.

To measure a circuit's power consumption, a small (e.g., 50 ohm) resistor is inserted in series with the power or ground input. The voltage difference across the resistor divided by the resistance yields the current. Well-equipped electronics labs have equipment that can digitally sample voltage differences at extraordinarily high rates (over 1GHz) with excellent accuracy (less than 1% error). Devices capable of sampling at 20MHz or faster and transferring the data to a PC can be bought for less than $400.

Simple Power Analysis (SPA) Attacks

Simple Power Analysis is generally based on looking at the visual representation of the power consumption of a unit while an encryption operation is being performed. Simple Power Analysis is a technique that involves direct interpretation of power consumption measurements collected during cryptographic operations. SPA can yield information about a device's operation as well as key material.

The attacker directly observes a system's power consumption. The amount of power consumed varies depending on the microprocessor instruction performed. Large features such as DES rounds, RSA operations, etc. may be identified, since the operations performed by the microprocessor vary significantly during different parts of these operations. SPA analysis can, for example, be used to break RSA implementations by revealing differences between multiplication and squaring operations. Similarly, many DES implementations have visible differences within permutations and shifts, and can thus be broken using SPA.

Because SPA can reveal the sequence of instructions executed, it can be used to break cryptographic implementations in which the execution path depends on the data being processed, such as: DES key schedule, DES permutations, Comparisons, Multipliers and Exponentiators. Most cryptographic units, that were tested, were found to be vulnerable to SPA attacks, it is not difficult to design a system that will not be vulnerable to such attacks.

Differential Power Analysis (DPA) Attacks

Differential Power Analysis Attacks are harder to prevent. They consist not only of visual but also statistical analysis and error-correction statistical methods, to obtain information about the keys. DPA usually consists of data collection and data analysis stages that make extensive use of statistical functions for noise filtering as well as for gaining additional information about the processes that the unit is performing.

In addition to large-scale power variations due to the instruction sequence, there are effects correlated to data values being manipulated. These variations tend to be smaller and are sometimes overshadowed by measurement errors and other noise. In such cases, it is still possible to break the system using statistical functions tailored to the target algorithm. Because DPA automatically locates correlated regions in a device's power consumption, the attack can be automated and little or no information about the target implementation is required.

In general terms, to implement a DPA attack, an attacker first observes m encryption operations and captures power traces T[1::m][1::k] containing k samples each. In addition, the attacker records the ciphertexts C[1::m]. No knowledge of the plaintext is required. DPA analysis uses power consumption measurements and statistical methods to determine whether a key block guess K is correct. Analyzing an outer DES operation first, using the resulting key to decrypt the ciphertexts, and attacking the next DES sub-key can find Triple-DES keys. DPA can use known plaintext or known ciphertext and find encryption or decryption keys.

Several improvements can be applied to the data collection and DPA analysis processes to reduce the number of samples required or to circumvent countermeasures. For example, it is helpful to apply corrections for the measurement variance, yielding the significance of the variations instead of their magnitude. One variant of this approach, automated template DPA, can find DES keys using fewer than 15 traces from most smart cards.

With regards to asymmetric ciphers, public key algorithms can be analyzed using DPA by correlating candidate values for computation intermediates with power consumption measurements. For modular exponentiation operations, it is possible to test exponent bit guesses by testing whether predicted intermediate values are correlated to the actual computation. Chinese Remainder Theorem RSA implementations can also be analyzed, for example, by defining selection functions over the CRT reduction or recombination processes. In general, signals leaking during asymmetric operations tend to be much stronger than those from many symmetric algorithms because of the relatively high computational complexity of multiplication operations.

High-Order DPA (HO-DPA) involves looking at power consumptions between several sub-operations of the encryption operation (and not just on the operation in general). Also, while the DPA techniques described above analyze information across a single event between samples, high-order DPA may be used to correlate information between multiple cryptographic sub-operations. Worth mentioning is that there is no known unit that is vulnerable to HO-DPA and that is not vulnerable to DPA as well. Yet, what is done to prevent DPA must also work against HO-DPA. In other words, the precautions that are taken to prevent DPA should be ones that work against HO-DPA as well, no systems are currently known that are resistant to DPA and are not resistant to HO-DPA.

Differential Fault Analysis (DFA) Attacks

Fault analysis relates to the ability to investigate ciphers and extract keys by generating faults in a system that is in the possession of the attacker, or by natural faults that occur. Faults are most often caused by changing the voltage, tampering with the clock, or by applying radiation of various types.

The attacks are based on encrypting the same piece of data (which is not necessarily known to the attacker) twice and comparing the results. A one-bit difference indicates a fault in one of the operations. Now, a short computation can be applied for DES, for example, to identify the round in which the error has occurred. A whole set of operations can now be carried out to recover one DES sub-key which is the sub-key of the last round. When this sub-key is known, the attacker can either guess the missing 8 bits (the last sub-key uses 48 bits) for which there are only 256 options, or simply peel off the last round for which he knows the sub-key and perform the attack on the reduced DES. This second method can be used also against Triple-DES. Often, DFA can be combined with other attacks as differential-key attacks or differential related key cryptanalysis.

Another type of Fault Analysis is the Non-Differential Fault Analysis, but this is based on causing permanent damage to devices for the purpose of extracting symmetric keys (such as of DES). It must be mentioned that a trait of such attacks is that they do not require correct ciphertexts (hence, ciphertexts that were produced before the damage to the unit has occurred). This leads to the attacker being able to make use of natural faulty units (that are malfunctioning since being manufactured), without himself tampering with them.

Preventing Side Channel Attacks

These techniques should be evaluated when defining the precautions to be taken by designers of cryptographic modules in ensuring that, to some extent, the product has the ability to resist side-channel attacks.

General Countermeasures Against All Attacks

General Data-Independent Calculations

In general, all operations that are performed by the module shall be data independent in their time consumption. In other words, the time that operations take must be totally independent of the input data or the key data. Whenever different sub-operations are performed according to input or key bits, these sub operations should take the same number of clock cycles.

The general feature of making the time needed for operation execution fixed for every piece of data prevents all timing attacks. This is because these attacks are based on variations in the computation time according to input and key bits. The only input property that may have an effect on the time the operation takes is the length of the exponent in exponentiation operations. However, the length of the exponent is information with no meaningful value for the attacker, and is mostly broadly known anyway.

Blinding

Techniques used for blinding signatures can be adapted to prevent attackers from knowing the input to the modular exponentiation function. This should help against any type of side-channel attack.

Even with blinding, the distribution will reveal the average time per operation, which can be used to infer the Hamming weight of the exponent. If anonymity is important or if further masking is required, a random multiple can be added to the exponent before each modular exponentiation. If this is done, care must be taken to ensure that the addition process itself does not have timing characteristics, which may reveal the random multiple. This technique may be helpful in preventing attacks that gain information leaked during the modular exponentiation operation due to electromagnetic radiation, system performance fluctuations, changes in power consumption, etc. since the exponent bits change with each operation.

Avoiding Conditional Branching and Secret Intermediates

Avoiding procedures that use secret intermediates or keys for conditional branching operations will mask many SPA characteristics. Software implementation of critical code shall not contain branching statements. Similarly, these will not contain conditional execution statements, such as IF clauses. Calculations should be performed using functions that utilize elementary operations (such as AND, OR and XOR) and not using branching and conditional execution of portions of the code.

This feature can make it extremely difficult to guess input and key values using measurements of time or power consumption. Conditional execution, which depends on input and key data, can easily reveal properties of this data if the attacker measures the time or power taken to perform certain actions. When all the lines of code are always running regardless of the input and key bits, the time and power taken to perform these actions does not depend on the data and therefore does not reveal any of its properties. This feature prevents all types of timing attacks on asymmetric ciphers as well as some power consumption attacks.

Licensing Modified Algorithms

The most effective general solution is to design and implement cryptosystems with the assumption that information will leak. A few companies develop approaches for securing existing cryptographic algorithms (including RSA, DES, DSA, Diffie-Hellman, El Gamal, and Elliptic Curve systems) to make systems remain secure even though the underlying circuits may leak information.

Countermeasures Against Timing Attacks

Adding Delays

The most obvious way to prevent timing attacks is to make all operations take exactly the same amount of time. Unfortunately this is often difficult. If a timer is used to delay returning results until a pre-specified time, factors such as the system responsiveness or power consumption may still change when the operation finishes in a way that can be detected. Fixed time implementations are likely to be slow; many performance optimizations cannot be used since all operations must take as long as the slowest operation.

When random delays are added, although these random delays do increase the number of ciphertexts required, attackers can compensate by collecting more measurements. The number of samples required increases roughly as the square of the timing noise. So, random delays can make the attack a bit more difficult, but still possible.

Time Equalization of Multiplication and Squaring

The time taken by the unit for the performance of multiplication and for the performance of exponentiation actions should be set to be similar. Due to this quality, an attacker will not be able to learn if, when and how many multiplications are made and how many exponentiations.

The equalization can be caused by always performing both operations (multiplication and exponentiation), regardless of the operation that is required at any given time. At any stage where one of the operations is required to run, both should be executed and the aftermath of the unnecessary operation is to be silently ignored. This technique prevents timing attacks against the exponentiation operations that are performed as a part of asymmetric encryption operations and which are subject to the most common attacks.

Countermeasures Against Power Analysis Attacks

Power Consumption Balancing

Power consumption balancing techniques should be applied when possible. Dummy registers and gates should be added on which (algorithm-wise) useless operations are made to balance power consumption into a constant value. Whenever an operation is performed in hardware, a complementary operation should be performed on a dummy element to assure that the total power consumption of the unit remains balanced according to some higher value.

Such techniques, by which the power consumption (as viewed from outside the module) is constant and independent on input and key bits, prevents all sorts of power consumption attacks such as SPA and DPA.

Reduction of Signal Size

One approach to preventing DPA attacks is by reducing signal sizes, such as by using constant execution path code, choosing operations that leak less information in their power consumption, balancing Hamming Weights and state transitions, or by physically shielding the device.

Unfortunately, such signal size reduction generally cannot reduce the signal size to zero, as an attacker with an infinite number of samples will still be able to perform DPA on the (heavily-degraded) signal.

Addition of Noise

Another approach against DPA involves introducing noise into power consumption measurements. Like signal size reductions, adding noise increases the number of samples required for an attack, possibly to an unfeasibly large number. In addition, execution timing and order can be randomized to generate a similar effect. Again, noise alone only increases the number of samples required, however if this increase is high enough to make the sampling unfeasible due to the number of samples required, the countermeasure works.

One suggested solution to prevent DPA attacks using noise is by adding random calculations that increase the noise level enough to make the DPA bias spikes undetectable. The results presented in give some indication of how much noise needs to be added. The main goal is to add enough random noise to stop an attack, but yet to add just a minimal overhead.

Shielding

In practice, aggressive physical shielding can make attacks unfeasible but adds significantly to a device's cost and size.

Modification of the Algorithms Design

A final approach against DPA attacks involves designing cryptosystems with realistic assumptions about the underlying hardware. Nonlinear key update procedures can be employed to ensure that power traces cannot be correlated between transactions. As a simple example, hashing a 160-bit key with SHA before using it as a key should effectively destroy partial information an attacker might have gathered about the key. Similarly, aggressive use of exponent and modulus modification processes in public key schemes can be used to prevent attackers from accumulating data across large numbers of operations.

This may solve the problem, but it does require design changes in the algorithms and protocols themselves, which are likely to make the resulting product noncompliant with standards and specifications.

Countermeasures Against Fault Attacks

Running the Encryption Twice

A possible solution against DFA is for the unit to run the encryption twice and output the results only if these two are identical. The main problem with this approach is that it increases computation time. Also, the probability that the fault will not occur twice is not sufficiently small. Since the fault may still occur twice (especially if the fault was caused artificially), this countermeasure will only make the attack harder to implement (requiring more samples), but not impossible.

Timing Attacks

Timing attacks enable an attacker to extract secrets maintained in a security system by observing the time it takes the system to respond to various queries. For example, Kocher designed a timing attack to expose secret keys used for RSA decryption. Until now, these attacks were only applied in the context of hardware security tokens such as smartcards. It is generally believed that timing attacks cannot be used to attack general purpose servers, such as web servers, since decryption times are masked by many concurrent processes running on the system. It is also believed that common implementations of RSA are not vulnerable to timing attacks.

We challenge both assumptions by developing a remote timing attack against OpenSSL, an SSL library commonly used in web servers and other SSL applications. Our attack client measures the time an OpenSSL server takes to respond to decryption queries. The client is able to extract the private key stored on the server. The attack applies in several environments.

Network

We successfully mounted our timing attack between two machines on our campus network. The attacking machine and the server were in different buildings with three routers and multiple switches between them. With this setup we were able to extract the SSL private key from common SSL applications such as a web server (Apache+mod SSL) and a SSL-tunnel.

Interprocess

We successfully mounted the attack between two processes running on the same machine. A hosting center that hosts two domains on the same machine might give management access to the admins of each domain. Since both domains are hosted on the same machine, one admin could use the attack to extract the secret key belonging to the other domain.

Virtual Machines

A Virtual Machine Monitor (VMM) is often used to enforce isolation between two Virtual Machines (VM) running on the same processor. One could protect an RSA private key by storing it in one VM and enabling other VM's to make decryption queries. For example, a web server could run in one VM while the private key is stored in a separate VM. This is a natural way of protecting secret keys since a break-in into the web server VM does not expose the private key. Our results show that when using OpenSSL the network server VM can extract the RSA private key from the secure VM, thus invalidating the isolation provided by the VMM. This is especially relevant to VMM projects such as Microsoft's NGSCB architecture (formerly Palladium). We also note that NGSCB enables an application to ask the VMM (aka Nexus) to decrypt (aka unseal) application data. The application could expose the VMM's secret key by measuring the time the VMM takes to respond to such requests.

Many crypto libraries completely ignore the timing attack and have no defenses implemented to prevent it. For example, libgcrypt (used in GNUTLS and GPG) and Cryptlib do not defend against timing attacks. OpenSSL 0.9.7 implements a defense against the timing attack as an option. However, common applications such as mod SSL, the Apache SSL module, do not enable this option and are therefore vulnerable to the attack. These examples show that timing attacks are a largely ignored vulnerability in many crypto implementations. We hope the results of this paper will help convince developers to implement proper defenses. Interestingly, Mozilla's NSS crypto library properly defends against the timing attack. We note that most crypto acceleration cards also implement defenses against the timing attack. Consequently, network servers using these accelerator cards are not vulnerable.

We chose to tailor our timing attack to OpenSSL since it is the most widely used open source SSL library. The OpenSSL implementation of RSA is highly optimized using Chinese Remainder, Sliding Windows, Montgomery multiplication, and Karatsuba's algorithm. These optimizations cause both known timing attacks on RSA to fail in practice. Consequently, we had to devise a new timing attack based on that is able to extract the private key from an OpenSSL based server. As we will see, the performance of our attack varies with the exact environment in which it is applied. Even the exact compiler optimizations used to compile OpenSSL can make a big difference.

Timing attacks are related to a class of attacks called side-channel attacks. These include power analysis and attacks based on electromagnetic radiation. Unlike the timing attack, these extended side channel attacks require special equipment and physical access to the machine. In this paper we only focus on the timing attack. We also note that our attack targets the implementation of RSA decryption in OpenSSL. Our timing attack does not depend upon the RSA padding used in SSL and TLS.

OpenSSL's Implementation of RSA

OpenSSL Decryption

At the heart of RSA decryption is a modular exponentiation $m = c^d \bmod N$ where $N = pq$ is the RSA modulus, d is the private decryption exponent, and c is the ciphertext being decrypted. OpenSSL uses the Chinese Remainder Theorem (CRT) to perform this exponentiation. With Chinese remaindering, the function $m = c^d \bmod N$ is computed in two steps. First, evaluate $m_1 = c^{d_1} \bmod p$ and $m_2 = c^{d_2} \bmod q$ (here d_1 and d_2 are precomputed from d). Then, combine m_1 and m_2 using CRT to yield m.

RSA decryption with CRT gives up to a factor of four speedup, making it essential for competitive RSA implementations. RSA with CRT is not vulnerable to Kocher's original timing attack. Nevertheless, since RSA with CRT uses the factors of N, a timing attack can expose these factors. Once the factorization of N is revealed it is easy to obtain the decryption key by computing $d = e^{-1} \bmod (p - 1)(q - 1)$.

Exponentiation

During an RSA decryption with CRT, OpenSSL computes $c^{d_1} \bmod p$ and $c^{d_2} \bmod q$. Both computations are done using the same code. For simplicity we describe how OpenSSL computes g d mod q for some g, d, and q.

The simplest algorithm for computing g^d mod q is square and multiply. The algorithm squares g approximately $\log_2$ d times, and performs approximately $\frac{\log_2 d}{2}$ additional multiplications by g. After each step, the product is reduced modulo q.

OpenSSL uses an optimization of square and multiply called sliding windows exponentiation. When using sliding windows a block of bits (window) of d are processed at each iteration, where as Simple Square-and multiply processes only one bit of d per iteration. Sliding windows requires pre-computing a multiplication table, which takes time proportional to 2 w−1+1 for a window of size w. Hence, there is an optimal window size that balances the time spent during pre-computation vs. actual exponentiation. For a 1024-bit modulus OpenSSL uses a window size of five so that about five bits of the exponent d are processed in every iteration.

For our attack, the key fact about sliding windows is that during the algorithm there are many multiplications by g, where g is the input cipher text. By querying on many inputs g the attacker can expose information about bits of the factor q. We note that a timing attack on sliding windows is much harder than a timing attack on square-and-multiply since there are far fewer multiplications by g in sliding windows. As we will see, we had to adapt our techniques to handle sliding windows exponentiation used in OpenSSL.

Montgomery Reduction

The sliding windows exponentiation algorithm performs a modular multiplication at every step. Given two integers x, y, computing xy mod q is done by first multiplying the integers x * y and then reducing the result modulo q. Later we will see each reduction also requires a few additional multiplications. We first briefly describe OpenSSL's modular reduction method and then describe its integer multiplication algorithm.

Naively, a reduction modulo q is done via multi-precision division and returning the remainder. This is quite expensive. In 1985 Peter Montgomery discovered a method for implementing a reduction modulo q using a series of operations efficient in hardware and software.

Montgomery reduction transforms a reduction modulo q into a reduction modulo some power of 2 denoted by R. A reduction modulo a power of 2 is faster than a reduction modulo q as many arithmetic operations can be implemented directly in hardware. However, in order to use Montgomery reduction all variables must first be put into Montgomery form. The Montgomery form of number x is simply xR mod q. To multiply two numbers a and b in Montgomery form we do the following. First, compute their product as integers: aR * bR = cR^2. Then, use the fast Montgomery reduction algorithm to compute cR^2 * R^{-1} = cR mod q. Note that the result cR mod q is in Montgomery form, and thus can be directly used in subsequent Montgomery operations. At the end of the exponentiation algorithm the output is put back into standard (non-Montgomery) form by multiplying it by R^{-1} mod q. For our attack, it is equivalent to use R and R^{-1} mod N, which is public.

Hence, for the small penalty of converting the input g to Montgomery form, a large gain is achieved during modular reduction. With typical RSA parameters the gain from Montgomery reduction outweighs the cost of initially putting numbers in Montgomery form and converting back at the end of the algorithm.

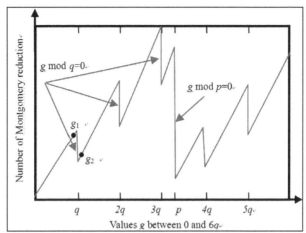

Number of extra reductions in a Montgomery reduction as a function of the input g.

The key relevant fact about a Montgomery reduction is at the end of the reduction one checks if the output cR is greater than q. If so, one subtracts q from the output, to ensure that the output cR is in the range (o, q). This extra step is called an extra reduction and causes a timing difference for different inputs. Schindler noticed that the probability of an extra reduction during an exponentiation $g^d \bmod q$ is proportional to how close g is to q. Schindler showed that the probability for an extra reduction is:

$$\Pr[\text{Extra Reduction}] = \frac{g \bmod q}{2R}$$

Consequently, as g approaches either factor p or q from below, the number of extra reductions during the exponentiation algorithm greatly increases. At exact multiples of p or q, the number of extra reductions drops dramatically. Figure shows this relationship, with the discontinuities appearing at multiples of p and q. By detecting timing differences that result from extra reductions we can tell how close g is to a multiple of one of the factors.

Multiplication Routines

RSA operations, including those using Montgomery's method, must make use of a multi-precision integer multiplication routine. OpenSSL implements two multiplication routines: Karatsuba (sometimes called recursive) and "normal". Multi-precision libraries represent large integers as a sequence of words. OpenSSL uses Karatsuba multiplication when multiplying two numbers with an equal number of words. Karatsuba multiplication takes time $O\left(n^{\log_2 3}\right)$ which is $O(n^{1.58})$. OpenSSL uses normal multiplication, which runs in time O(nm), when multiplying two numbers with an unequal number of words of size n and m. Hence, for numbers that are approximately the same size (i.e. n is close to m) normal multiplication takes quadratic time.

Thus, OpenSSL's integer multiplication routine leaks important timing information. Since Karatsuba is typically faster, multiplication of two unequal size words takes longer than multiplication of two equal size words. Time measurements will reveal how frequently the operands given to the multiplication routine have the same length. We use this fact in the timing attack on OpenSSL.

In both algorithms, multiplication is ultimately done on individual words. The underlying word multiplication algorithm dominates the total time for a decryption. For example, in OpenSSL the underlying word multiplication routine typically takes 30% – 40% of the total runtime. The time to multiply individual words depends on the number of bits per word. As we will see in experiment 3 the exact architecture on which OpenSSL runs has an impact on timing measurements used for the attack. In our experiments the word size was 32 bits.

Comparison of Timing Differences

So far we identified two algorithmic data dependencies in OpenSSL that cause time variance in RSA decryption: (1) Schindler's observation on the number of extra reductions in a Montgomery reduction, and (2) the timing difference due to the choice of multiplication routine, i.e. Karatsuba vs. normal. Unfortunately, the effects of these optimizations counteract one another.

Consider a timing attack where we decrypt a ciphertext g. As g approaches a multiple of the factor q from below, equation (1) tells us that the number of extra reductions in a Montgomery reduction increases. When we are just over a multiple of q, the number of extra reductions decreases dramatically. In other words, decryption of g < q should be slower than decryption of g > q.

The choice of Karatsuba vs. normal multiplication has the opposite effect. When g is just below a multiple of q, then OpenSSL almost always uses fast Karatsuba multiplication. When g is just over a multiple of q then g mod q is small and consequently most multiplications will be of integers with different lengths. In this case, OpenSSL uses normal multiplication which is slower. In other words, decryption of g < q should be faster than decryption of g > q — the exact opposite of the effect of extra reductions in Montgomery's algorithm. Which effect dominates is determined by the exact environment. Our attack uses both effects, but each effect is dominant at a different phase of the attack.

A Timing Attack on OpenSSL

Our attack exposes the factorization of the RSA modulus. Let $N = pq$ with $q < p$. We build approximations to q that get progressively closer as the attack proceeds. We call these approximations guesses. We refine our guess by learning bits of q one at a time, from most significant to least. Thus, our attack can be viewed as a binary search for q. After recovering the half-most significant bits of q, we can use Coppersmith's algorithm to retrieve the complete factorization.

Initially our guess g of q lies between 2^{512} (i.e. $2^{\log_2 N/2}$) and 2^{511} (i.e. $2^{\log_2(N/2)-1}$). We then time the decryption of all possible combinations of the top few bits (typically 2-3). When plotted, the decryption times will show two peaks: one for q and one for p. We pick the values that bound the first peak, which in OpenSSL will always be q.

Suppose we already recovered the top $i-1$ bits of q. Let g be an integer that has the same top $i - 1$ bits as q and the remaining bits of g are 0. Then $g < q$. At a high level, we recover the i'th bit of q as follows:

- Step 1 - Let g_{hi} be the same value as g, with the i'th bit set to 1. If bit i of q is 1, then $g < g_{hi} < q$. Otherwise, $g < q < g_{hi}$.

- Step 2 - Compute $u_g = gR^{-1} \bmod N$ and $u_{g_{hi}} = g_{hi}R^{-1} \bmod N$. This step is needed because RSA decryption with Montgomery reduction will calculate $u_g R = g$ and $u_{g_{hi}} R = g_{hi}$ to put u_g and $u_{g_{hi}}$ in Montgomery form before exponentiation during decryption.

- Step 3 - We measure the time to decrypt both u_g and $u_{g_{hi}}$. Let t_1 = DecryptTime(u_g) and t_2 = DecryptTime($u_{g_{hi}}$).

- Step 4 - We calculate the difference $\Delta = |t_1 - t_2|$. If $g < q < g_{hi}$ then, the difference Δ will be "large", and bit i of q is 0. If $g < g_{hi} < q$, the difference Δ will be "small", and bit i of q is 1. We use previous Δ values to know what to consider "large" and "small". Thus we use the value $|t_1 - t_2|$ as an indicator for the i'th bit of q.

When the i'th bit is 0, the "large" difference can either be negative or positive. In this case, if $t_1 - t_2$ is positive then DecryptTime(g) > DecryptTime(ghi), and the Montgomery reductions dominated the time difference. If $t_1 - t_2$ is negative, then DecryptTime(g) < DecryptTime(ghi), and the multi-precision multiplication dominated the time difference.

Formatting of RSA plaintext, e.g. PKCS 1, does not affect this timing attack. We also do not need the value of the decryption, only how long the decryption takes.

Exponentiation Revisited

We would like $\left|t_{g1} - t_{g2}\right| \gg \left|t_{g3} - t_{g4}\right|$ when $g_1 < q < g_2$ and $g_3 < g_4 < q$. Time measurements that have this property we call a strong indicator for bits of q, and those that do not are a weak indicator for bits of q. Square and multiply exponentiation results in a strong indicator because there are approximately $\dfrac{\log_2 d}{2}$ multiplications by g during decryption. However, in sliding windows with window size w (w = 5 in OpenSSL) the expected number of multiplications by g is only:

$$E[\# \text{ multiply by } g] \approx \frac{\log_2 d}{2^{w-1}(w+1)}$$ resulting in a weak indicator.

To overcome this we query at a neighborhood of values g, g +1, g +2, ..., g +n, and use the result as the decrypt time for g (and similarly for g_{hi}). The total decryption time for g or g_{hi} is then:

$$T_g = \sum_{i=0}^{n} \text{DecryptTime}(g+i)$$

We define T_g as the time to compute g with sliding windows when considering a neighborhood of values. As n grows, $\left|T_g - T_{g_{hi}}\right|$ typically becomes a stronger indicator for a bit of q (at the cost of additional decryption queries).

Cryptographic Key Management

Public-key encryption schemes are secure only if the authenticity of the public key is assured. A public-key certificate scheme provides the necessary security. A simple public-key algorithm is Diffie-Hellman key exchange. This protocol enables two users to establish a secret key using a public-key scheme based on discrete logarithms. The protocol is secure only if the authenticity of the two participants can be established. Elliptic curve arithmetic can be used to develop a variety of elliptic curve cryptography (ECC) schemes, including key exchange, encryption, and digital signature. For purposes of ECC, elliptic curve arithmetic involves the use of an elliptic curve equation defined over a finite field.

Key Management

We examine the problem of the distribution of secret keys. One of the major roles of public-key encryption has been to address the problem of key distribution. There are actually two distinct aspects to the use of public-key cryptography in this regard. The distribution of public keys, the use of public-key encryption to distribute secret keys.

Distribution of Public Keys

Several techniques have been proposed for the distribution of public keys. Virtually all these proposals can be grouped into the following general schemes like public announcement, publicly available directory, public-key authority and public-key certificates.

Public Announcement of Public Keys

On the face of it, the point of public-key encryption is that the public key is public. Thus, if there is some broadly accepted public-key algorithm, such as RSA, any participant can send his or her public key to any other participant or broadcast the key to the community at large.

Uncontrolled Public-Key Distribution.

For example, because of the growing popularity of PGP (pretty good privacy), which makes use of RSA, many PGP users have adopted the practice of appending their public key to messages that they send to public forums, such as USENET newsgroups and Internet mailing lists.

Although this approach is convenient, it has a major weakness. Anyone can forge such a public announcement. That is, some user could pretend to be user A and send a public key to another participant or broadcast such a public key. Until such time as user A discovers the forgery and alerts other participants, the forger is able to read all encrypted messages intended for A and can use the forged keys for authentication.

Publicly Available Directory

A greater degree of security can be achieved by maintaining a publicly available dynamic directory of public keys. Maintenance and distribution of the public directory would have to be the responsibility of some trusted entity or organization. Such a scheme would include the elements such as the authority maintains a directory with a {name, public key} entry for each participant. Each participant registers a public key with the directory authority. Registration would have to be in person or by some form of secure authenticated communication. A participant may replace the existing key with a new one at any time, either because of the desire to replace a public key that has already been used for a large amount of data, or because the corresponding private key has been compromised in some way. Participants could also access the directory electronically. For this purpose, secure, authenticated communication from the authority to the participant is mandatory.

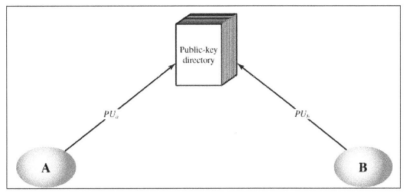

Public-Key Publication.

Public-Key Authority

Stronger security for public-key distribution can be achieved by providing tighter control over the distribution of public keys from the directory. A typical scenario is illustrated in Figure, which is based on a figure. As before, the scenario assumes that a central authority maintains a dynamic directory of public keys of all participants. In addition, each participant reliably knows a public key for the authority, with only the authority knowing the corresponding private key. The following steps occur:

- A sends a time stamped message to the public-key authority containing a request for the current public key of B.

- The authority responds with a message that is encrypted using the authority's private key, PRauth. Thus, A is able to decrypt the message using the authority's public key. Therefore, A is assured that the message originated with the authority. The message includes the originated with the authority. The message includes the following:

  ○ B's public key, PUb which A can use to encrypt messages destined for B.

  ○ The original request, to enable A to match this response with the corresponding earlier request and to verify that the original request was not altered before reception by the authority.

  ○ The original timestamp, so A can determine that this is not an old message from the authority containing a key other than B's current public key.

- A stores B's public key and also uses it to encrypt a message to B containing an identifier of A (IDA) and a nonce (N_1), which is used to identify this transaction uniquely.

- B retrieves A's public key from the authority in the same manner as A retrieved B's public key. At this point, public keys have been securely delivered to A and B, and they may begin their protected exchange. However, two additional steps are desirable: B sends a message to A encrypted with PUa and containing A's nonce (N_1) as well as a new nonce generated by B (N_2), Because only B could have decrypted.

- Message (3), the presence of N_1 in message (6) assures A that the correspondent is B.

- A returns N_2, encrypted using B's public key, to assure B that its correspondent is A.

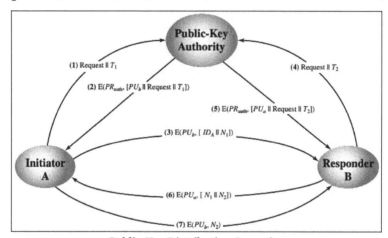

Public-Key Distribution Scenario.

Thus, a total of seven messages are required. However, the initial four messages need be used only infrequently because both A and B can save the other's public key for future use, a technique known as caching. Periodically, a user should request fresh copies of the public keys of its correspondents to ensure currency.

Public-Key Certificates

The scenario of Figure above is attractive, yet it has some drawbacks. The public-key authority could be somewhat of a bottleneck in the system, for a user must appeal to the authority for a public key for every other user that it wishes to contact. As before, the directory of names and public keys maintained by the authority is vulnerable to tampering.

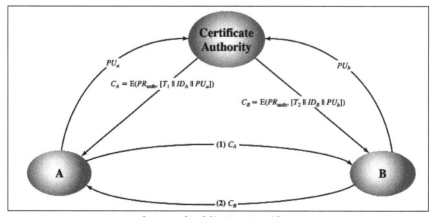

Exchange of Public-Key Certificates.

An alternative approach, use certificates that can be used by participants to exchange keys without contacting a public-key authority, in a way that is as reliable as if the keys were obtained directly from a public-key authority. In essence, a certificate consists of a public key plus an identifier of the key owner, with the whole block signed by a trusted third party.

Typically, the third party is a certificate authority, such as a government agency or a financial institution that is trusted by the user community. A user can present his or her public key to the authority in a secure manner, and obtain a certificate. The user can then publish the certificate. Anyone needed this user's public key can obtain the certificate and verify that it is valid by way of the attached trusted signature. A participant can also convey its key information to another by transmitting its certificate. Other participants can verify that the certificate was created by the authority. We can place the following requirements on this scheme:

- Any participant can read a certificate to determine the name and public key of the certificate's owner.

- Any participant can verify that the certificate originated from the certificate authority and is not counterfeit.

- Only the certificate authority can create and update certificates.

- Any participant can verify the currency of the certificate.

Application must be in person or by some form of secure authenticated communication. For participant A, the authority provides a certificate of the form:

$$C_A = E\left(PR_{auth}, \; \left[T_1 \| ID_A \| PU_a\right]\right)$$

Where PRauth is the private key used by the authority and T is a timestamp. A may then pass this certificate on to any other participant, who reads and verifies the certificate as follows:

$$D\left(PU_{auth}, \; C_A\right) = D\left(PU_{auth}, \; E\left(PR_{auth}, \; \left[T \| ID_A \| PU_a\right]\right)\right) = \left(T \| ID_A \| PU_a\right).$$

Distribution of Secret Keys using Public-Key Cryptography

Once public keys have been distributed or have become accessible, secure communication that thwarts eavesdropping, tampering, or both is possible. However, few users will wish to make exclusive use of public-key encryption for communication because of the relatively slow data rates that can be achieved. Accordingly, public-key encryption provides for the distribution of secret keys to be used for conventional encryption.

Simple Secret Key Distribution

Merkle proposed simple secrete key distribution in 1979. It generates a new temporary public key pair .A sends B the public key and their identity. B generates a session key K sends it to A encrypted using the supplied public key. A decrypts the session key and both problem is that an opponent can intercept and impersonate both halves of protocol.

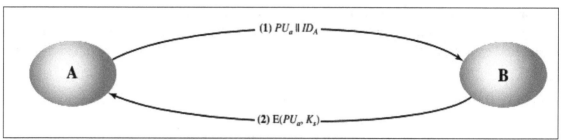

Simple Use of Public-Key Encryption to Establish a Session Key.

A and B can now securely communicate using conventional encryption and the session key Ks. At the completion of the exchange, both A and B discard Ks. Despite its simplicity, this is an attractive protocol. No keys exist before the start of the communication and none exist after the completion of communication. Thus, the risk of compromise of the keys is minimal. At the same time, the communication is secure from eavesdropping.

The protocol depicted in Figure above is insecure against an adversary who can intercept messages and then either relay the intercepted message or substitute another message. Such an attack is known as a man-in-the-middle attack. In this case, if an adversary, E, has control of the intervening communication channel, then E can compromise the communication in the following fashion without being detected:

- A generates a public/private key pair $\{PU_a, PR_a\}$ and transmits a message intended for B consisting of PU_a and an identifier of A, ID_A.

- E intercepts the message, creates its own public/private key pair $\{PU_e, PR_e\}$ and transmits $PU_e||ID_A$ to B.

- B generates a secret key, K_s, and transmits $E(PU_e, K_s)$.

- E intercepts the message, and learns K_s by computing $D(PR_e, E(PU_e, K_s))$.

- E transmits $E(PU_a, K_s)$ to A.

The result is that both A and B know K_s and are unaware that K_s has also been revealed to E. A and B can now exchange messages using K_s E no longer actively interferes with the communications channel but simply eavesdrops. Knowing K_s E can decrypt all messages, and both A and B are unaware of the problem. Thus, this simple protocol is only useful in an environment where the only threat is eavesdropping.

Secret Key Distribution with Confidentiality and Authentication

Based on an approach suggested in Figure it provides protection against both active and passive attacks. We begin at a point when it is assumed that A and B have exchanged public keys by one of the schemes described earlier in this section. Then the following steps occur:

- A uses B's public key to encrypt a message to B containing an identifier of A (IDA) and a nonce (N_1), which is used to identify this transaction uniquely.

- B sends a message to A encrypted with PU a and containing A's nonce (N_1) as well as a new nonce generated by B (N_2). Because only B could have decrypted message (1), the presence of N_1 in message (2) assures A that the correspondent is B.

- A returns N_2 encrypted using B's public key, to assure B that its correspondent is A.

- A selects a secret key K_s and sends M = E(PU_b, E(PR_a, K_s)) to B. Encryption of this message with B's public key ensures that only B can read it; encryption with A's private key ensures that only A could have sent it.

- B computes D(PU_a, D(PR_b, M)) to recover the secret key.

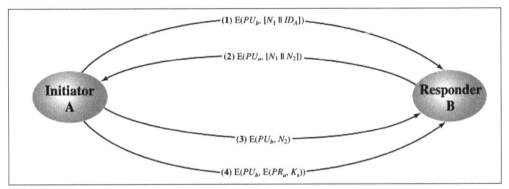

Public-Key Distribution of Secret Keys.

Notice that the first three steps of this scheme are the same as the last three steps of Figure. The result is that this scheme ensures both confidentiality and authentication in the exchange of a secret key.

Hybrid Key Distribution

Yet another way to use public-key encryption to distribute secret keys is a hybrid approach in use on IBM mainframes. This scheme retains the use of a key distribution center (KDC) that shares a secret master key with each user and distributes secret session keys encrypted with the master key. A public key scheme is used to distribute the master keys. The following rationale is provided for using this three-level approach such as Performance: There are many applications, especially transaction-oriented applications, in which the session keys change frequently. Distribution of session keys by public-key encryption could degrade overall system performance because of the relatively high computational load of public-key encryption and decryption. With a three-level hierarchy, public-key encryption is used only occasionally to update the master key between a user and the KDC and Backward compatibility: The hybrid scheme is easily overlaid on an existing KDC scheme, with minimal disruption or software changes.

Cryptographic Key

In cryptography, a key is a string of characters used within an encryption algorithm for altering data so that it appears random. Like a physical key, it locks (encrypts) data so that only someone with the right key can unlock (decrypt) it. The original data is known as the *plaintext*, and the data after the key encrypts it is known as the *ciphertext*.

The formula: plaintext + key = ciphertext

Keys in Early Forms of Encryption

Before the advent of computers, ciphertext was often created by simply replacing one letter with another letter in the plaintext, a method known as a "substitution cipher." For instance, suppose that someone sends a message reading "Hello" to another person, and each letter is replaced with the one after it in the alphabet: "Hello" becomes "Ifmmp."

H	E	L	L	O
+1	+1	+1	+1	+1
I	F	M	M	P

"Ifmmp" looks like a nonsensical string of letters, but if someone knows the key, they can substitute the proper letters and decrypt the message as "Hello." For this example, the key is (*letter*) - 1, moving each letter down one spot in the alphabet to arrive at the real letter.

I	F	M	M	P
-1	-1	-1	-1	-1
H	E	L	L	O

Such ciphers are relatively easy to break with simple statistical analysis, since certain letters will appear more often than others in any given text (for instance E is the most common letter in the English language). To combat this, cryptographers developed a system called the one-time pad.

A one-time pad is a single-use-only key that has at least as many values as the plaintext has characters. In other words, each letter will be replaced by a letter that's a unique number of letters removed from it in the alphabet. For example, suppose someone has to encrypt the message "Hello," and they use a one-time pad with the values 7, 17, 24, 9, 11.

H	E	L	L	O
7	17	24	9	11

Whereas before we simply moved up one position for each letter (letter + 1), now we move a different number of places in the alphabet for each letter. We add 7 to the first letter, H; we add 17 to the second letter; and so on. For any calculations that take us past Z, we simply go back to the beginning of the alphabet and keep adding.

H	E	L	L	O
7	17	24	9	11
O	V	J	U	Z

Starting from the plaintext "Hello," we now have the ciphertext "Ovjuz," using the key "7, 17, 24, 9, 11." For communication via a one-time pad to work, both sides of the conversation have to use the same key for each individual message (symmetric encryption), although a different key is used every time there's a new message. Although to any third parties "Ovjuz" looks like random nonsense, the person who receives the ciphertext "Ovjuz" will know to use the key "7, 17, 24, 9, 11" to decrypt it (subtracting instead of adding):

O	V	J	U	Z

7	17	24	9	11
H	E	L	L	O

Thus, a simple message can be altered by a string of random data, a key, in order to be encrypted or decrypted.

Keys in Modern Encryption

Although the above examples of early cryptography illustrate how using a random string of information to turn plaintext into ciphertext works, cryptographic keys today are far more complex. For instance, the public key for cloudflare.com is: 04 CE D7 61 49 49 FD 4B 35 8B 1B 86 BC A3 C5 BC D8 20 6E 31 17 2D 92 8A B7 34 F4 DB 11 70 4E 49 16 61 FC AE FA 7F BA 6F 0C 05 53 74 C6 79 7F 81 12 8A F7 E2 5E 6C F5 FA 10 69 6B 67 D9 D5 96 51 B0.

This is much more complex than the "7 17 24 9 11" key we used above to encrypt "Hello." Instead of simply adding or subtracting, modern encryption uses complex mathematical formulas known as *algorithms*. And instead of a simple string of random numbers for a key, modern keys are typically randomized even further. This is the case for several reasons:

- Computers are capable of far more complicated calculations in a shorter amount of time than human cryptographers, making more complex encryption not only possible, but necessary.

- Computers can alter information at the binary level, the 1s and 0s that make up data, not just at the level of individual letters and numbers.

- If encrypted data is not randomized enough, a computer program will be able to decrypt it. True randomness is extremely important for truly secure encryption. Although it is not possible to write a program that produces truly random data 100% of the time, computers are much better at it than humans are on their own.

Combined with an encryption algorithm, a cryptographic key will scramble a text beyond human recognition. As an example, let's encrypt the message "Hello" with the cloudflare.com public key. Using an encryption algorithm with that key, we get "KZoKVey8l1c=" as the ciphertext.

How are Keys used in SSL Encryption (HTTPS)?

There are two kinds of encryption: symmetric encryption and asymmetric encryption, also known as public key encryption. In symmetric encryption, both sides of a conversation use the same key for turning plaintext into ciphertext and vice versa.

In asymmetric or public key encryption, the two sides of the conversation each use a different key. One key is called the public key, and one key is called the private key – thusly named because one of the parties keeps it secret and never shares it with anyone. When plaintext is encrypted with the public key, only the private key can decrypt it, not the public key. It works the other way, too: When plaintext is encrypted with the private key, only the public key can decrypt it.

SSL (or TLS, as it is called today), is an encryption protocol used to keep Internet communications secure, and a website that is served over HTTPS instead of HTTP uses this kind of encryption. In TLS/SSL, a website or web application will have both a public key and a private key. The public key is shared publicly in the website's SSL certificate for anyone to see. The private key is installed on the origin server and never shared.

TLS/SSL communication sessions begin with a TLS handshake, during which the website and the client use the public key and the private key in order to generate new keys, which are called session keys. These session keys are then used by both sides to encrypt their messages back and forth. Thus, TLS starts with asymmetric encryption (with two keys) and moves to symmetric encryption (with one key). Both sides use the same keys during the communication session, but when they start a new session, they will generate new keys together.

Cryptographic Hardware and Software

Modern cryptographic algorithms can be implemented using dedicated cryptographic hardware or software running on general-purpose hardware. For various reasons, dedicated cryptographic hardware provides a better solution for most applications. The table below lists reasons why hardware-based cryptographic solutions are more desirable.

Hardware-based cryptography	Software-based cryptography
1. Uses dedicated hardware, thus much faster to execute.	1. Uses shared hardware, thus slower to execute.
2. Not dependent on the operating system. Supported by dedicated software to operate the hardware.	2. Dependent on the security levels and features of the operating system and supported software.
3. Can use factory provisioning and securely store keys and other data in dedicated secure memory locations.	3. No dedicated secure memory locations available. Thus, suspectible to stealing or manipulation of keys and data.
4. Maxim's hardware implementations have protections built in against reverse-engineering, such as PUF (ChipDNA).	4. Software implementations can be easier to reverse-engineer.
5. In a hardware system, special care is taken to hide and protect the vital information, such as private keys, to make it more difficult to access.	5. In a general-purpose system where software cryptography is implemented, there are more ways to snoop to and access vital information. An example would be intercepting the private key in transit within the computer's system.

Secure Boot and Secure Download

Among the everyday IoT devices that use embedded hardware are:

- Home devices: Wi-Fi cameras, IoT thermostats, and smoke detectors.

- Medical devices.

- Wearables, fitness trackers, or smart watches.

- Industrial machines such as robotic arms in factories.

Almost all of these devices contain boot firmware or downloadable data that access the internet, which puts them at risk. Boot firmware is essentially saved in non-volatile memory inside the device. It's the brains of the device. This software is updated from time to time to correct and enhance certain features. This can be anything from a new intruder detection algorithm for a Wi-Fi camera or the angle of an industrial robot arm for better positioning of a weld.

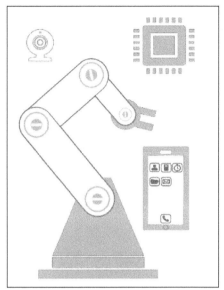

IoT devices, such as a robotic arm in a factory, have embedded hardware that could pose a security risk.

Why Protect IoT Device Firmware or Data?

IoT devices must be trustworthy, which means the device firmware and critical data must be verified to be genuine. In a perfect world, boot firmware and configuration data would be locked down at the factory, but customers have come to expect firmware updates and reconfiguration to be available over the internet. And that's the problem—malicious actors can use these network interfaces as a conduit for malware.

If someone gains control of an IoT device, they may take control of the device for malicious purposes. For this reason, any code that purports to come from an authorized source must be authenticated before it's allowed to be used.

An attacker may deliver malware to an IoT device by various means:

- If the attacker can gain physical access to the device, then malware may be introduced via a physical connection (such as USB, Ethernet, etc).

- Operating systems often exhibit vulnerabilities that are closed as they're discovered by means of a patch. If an attacker can access an unpatched system, they may be able to introduce malware.

- Frequently, IoT devices will contact update servers to determine if updated firmware or configuration data is available. An attacker may intercept the DNS request and redirect the IoT device to a malicious source that hosts the malware or corrupt configuration data.

- The authentic website may be misconfigured in such a way to allow an attacker to take control of the website and replace authentic firmware with one that contains the attacker's malware.

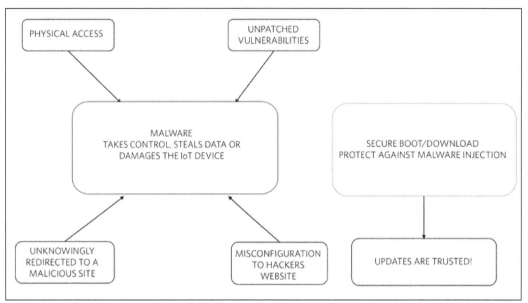

Attackers can infiltrate an unprotected IoT device versus a secured IoT device.

We can prevent infiltration and protect against malware injection by using secure boot and secure download. Thus, the IoT device can trust the updates being received from the command/control center. Protecting from malware injection with secure boot/download means the IoT device can trust the updates received from the command/control center.

Note that if a command/control center wants to fully trust the IoT device, there's an additional step that involves authenticating the IoT device's data. How do we go about protecting these devices by using secure boot and secure download?

Authentication and Integrity of the Firmware

Authentication and integrity can provide a way to:

- Ensure that the targeted embedded device runs only authorized firmware or configuration data.

- Confirm that the data is trusted and not subsequently modified.

- Allow cryptography to be used to prove that data is both authentic and has integrity.

- Utilize cryptographic digital signatures, like a seal or manual signature at the bottom of a letter.

With authentication and integrity, the firmware and configuration data are loaded during the manufacturing phase and all subsequent updates are digitally signed. This way, the digital signature enables trust during the device's entire lifetime. These features of digital signature are paramount to providing security:

- The digital signature used must be computed by a cryptographic algorithm.

- To bring the highest level of security, the algorithms need to be public and well-proven.

Asymmetric Cryptography Applied to Secure Boot/Download

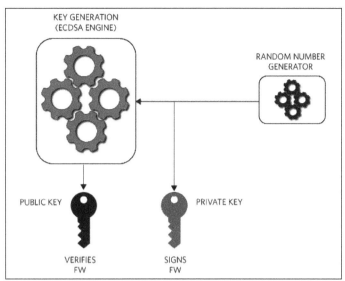

Asymmetric cryptography includes ECDSA key generation.

Asymmetric cryptography uses a public/private key pair for algorithm computations:

- The start of any key-pair generation includes selecting a random number to be used as the private key.

- The random number is input into the key generator and the computation begins outputting a public key.

- The public key is made public (it can be distributed freely to all without any security risk).

- However, the private key is critical information that must be kept confidential.

The fundamental principles of secure download in asymmetric cryptography are:

- The firmware developer uses the private key for signing.

- An embedded device (or an IoT device) uses the public key for verification.

So why use asymmetric key cryptography?

- The advantage is that no private key is stored on the embedded device.

- When using asymmetric cryptography, there's no way an attacker can retrieve the private key.

- Lastly, the algorithm chosen (i.e., ECDSA) makes it mathematically infeasible to derive the private key from the public key.

Secure Boot and Secure Download using DS28C36

A number of embedded devices don't have a secure microcontroller with the computational capacity to perform the required calculations to verify the authenticity and integrity of downloaded firmware or data. One cost-effective hardware-based IC solution is the DS28C36 DeepCover secure authenticator.

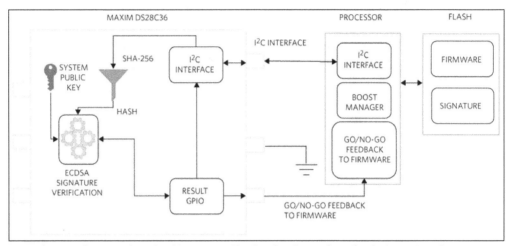

Secure boot and secure download in a cost-effective, hardware-based solution using the DS28C36.

Steps for secure boot and secure download:

- A system public-private key pair for the secure boot or secure download function is established at the R&D facility. The system private key of this pair is used to sign firmware or data that ultimately is verified by the DS28C36 embedded in the end system. This system private key never leaves the controlled development environment. The system public key of this pair is installed in the DS28C36 in a key register location that has an "authority key" attribute, which is a configurable setting in the DS28C36.

- The system private key is used to compute the digital signature of the firmware or data.

- The DS28C36 with the pre-programmed system public key is located on the interface to the host processor.

- When firmware is required to be run by the processor, it's first retrieved by the processor boot manager and delivered to the DS28C36 in sequential 64-byte blocks to compute a SHA-256 hash.

- After the DS28C36 completes the SHA-256 hash computation, the processor delivers the ECDSA signature of the firmware or data that was computed in the development environment and appended to the file.

- After the DS28C36 receives the ECDSA signature, the processor sends commands to use the preinstalled system public key to perform a signature verification.

- If the DS28C36 verifies the signature, a pass result parameter byte and a GPIO pin set to logic 0 is delivered to the processor. The status of this pin and parameter byte result acts as a go/no-go result to the processor to run the now known trusted firmware or data update.

- In addition, if the command/control center would like to trust the DS28C36, an extra ECDSA signature engine is optionally available.

We have shown a proven security solution for secure boot or secure download using the DS28C36 that addresses threats to IoT devices. This secure authenticator IC offloads the heavy computational math involved to prove both authenticity and integrity of firmware or data updates.

Bidirectional Authentication for IP Protection

Bidirectional (or mutual) authentication is an important part of secure communication. Both parties of communication should be certain that their counterpart can be trusted. This can be accomplished by proving possession of private information. This information can be shared between the parties, or kept completely private, as long as there's the ability to prove possession.

Symmetric authentication systems require information to be shared among all participants in a communication. This information is usually called a "secret." A secret is a piece of information not generally known; it's known only to those who need it. The secret is used in concert with a symmetric authentication algorithm such as SHA, along with other data shared between participants. The ability to generate a matching signature on both sides of communication proves possession of the secret.

Asymmetric authentication systems (like ECDSA) employ hidden information that's not shared between parties (known as a "private key"), but is used to produce information that can be known to the public (known as a "public key"). Proper use of the public key proves possession of the private key because the private key is needed to unlock a message locked by the public key and vice versa.

Slave Authentication

To authenticate a slave device in a master-slave configuration, a piece of random data (also known as a "challenge") is sent to a slave. Along with any shared data between the devices, the challenge is run through a signing operation with a secret or private key to produce a "response" signature. The response signature can be verified by the master because the master is in possession of the shared secret, or a public key that corresponds to the slave's private key. The general flow of this process is shown in figure.

Authentication generally depends on algorithms that produce signatures proving possession of a participant's hidden information but make it difficult to discover the information itself. These are known as one-way functions. SHA and ECDSA are examples of such algorithms.

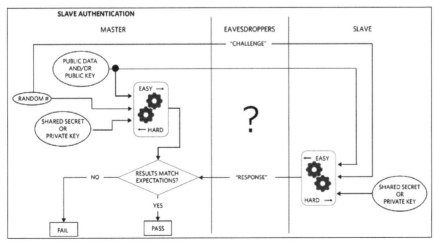

Slave device authentication in a master-slave system.

Master Authentication

To prove all parties can be trusted, the master must also need to prove authenticity to the slave. An example of this process is shown in the form of an authenticated write.

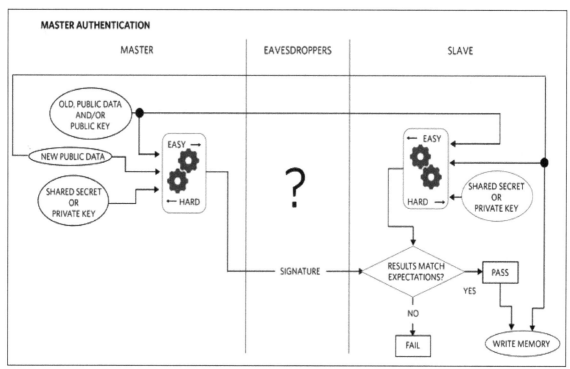

A master writes new data into a slave device.

In *Figure*, the master is writing new data into a slave device. However, to complete the write, the slave must verify authenticity of the information by requiring the master to produce a signature based on that information, as well as the master's hidden data (secret or private key). By using either a shared secret or the public key corresponding to the master's private key, the slave can verify that the signature is authentic.

The use of one-way functions may allow any eavesdroppers to see all data being transmitted, but it prevents them from determining the hidden information that produced the signatures associated with the data. Without this hidden information, eavesdroppers can't become impersonators.

This two-way authentication model can easily be used to make sure that intellectual property (IP) stored in a device will be well-protected from counterfeiters.

TRNG Output and Typical Use

Maxim's ChipDNA secure authenticators have a built-in true random number generator (TRNG). This is used by the device for internal purposes. But they also have a command that sends out the TRNG output if the user requests it. At this time, the maximum length of the TRNG output length is 64 bytes. This hardware NIST-compliant random number source can be used for cryptographic needs such as "challenge (nonce)" generation by a host processor.

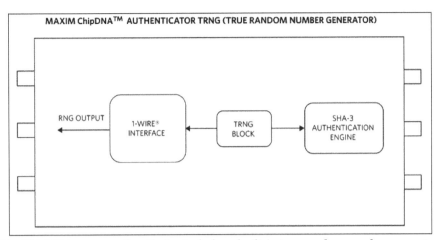

The ChipDNA secure authenticator includes a built-in true random number generator.

Cryptographic Hardware Accelerators

A Cryptographic Hardware Accelerator can be:

- Integrated into the soc as a separate processor, as special purpose CPU (aka Core).

- Integrated in a W Coprocessor on the circuit board.

- Contained on a Chip on an extension circuit board, this can be connected to the mainboard via some BUS, e.g. PCI.

- An W ISA extension like e.g. W AES instruction set and thus integral part of the CPU (in that case a kernel driver is not needed).

The purpose is to load off the very computing intensive tasks of encryption/decryption and compression/decompression. The acceleration is usually achieved by doing certain arithmetic calculation in hardware. Its use in application usually involve a number of layers:

- The kernel needs a hardware-specific driver to use its capabilities. It is usually built into the kernel for boards that support them, and allow access by services that run in kernel-mode.

- To use them in userspace, when the acceleration is not in the instruction set of the CPU, it is supported via a kernel driver (/dev/crypto or AF_ALG socket).

- The above steps provide the bare minimum to allow userspace use, but it is more usual to use them inside a crypto library, such as gnutls or openssl, allowing access by most apps linked to them.

Performance

Depending on which arithmetic calculations exactly are being done in the specific hardware, the results differ widely. You should not concern yourself with theoretical bla, bla but find out how a certain implementation performs in the task you want to do with it! You could want to:

- You could attach a USB drive to your device and mount a local filesystem like ext3 from it. Then you want to read from and write to this filesystem from the Internet over a secured protocol. Let's use sshfs. You would set up a sshfs.server on your device and a sshfs.client on the other end. Now how fast can you read/write to this with and without Cryptographic Hardware Accelerators? If the other end, the client, is a "fully grown PC" with a 2GHz CPU, it will probably perform fast enough to use the entire bandwidth of your Internet connection. If the server side is some embedded device, with let's say some 400MHz MIPS CPU, it could benefit highly from some integrated (and supported!) acceleration. You probably want enough performance, that you can use your entire bandwidth. Well, now go and find some benchmark showing you precisely the difference with enabled/disabled acceleration. Because you will not be able to extrapolate this information from specifications you find on this page or on the web.

- You could want to run an OpenVPN or an OpenConnect server on your router/embedded device, instead of using WEP/WPA/WPA2. There will be no reading from/writing to a USB device. Find benchmarks that show you exactly the performance for this purpose. You won't be able to extrapolate this information from other benchmarks.

- Think of other practical uses, and find specific benchmarks.

Finding out what's Available in the Kernel

If your boards supports hardware crypto acceleration, the respective drivers should already be built into the kernel. Some crypto engines have their own packages, and these may need to be installed first.

To see all of the available crypto drivers running on your system (this means *after* installing the packages, if needed), take a look at /proc/crypto.

```
# cat /proc/crypto
name         : cbc(aes)
driver       : mv-cbc-aes
module       : kernel
priority     : 300
refcnt       : 1
selftest     : passed
internal     : no
type         : skcipher
async        : yes
blocksize    : 16
min keysize  : 16
max keysize  : 32
ivsize       : 16
```

```
chunksize     : 16
walksize      : 16
name          : cbc(aes)
driver        : cbc-aes-neonbs
module        : kernel
priority      : 250
refcnt        : 1
selftest      : passed
internal      : no
type          : skcipher
async         : yes
blocksize     : 16
min keysize   : 16
max keysize   : 32
ivsize        : 16
chunksize     : 16
walksize      : 16
name          : sha256
driver        : mv-sha256
module        : kernel
priority      : 300
refcnt        : 1
selftest      : passed
internal      : no
type          : ahash
async         : yes
blocksize     : 64
digestsize    : 32
name          : sha256
driver        : sha256-neon
module        : kernel
priority      : 250
refcnt        : 2
```

```
selftest      : passed

internal      : no

type          : shash

blocksize     : 64

digestsize    : 32

name          : sha256

driver        : sha256-asm

module        : kernel

priority      : 150

refcnt        : 1

selftest      : passed

internal      : no

type          : shash

blocksize     : 64

digestsize    : 32

name          : sha256

driver        : sha256-generic

module        : sha256_generic

priority      : 100

refcnt        : 1

selftest      : passed

internal      : no

type          : shash

blocksize     : 64

digestsize    : 32
```

This was edited to only show AES-CBC and SHA256. Both AF_ALG and /dev/crypto interfaces allow userspace access to any crypto driver offering symmetric-key ciphers, and digest algorithms. That means hardware acceleration, but also software-only drivers. The use of software drivers is almost always slower than implementing it in userspace, as the context switches slow things down considerably.

To identify hardware-drivers, look for drivers with types `skcipher` and `shash`, having priority >= 300, but beware that AES-NI and similar CPU instructions will have a high priority as well, and do not need /dev/crypto or AF_ALG to be used.

Notice in this case, that are two drivers offering `cbc(aes)`: `cbc-aes-neonbs`(software driver, using neon asm instruction, and `mv-cbc-aes`(Marvell CESA, hw accelerated), and four offering `sha256: sha256-generic`(soft, generic C code), `sha256-asm`(soft, basic arm asm), `sha256-neon` (soft, using neon asm instruction), and `mv-sha256` (Marvell CESA). The kernel will export the one with the highest priority for each algorithm. In this case, it would be the hw accelerated Marvell CESA drivers: mv-cbc-aes, and mv-sha256.

For IPsec ESP, which is done by the Kernel, this will be enough to tell you if you are able to use the crypto accelerator, and you don't need to do anything further. Just make sure you're using the same algorithm made available by your crypto driver.

Enabling the Userspace Interface

The crypto drivers enable the algorithms for kernel use. To be able to access them from userspace, another driver needs to be used. In OpenWrt, there are two of them: `cryptodev`, and `AF_ALG`. Opinions on the subject may vary, but /dev/crypto has the speed advantage here.

Cryptodev

Cryptodev uses a `/dev/crypto` device to export the kernel algorithms. In OpenWrt 19.07 and later, it is provided by the `kmod-cryptodev`, and is installed automatically when you install `libopenssl-devcrypto`.

In OpenWrt 18.06.x and earlier, /dev/crypto required compiling the driver yourself. Run `make menuconfig` and select:

- kmod-crypto-core: m

    ○ kmod-cryptodev: m

Installing the `kmod-cryptodev` package will create a `/dev/crypto` device, even if you don't have any hw-crypto. `/dev/crypto` will export kernel crypto drivers regardless of being implemented in software or hardware. Use of kernel software drivers may severely slow crypto performance! Don't install this package unless you know you have `hw-crypto` drivers installed.

AF_ALG

The AF_ALG interface uses sockets to allow access to the kernel crypto algorithms, so you won't see anything in the filesystem. It is provided by the `kmod-crypto-user` package.

Checking Openssl Support

Openssl supports hardware crypto acceleration through an engine. You may find out what engines are available, along with the enabled algorithms, and configuration commands by running `openssl engine -t -c`:

```
(devcrypto) /dev/crypto engine

 [DES-CBC, DES-EDE3-CBC, BF-CBC, AES-128-CBC, AES-192-CBC, AES-256-CBC, AES-
128-CTR, AES-192-CTR, AES-256-CTR, AES-128-ECB, AES-192-ECB, AES-256-ECB, CA-
MELLIA-128-CBC,
```

```
CAMELLIA-192-CBC, CAMELLIA-256-CBC,MD5, SHA1, RIPEMD160, SHA224, SHA256, SHA384,
SHA512]
```

    [available]

```
(rdrand) Intel RDRAND engine
```

 [RAND]

    [available]

```
(dynamic) Dynamic engine loading support
```

    [unavailable]

For openssl-1.0.2 and earlier, the engine was called `cryptodev`. It was renamed to `devcrypto` in openssl 1.1.0. In this example, engine 'devcrypto' is available, showing the list of algorithms available.

Starting in OpenSSL 1.1.0, an AF_ALG engine can be used. In OpenWrt 19.07, it is packaged as `libopenssl-afalg`, but it requires a custom built: the package will not show up under 'Libraries', 'SSL', 'libopenssl' unless you go to 'Global build settings', 'Kernel build options', and select 'Compile the kernel with asynchronous IO support'. This engine supports only AES-CBC, and needs to be enabled in `/etc/ssl/openssl.cnf`, but it does not accept the CIPHERS, DIGESTSS, or `USE_SOFTDRIVERS` options.

In OpenWrt 19.07, the shipped `/etc/ssl/openssl.cnf` already has the basic engine configuration sections for both the devcrypto and the orignal afalg engines. To enable them, uncomment the respective lines under the `[engines]` section.

Shortly after 19.07.0 was released, an alternate AF_ALG engine was added, `libopenssl-afalg_sync` that is basically a mirror of the devcrypto engine, but using the AF_ALG interface. It accepts all of the options, and is configured the same way as the `devcrypto` engine. You may follow the steps below, just configure it under `afalg`, instead of `devcrypto`. As of 19.07.0, the `openssl.cnf` file does not have the CIPHERS, DIGESTS and USE_ SOFTDRIVERS options listed, but you can just copy them from the [devcrypto] section. Note that the OpenWrt package is called `afalg_sync`, but for openssl the engine it is simply `afalg`. It can't coexist with the original engine. its creator, cotequeiroz, states that the afalg_sync (as of v1.0.1) performance is better than the original afalg engine, but poorer than devcrypto.

Checking Openssl Support for AES-NI hw Crypto on x86_64 (Normal PC Hardware)

OpenSSL in OpenWrt on x86 supports AES-NI CPU instructions natively and should use them automatically where available. You can try two different commands and see if performance is different. This should use AES-NI and should have bigger performance:

```
openssl speed -elapsed -evp aes-128-cbc
```

This has a runtime switch that disables use of AES-NI in openSSL and should therefore have lower performance.

```
OPENSSL_ia32cap="~0x200000200000000" openssl speed -elapsed -evp aes-128-cbc
```

This is an example of the results, showing the OpenSSL with AES-NI support (faster).

```
root@routegateway:~# openssl speed -elapsed -evp aes-128-cbc

You have chosen to measure elapsed time instead of user CPU time.

Doing aes-128-cbc for 3s on 16 size blocks: 117879925 aes-128-cbc's in 3.00s

Doing aes-128-cbc for 3s on 64 size blocks: 39584711 aes-128-cbc's in 3.00s

Doing aes-128-cbc for 3s on 256 size blocks: 10062149 aes-128-cbc's in 3.00s

Doing aes-128-cbc for 3s on 1024 size blocks: 2530718 aes-128-cbc's in 3.00s

Doing aes-128-cbc for 3s on 8192 size blocks: 318704 aes-128-cbc's in 3.00s

Doing aes-128-cbc for 3s on 16384 size blocks: 158373 aes-128-cbc's in 3.00s

OpenSSL 1.1.1g  21 Apr 2020

built on: Sun Aug  2 16:16:00 2020 UTC

options:bn(64,64) rc4(16x,int) des(int) aes(partial) blowfish(ptr)

compiler: x86_64-openwrt-linux-musl-gcc -fPIC -pthread -m64 -Wa,--noexecstack
-Wall -O3 -pipe -fno-caller-saves -fno-plt -fhonour-copts -Wno-error=unused-
but-set-variable  -Wno-error=unused-result  -Wformat  -Werror=format-security
-fstack-protector -D_FORTIFY_SOURCE=1 -Wl,-z,now -Wl,-z,relro -O3 -fpic -ffunc-
tion-sections -fdata-sections -znow -zrelro -DOPENSSL_USE_NODELETE -DL_ENDI-
AN -DOPENSSL_PIC -DOPENSSL_CPUID_OBJ -DOPENSSL_IA32_SSE2 -DOPENSSL_BN_ASM_MONT
-DOPENSSL_BN_ASM_MONT5 -DOPENSSL_BN_ASM_GF2m -DSHA1_ASM -DSHA256_ASM -DSHA512_
ASM -DKECCAK1600_ASM -DRC4_ASM -DMD5_ASM -DAESNI_ASM -DVPAES_ASM -DGHASH_ASM
-DECP_NISTZ256_ASM -DX25519_ASM -DPOLY1305_ASM -DNDEBUG

The 'numbers' are in 1000s of bytes per second processed.
```

type	16 bytes	64 bytes	256 bytes	1024 bytes	8192 bytes	16384 bytes
aes-128-cbc	628692.93k	844473.83k	858636.71k	863818.41k	870274.39k	864927.74k

and this is the result without AES-NI support (slower).

```
root@routegateway:~# OPENSSL_ia32cap="~0x200000200000000" openssl speed -elapsed
-evp aes-128-cbc

You have chosen to measure elapsed time instead of user CPU time.

Doing aes-128-cbc for 3s on 16 size blocks: 37905593 aes-128-cbc's in 3.00s

Doing aes-128-cbc for 3s on 64 size blocks: 10779104 aes-128-cbc's in 3.00s

Doing aes-128-cbc for 3s on 256 size blocks: 2769347 aes-128-cbc's in 3.00s

Doing aes-128-cbc for 3s on 1024 size blocks: 702288 aes-128-cbc's in 3.00s

Doing aes-128-cbc for 3s on 8192 size blocks: 88129 aes-128-cbc's in 3.00s

Doing aes-128-cbc for 3s on 16384 size blocks: 44055 aes-128-cbc's in 3.00s
```

```
OpenSSL 1.1.1g  21 Apr 2020

built on: Sun Aug  2 16:16:00 2020 UTC

options:bn(64,64) rc4(16x,int) des(int) aes(partial) blowfish(ptr)

compiler: x86_64-openwrt-linux-musl-gcc -fPIC -pthread -m64 -Wa,--noexecstack
-Wall -O3 -pipe -fno-caller-saves -fno-plt -fhonour-copts -Wno-error=unused-
but-set-variable  -Wno-error=unused-result  -Wformat  -Werror=format-security
-fstack-protector -D_FORTIFY_SOURCE=1 -Wl,-z,now -Wl,-z,relro -O3 -fpic -ffunc-
tion-sections -fdata-sections -znow -zrelro -DOPENSSL_USE_NODELETE -DL_ENDI-
AN -DOPENSSL_PIC -DOPENSSL_CPUID_OBJ -DOPENSSL_IA32_SSE2 -DOPENSSL_BN_ASM_MONT
-DOPENSSL_BN_ASM_MONT5 -DOPENSSL_BN_ASM_GF2m -DSHA1_ASM -DSHA256_ASM -DSHA512_
ASM -DKECCAK1600_ASM -DRC4_ASM -DMD5_ASM -DAESNI_ASM -DVPAES_ASM -DGHASH_ASM
-DECP_NISTZ256_ASM -DX25519_ASM -DPOLY1305_ASM -DNDEBUG

The 'numbers' are in 1000s of bytes per second processed.
```

type	16 bytes	64 bytes	256 bytes	1024 bytes	8192 bytes	16384 bytes
aes-128-cbc	202163.16k	229954.22k	236317.61k	239714.30k	240650.92k	240599.04k

Using the Libopenssl-Devcrypto Package

Starting with 19.x branch, the `/dev/crypto` support can be packaged separately from the main openssl library, as the `libopenssl-devcrypto` package. The engine is not enabled by default, even when the package is installed. It requires editing the `/etc/ssl/openssl.cnf`, as follows.

Configuring the Devcrypto Engine

When using the standalone package, this becomes mandatory. If the engine is built into libcrypto, it is only optional. To configure the engine, you must first add a line to the default section (i.e. the first, unnamed section), adding the following line, which tells which section is used to configure the library. The sections are lines within brackets [ ]:

```
# this points to the main library configuration section

openssl_conf = openssl_def
```

This will point the main openssl configuration to be done in a section called `openssl_def`. Then, that section needs to be created, anywhere past the last line in the unnamed section. I'd just add it to the very end of the file. It will add an engine configuration section, where you can add a section for every engine you're configuring, and finally, a section to configure the engine itself. In this example, we are configuring just the /dev/crypto engine:

```
[openssl_def]

# this is the main library configuration section

engines=engine_section

[engine_section]
```

```
# this is the engine configuration section, where the engines are listed
devcrypto=devcrypto_section

[devcrypto_section]
# this is the section where the devcrypto engine commands are used
CIPHERS=ALL

DIGESTS=NONE
```

You can use the -vv option of the `openssl` engine command to view the available configuration commands, along with a description of each command. Notice the line disabling all digests. Digests are computed fairly fast in software, and to use hardware crypto requires a context switch, which is an "expensive" operation. So in order to be worth using an algorithm, it needs to be much faster than software to offset the cost of the context switch. Efficiency depends on the length of each operation. For ciphers, it is faster to use hardware than software in chunks of 1000 bytes or more, depending on your hardware. For digests, the size has to be 10x greater. Considering an MTU of 1500 bytes, which is the de facto limit on TLS encryption block limit, it will not be worth to enable digests. You can use a different configuration file for every application, by setting the environment variable `OPENSSL_CONF` to the full path of the configuration file to be used.

Showing /dev/crypto Algorithm Information

There's a command for the devcrypto engine, not to be used in `openssl.cnf`, that will show some useful information about the algorithms available. It shows a list of engine-supported algorithms, if it can be used (a session can be opened) with /dev/crypto or not, along with the corresponding kernel driver, and if it hw-accelerated or no. To use it, run:

```
# openssl engine -pre DUMP_INFO devcrypto

(devcrypto) /dev/crypto engine

Information about ciphers supported by the /dev/crypto engine:

Cipher DES-CBC, NID=31, /dev/crypto info: id=1, driver=mv-cbc-des (hw acceler-
ated)

Cipher DES-EDE3-CBC, NID=44, /dev/crypto info: id=2, driver=mv-cbc-des3-ede (hw
accelerated)

Cipher BF-CBC, NID=91, /dev/crypto info: id=3, CIOCGSESSION (session open call)
failed

Cipher CAST5-CBC, NID=108, /dev/crypto info: id=4, CIOCGSESSION (session open
call) failed

Cipher AES-128-CBC, NID=419, /dev/crypto info: id=11, driver=mv-cbc-aes (hw ac-
celerated)

Cipher AES-192-CBC, NID=423, /dev/crypto info: id=11, driver=mv-cbc-aes (hw ac-
celerated)

Cipher AES-256-CBC, NID=427, /dev/crypto info: id=11, driver=mv-cbc-aes (hw ac-
celerated)
```

```
Cipher RC4, NID=5, /dev/crypto info: id=12, CIOCGSESSION (session open call)
failed

Cipher AES-128-CTR, NID=904, /dev/crypto info: id=21, driver=ctr-aes-neonbs
(software)

Cipher AES-192-CTR, NID=905, /dev/crypto info: id=21, driver=ctr-aes-neonbs
(software)

Cipher AES-256-CTR, NID=906, /dev/crypto info: id=21, driver=ctr-aes-neonbs
(software)

Cipher AES-128-ECB, NID=418, /dev/crypto info: id=23, driver=mv-ecb-aes (hw ac-
celerated)

Cipher AES-192-ECB, NID=422, /dev/crypto info: id=23, driver=mv-ecb-aes (hw ac-
celerated)

Cipher AES-256-ECB, NID=426, /dev/crypto info: id=23, driver=mv-ecb-aes (hw ac-
celerated)


Information about digests supported by the /dev/crypto engine:

Digest MD5, NID=4, /dev/crypto info: id=13, driver=mv-md5 (hw accelerated), CI-
OCCPHASH capable

Digest SHA1, NID=64, /dev/crypto info: id=14, driver=mv-sha1 (hw accelerated),
CIOCCPHASH capable

Digest RIPEMD160, NID=117, /dev/crypto info: id=102, driver=unknown. CIOCGSES-
SION (session open) failed

Digest SHA224, NID=675, /dev/crypto info: id=103, driver=sha224-neon (soft-
ware), CIOCCPHASH capable

Digest SHA256, NID=672, /dev/crypto info: id=104, driver=mv-sha256 (hw acceler-
ated), CIOCCPHASH capable

Digest SHA384, NID=673, /dev/crypto info: id=105, driver=sha384-neon (soft-
ware), CIOCCPHASH capable

Digest SHA512, NID=674, /dev/crypto info: id=106, driver=sha512-neon (soft-
ware), CIOCCPHASH capable
```

Measuring the Algorithm Speed

As stated above, the best way to determine the speed is benchmarking the actual application you're using. If that›s not feasible, `openssl speed` can be used to compare the algorithm speed with and without the engine. To measure the speed without the engine, set `CIPHERS=NONE` and `DI-GESTS=NONE` in `/etc/ssl/openssl.cnf`. You must use the `-elapsed` option to get a reasonable calculation. That's because the speed command will use the CPU user time by default. When using the engine, most all of the processing will be done in kernel time, and the user time will be close to zero, yielding an exaggerated result. This is the measurement of the AES-256-CTR algorithm, implemented 100% in software (you must configure `USE_SOFTDRIVERS=1` in `openssl.cnf` to be able to use software drivers with devcrypto).

```
# time openssl speed -evp aes-256-ctr

Doing aes-256-ctr for 3s on 16 size blocks: 1506501 aes-256-ctr's in 0.32s

Doing aes-256-ctr for 3s on 64 size blocks: 830921 aes-256-ctr's in 0.18s

Doing aes-256-ctr for 3s on 256 size blocks: 526267 aes-256-ctr's in 0.15s

Doing aes-256-ctr for 3s on 1024 size blocks: 167828 aes-256-ctr's in 0.07s

Doing aes-256-ctr for 3s on 8192 size blocks: 22723 aes-256-ctr's in 0.00s

Doing aes-256-ctr for 3s on 16384 size blocks: 11400 aes-256-ctr's in 0.00s

OpenSSL 1.1.1b  26 Feb 2019

built on: Wed Dec 13 18:43:03 2017 UTC

options:bn(64,32) rc4(char) des(long) aes(partial) blowfish(ptr)

compiler: arm-openwrt-linux-muslgnueabi-gcc -fPIC -pthread -Wa,--noexecstack
-Wall -O3 -pipe -mcpu=cortex-a9 -mfpu=vfpv3-d16 -fno-caller-saves -fno-plt
-fhonour-copts    -Wno-error=unused-but-set-variable    -Wno-error=unused-result
-mfloat-abi=hard -Wformat -Werror=format-security -fstack-protector -D_FORTIFY_
SOURCE=1 -Wl,-z,now -Wl,-z,relro -O3 -fpic -ffunction-sections -fdata-sections
-znow -zrelro -DOPENSSL_USE_NODELETE -DOPENSSL_PIC -DOPENSSL_CPUID_OBJ -DOPENS-
SL_BN_ASM_MONT -DOPENSSL_BN_ASM_GF2m -DSHA1_ASM -DSHA256_ASM -DSHA512_ASM -DKE-
CCAK1600_ASM -DAES_ASM -DBSAES_ASM -DGHASH_ASM -DECP_NISTZ256_ASM -DPOLY1305_
ASM -DNDEBUG -DOPENSSL_PREFER_CHACHA_OVER_GCM

The 'numbers' are in 1000s of bytes per second processed.
```

type	16 bytes	64 bytes	256 bytes	1024 bytes	8192 bytes
16384 bytes					
aes-256-ctr	75325.05k	295438.58k	898162.35k	2455083.89k	infk
infk					

```
real    0m 18.04s

user    0m 0.72s

sys     0m 17.27s
```

Notice the infinite speeds. If you spend 0 seconds in CPU user time, and use that as a divisor, you'll get infinite. The speed command, with the addition of the -elapsed parameter will return a more realistic result:

```
# time openssl speed -evp aes-256-ctr -elapsed
```

type	16 bytes	64 bytes	256 bytes	1024 bytes	8192 bytes
16384 bytes					
aes-256-ctr	7975.70k	17403.54k	44777.30k	57178.79k	62076.25k
62395.73k					

```
real    0m 18.04s

user    0m 0.88s

sys     0m 17.11s
```

This is the result of the AES-256-CTR without the engine:

```
type                16 bytes      64 bytes     256 bytes    1024 bytes    8192 bytes
16384 bytes

aes-256-ctr         39684.36k     47027.86k    53044.99k    60888.06k     63548.07k
63706.45k

real    0m 18.04s

user    0m 17.98s

sys     0m 0.00s
```

In this case -elapsed does not matter much, as almost 100% of the execution time is spent in user-mode, and CPU user time would actually be a better measurement by not counting time spent in other processes. With that out of the way, let's see an actual hardware-implemented cipher:

```
# time openssl speed -evp aes-256-cbc -elapsed
```

```
The 'numbers' are in 1000s of bytes per second processed.

type                16 bytes      64 bytes     256 bytes    1024 bytes    8192 bytes
16384 bytes

aes-256-cbc         1551.04k      6126.44k     21527.81k    55995.05k     95027.20k
99936.94k

real    0m 18.04s

user    0m 0.21s

sys     0m 5.13s
```

For comparison, this is the same cipher, implemented by the libcrypto software:

```
# time openssl speed -evp aes-256-cbc -elapsed
```

```
type                16 bytes      64 bytes     256 bytes    1024 bytes    8192 bytes
16384 bytes

aes-256-cbc         39603.10k     47420.37k    50270.38k    51002.71k     51249.15k
51232.77k

real    0m 18.03s

user    0m 18.00s

sys     0m 0.01s
```

This is typical for a/dev/crypto cipher. There's a cost in CPU usage, the context switches needed to run the code in the kernel, represented by the 5.13s of system time used. That cost will not vary much with the size of the crypto operation. Because of that, for small batches, the use of hardware drivers will slow you down considerably. As the block size increases, /dev/crypto becomes the best choice. You must be aware of how the application uses the cipher. For example, AES-128-ECB is used by openssl to seed the rng, using 16-bytes calls.

Disabling Digests

Please, don't enable digests unless you know what you're doing. They are usually slower than software, except for large (> 10k) blocks. Some applications—openssh, for example—will not work with

/dev/crypto digests. This is a limitation of how the engine works. Openssh will save a partial digest, and then fork, duplicating that context, and working with successive copies of it, which is useful for HMAC, where the hash of the key remains constant. In the kernel, however, those contexts are still linked to the same session, so when one process calls another update, or closes that digest context, the kernel session is changed/closed for all of the instances, and you'll get a libcrypto failure. For well-behaved applications using large update blocks, you may enable digests. Use a separate copy of the `openssl.cnf` configuration file, and set `OPENSSL_CONF=_path_to_file` in the environment before running it (add it to the respective file in /etc/init.d/). Again, benchmarking the actual application you're using is the best way to gauge the impact of hardware crypto.

Cryptographic Hash Function

Hash Function produces a fingerprint of some file/message/data h = H(M) condenses a variable-length message M to a fixed-sized finger print .this is assumed to be public.

Requirements for Hash Functions

The hash function can be applied to any sized message M produces fixed-length output h is easy to compute h=H(M) for any message M, given h is infeasible to find x s.t. H(x)=h .one-way property given x is infeasible to find y s.t. H(y)=H(x) weak collision resistance is infeasible to find any x,y s.t. H(y)=H(x) strong collision resistance. These are the specifications for good hash functions. Essentially it must be extremely difficult to find 2 messages with the same hash, and the hash should not be related to the message in any obvious way (ie it should be a complex non-linear function of the message). There are quite a few similarities in the evolution of hash functions & block ciphers, and in the evolution of the design requirements on both.

Block Ciphers as Hash Functions

The block ciphers can be used as a hash functions using $H_0=0$ and zero-pad of final block compute: $H_i = E_{M_i} [H_{i-1}]$ and use final block as the hash value similar to CBC but without a key resulting hash is too small (64-bit) both due to direct birthday attack and to "meet-in-the-middle" attack other variants also susceptible to attack.

Hash Algorithms

The similarities in the evolution of hash functions & block ciphers are increasing power of brute-force attacks this leads to evolution in algorithms like DES to AES in block cipher and from MD4 & MD5 to SHA-1 & RIPEMD-160 in hash algorithms .likewise tend to use common iterative structure as do block ciphers.

MD5

MD5 is the current, and very widely used, member of Rivest's family of hash functions. It is designed by Ronald Rivest (the R in RSA) the latest in a series of MD2, MD4 it produces a 128-bit hash value until recently was the most widely used hash algorithm ,in recent times have both brute-force & cryptanalytic concerns specified as Internet standard RFC1321. The padded message is broken into 512-bit blocks, processed along with the buffer value using 4 rounds, and the result added to the input buffer to make the new buffer value. Repeat till run out of message, and use final buffer value as hash. nb. Due to padding always have a full final block (with length in it).

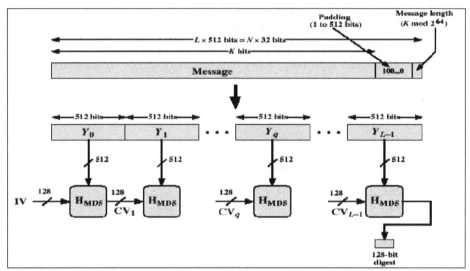

MD5 Overview.

MD5 Compression Function

Each round mixes the buffer input with the next "word" of the message in a complex, non-linear manner. A different non-linear function is used in each of the 4 rounds (but the same function for all 16 steps in a round). The 4 buffer words (a,b,c,d) are rotated from step to step so all are used and updated. g is one of the primitive functions F,G,H,I for the 4 rounds respectively. X[k] is the kth 32-bit word in the current message block. T[i] is the ith entry in the matrix of constants T. The addition of varying constants T and the use of different shifts helps ensure it are extremely difficult to compute collisions. Each round has 16 steps of the form:

$$a \ b + ((a + g(b,c,d) + X[k] + T[i]) <<< s)$$

a,b,c,d refer to the 4 words of the buffer, but used in varying permutations note this updates 1 word only of the buffer after 16 steps each word is updated 4 times. Where g(b,c,d) is a different nonlinear function in each round (F,G,H,I) T[i] is a constant value derived from sin.

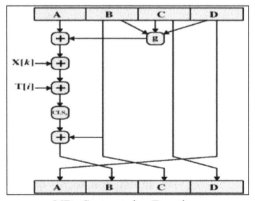

MD5 Compression Function.

MD4

MD4 is the precursor to MD5, and was widely used. It uses 3 instead of 4 rounds, and the round functions are a little simpler. In creating MD5 Rivels aimed to strengthen the algorithms by introducing the extra round and varying the constants used. MD5 design goals: collision resistant (hard to find collisions), direct security (no dependence on "hard" problems), fast, simple, compact, favours little-endian systems (e.g. PCs).

Strength of MD5

Some progress has been made analysing MD5, which along with the hash size of 128-bits means it's starting to look too small. Hence interest in hash functions that create larger hashes. MD5 hash is dependent on all message bits Rivest claims security is good as can be known attacks are Berson 92 attacked any 1 round using differential cryptanalysis (but can't extend) Boer & Bosselaers 93 found a pseudo collision (again unable to extend) Dobbertin 96 created collisions on MD compression function (but initial constants prevent exploit) conclusion is that MD5 looks vulnerable soon.

Secure Hash Algorithm (SHA)

The Secure Hash Algorithm (SHA) was developed by the National Institute of Standards and Technology (NIST) and published as a federal information processing standard (FIPS 180) in 1993; a revised version was issued as FIPS 180-1 in 1995 and is generally referred to as SHA-1. The actual standards document is entitled Secure Hash Standard. SHA is based on the hash function MD4 and its design closely models MD4. SHA-1 is also specified in RFC 3174, which essentially duplicates the material in FIPS 180-1, but adds a C code implementation.

SHA-1 produces a hash value of 160 bits. In 2002, NIST produced a revised version of the standard, FIPS 180-2, that defined three new versions of SHA, with hash value lengths of 256, 384, and 512 bits, known as SHA-256, SHA384, and SHA-512. These new versions have the same underlying structure and use the same types of modular arithmetic and logical binary operations as SHA-1. In 2005, NIST announced the intention to phase out approval of SHA-1 and move to a reliance on the other SHA versions by 2010. Shortly thereafter, a research team described an attack in which two separate messages could be found that deliver the same SHA-1 hash using 269 operations, far fewer than the 280 operations previously thought needed to find a collision with an SHA-1 hash. This result should hasten the transition to the other versions of SHA.

Table: Comparison of SHA Parameters.

	SHA-1	SHA-256	SHA-384	SHA-1 512
Message digest size	160	256	384	512
Message size	$<2^{64}$	$<2^{64}$	$<2^{128}$	$<2^{128}$
Block size	512	512	1024	1024
Word size	32	32	64	64
Number of steps	80	64	80	80
Security	80	128	192	256

- All sizes are measured in bits.

- Security refers to the fact that a birthday attack on a message digest of size n produces a collision with a work factor of approximately $2^{n/2}$.

SHA-512 Logic

The algorithm takes as input a message with a maximum length of less than 2128 bits and produces as output a 512-bit message digest. The input is processed in 1024-bit blocks. Figure depicts the overall processing of a message to produce a digest.

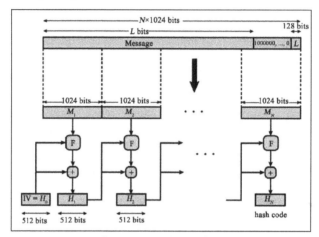

Message Digest Generation Using SHA-512.

The processing consists of the following steps:

Step 1: Append padding bits. The message is padded so that its length is congruent to 896 modulo 1024 [length 896 (mod 1024)]. Padding is always added, even if the message is already of the desired length. Thus, the number of padding bits is in the range of 1 to 1024. The padding consists of a single 1-bit followed by the necessary number of 0-bits.

Step 2: Append length. A block of 128 bits is appended to the message. This block is treated as an unsigned 128-bit integer (most significant byte first) and contains the length of the original message (before the padding). The outcome of the first two steps yields a message that is an integer multiple of 1024 bits in length. In Figure, the expanded message is represented as the sequence of 1024-bit blocks M1, M2,..., MN, so that the total length of the expanded message is N x 1024 bits.

Step 3: Initialize hash buffer. A 512-bit buffer is used to hold intermediate and final results of the hash function. The buffer can be represented as eight 64-bit registers (a, b, c, d, e, f, g, h). These registers are initialized to the following 64-bit integers (hexadecimal values):

a = 6A09E667F3BCC908

b = BB67AE8584CAA73B

c = 3C6EF372FE94F82B

c = A54FF53A5F1D36F1

e = 510E527FADE682D1

f = 9B05688C2B3E6C1F

g = 1F83D9ABFB41BD6B

h = 5BE0CDI9137E2179

These values are stored in big-endian format, which is the most significant byte of a word in the low-address (leftmost) byte position. These words were obtained by taking the first sixty-four bits of the fractional parts of the square roots of the first eight prime numbers.

Step 4: Process message in 1024-bit (128-word) blocks. The heart of the algorithm is a module that consists of 80 rounds; this module is labeled F in Figure. The logic is illustrated in figure.

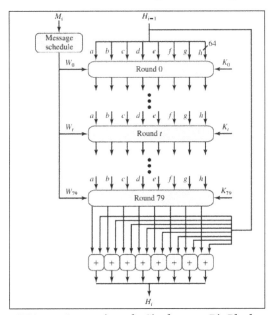

SHA-512 Processing of a Single 1024-Bit Block.

Each round takes as input the 512-bit buffer value abcdefgh, and updates the contents of the buffer. At input to the first round, the buffer has the value of the intermediate hash value, H_{i-1}. Each round t makes use of a 64-bit value W_t derived from the current 1024-bit block being processed (M_i) these values are derived using a message schedule described subsequently. Each round also makes use of an additive constant K_t where 0 t 79 indicates one of the 80 rounds. These words represent the first sixty-four bits of the fractional parts of the cube roots of the first eighty prime numbers. The constants provide a "randomized" set of 64-bit patterns, which should eliminate any regularities in the input data. The output of the eightieth round is added to the input to the first round (H_{i-1}) to produce H_i. The addition is done independently for each of the eight words in the buffer with each of the corresponding words in H_{i-1} using addition modulo 264.

Step 5: Output. After all N 1024-bit blocks have been processed, the output from the Nth stage is the 512-bit message digest. We can summarize the behavior of SHA-512 as follows:

$$H_0 = IV$$
$$H_i = SUM_{64}\left(H_{i-1},\ abcdefgh_i\right)$$
$$MD = H_N$$

Where,

- IV = initial value of the abcdefgh buffer, defined in step 3.

- $abcdefgh_i$ = the output of the last round of processing of the ith message block.

- N = the number of blocks in the message (including padding and length fields).

- SUM_{64} = Addition modulo 264 performed separately on each word of the pair of inputs.

- MD = final message digest value.

SHA-512 Round Function

Let us look in more detail at the logic in each of the 80 steps of the processing of one 512-bit block. Each round is defined by the following set of equations:

$$T_1 = h + Ch(e,f,g) + \left(\sum_1^{512} e\right) + W_t + K_t$$

$$T_2 = \left(\sum_0^{512} a\right) + Maj(a,b,c,)$$

$$a = T_1 + T_2$$

$$b = a$$

$$c = b$$

$$d = c$$

$$e = d + T_1$$

$$f = e$$

$$g = f$$

$$h = g$$

Where,

- t = step number; $0 \le t \le 79$.

- Ch (e, f, g) = (e AND f) $\oplus$ (NOT e AND g) the conditional function: If e then f else g.

- Maj(a, b, c) = (a AND b) $\oplus$ (a AND c) $\oplus$ (b AND c) the function is true only of the majority (two or three) of the arguments are true.

$$\left(\sum_0^{512} a\right) = ROTR^{28}(a) \oplus ROTR^{34}(a) \oplus ROTR^{39}(a)$$

$$\left(\sum_1^{512} e\right) = ROTR^{14}(e) \oplus ROTR^{18}(e) \oplus ROTR^{41}(e)$$

- $ROTR^n$ (x) = circular right shift (rotation) of the 64-bit argument x by n bits.

- W_t = a 64-bit word derived from the current 512-bit input block.

- K_t` = a 64-bit additive constant.

- + = addition modulo 2^{64}.

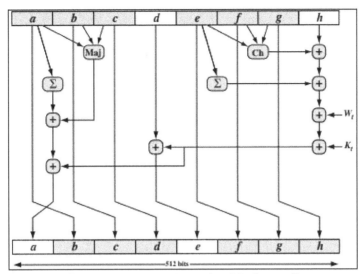

Elementary SHA-512 Operation (single round).

It remains to indicate how the 64-bit word values W_t are derived from the 1024-bit message. Figure illustrates the mapping. The first 16 values of W_t are taken directly from the 16 words of the current block. The remaining values are defined as follows:

$$W_t = \sigma_1^{512}\left(W_{t-2}\right) + W_{t-7} + \sigma_0^{512}\left(W_{t-15}\right) + W_{t-16}$$

Where,

$$\sigma_0^{512}\left(x\right) = ROTR^1\left(x\right) \oplus ROTR^8\left(x\right) \oplus SHR^7\left(x\right)$$
$$\sigma_1^{512}\left(x\right) = ROTR^{19}\left(x\right) \oplus ROTR^{61}\left(x\right) \oplus SHR^6\left(x\right)$$

- $ROTR^n$ (x) = Circular right shift (rotation) of the 64-bit argument x by n bits.

- SHR^n (x) = Left shift of the 64-bit argument x by n bits with padding by zeros on the right.

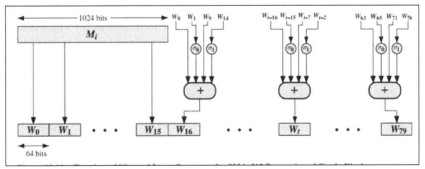

Creation of 80-word Input Sequence for SHA-512 Processing of Single Block.

Thus, in the first 16 steps of processing, the value of W_t is equal to the corresponding word in the message block. For the remaining 64 steps, the value of W_t consists of the circular left shift by one bit of the XOR of four of the preceding values of W_t, with two of those values subjected to shift and rotate operations. This introduces a great deal of redundancy and interdependence into the message blocks that are compressed, which complicates the task of finding a different message block that maps to the same compression function output.

Keyed Hash Functions as MACs

The desire to create a MAC using a hash function rather than a block cipher because hash functions are generally faster and not limited by export controls unlike block ciphers hash includes a key along with the message original proposal KeyedHash = Hash(Key|Message) some weaknesses were found with this eventually led to development of HMAC.

HMAC

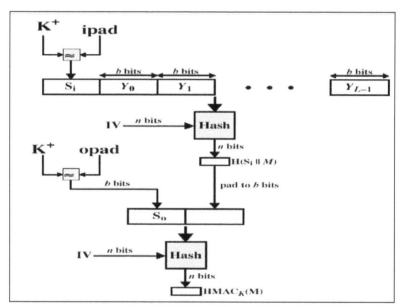

HMAC Overview.

The idea of a keyed hash evolved into HMAC, designed to overcome some problems with the original proposals. Further have a design that has been shown to have the same security as the underlying hash alg. The hash function need only be used on 3 more blocks than when hashing just the original message (for the two keys + inner hash). Choose the hash algorithm to use based on speed/security concerns. specified as Internet standard RFC2104 uses hash function on the message $HMAC_K$ = Hash [(K⁺XOR opad) || Hash [(K⁺ XOR ipad) || M)]] where K+ is the key padded out to size and opad, ipad are specified padding constants overhead is just 3 more hash calculations than the message needs alone any of MD5, SHA-1, RIPEMD-160 can be used.

HMAC Security

The Security of HMAC relates to that of the underlying hash algorithm attacking HMAC requires either: brute force attack on key use Birthday attack (but since keyed would need to observe a very large number of messages) choose hash function used based on speed verses security constraints.

Cryptographic Applications

Historically, cryptography was used to assure only secrecy. Wax seals, signatures, and other physical mechanisms were typically used to assure integrity of the media and authenticity of the sender. With the advent of electronic funds transfer, the applications of cryptography for integrity began to surpass its use for secrecy. Electronic cash came into being from cryptography, and the electronic credit card and debit card sprung into widespread use. The advent of public key cryptography introduced the possibility of digital signatures, and other related concepts such as electronic credentials. In the information age, cryptography has become one of the major methods for protection in all applications.

Cryptographic protocols have only recently come under intensive study, and as of this time, they are not sufficiently well developed to provide a great deal of assurance. There are several protocols that offer provable properties, primarily those designed for use with the OTP. The problem with proving properties of protocols under other schemes is that the mathematics is extremely complex for the RSA, and there is no sound mathematical basis for the DES. Much research is under way at this time in the field of protocol analysis and verification, and it is likely that once this field stabilizes, cryptographic protocols will follow suit.

Several special purpose cryptographic protocols have been developed and demonstrated sound. Most notably, the RSA key distribution protocol, a public key poker playing protocol, an OTP based dining cryptographers protocol, and the protocol used for verifying the nuclear test ban treaty.

A typical cryptographic protocol failure is encountered in the use of the RSA. It seems that if an attacker can choose the plaintext to be signed under an RSA signature system, observe the result of the signature, and then iterate the process, it is possible to get the signer to reveal the private key in a very small number of signatures (about 1 signature per bit of the key). Thus an unmodified RSA signature system requires a sound protocol to be safely used.

Secrecy in Transmission

Most current secrecy systems for transmission use a private key system for transforming transmitted information because it is the fastest method that operates with reasonable assurance and low overhead. If the number of communicating parties is small, key distribution is done periodically with a courier service and key maintenance is based on physical security of the keys over the period of use and destruction after new keys are distributed.

If the number of parties is large, electronic key distribution is usually used. Historically, key distribution was done with a special key-distribution-key (also known as a master-key) maintained by all parties in secrecy over a longer period of time than the keys used for a particular transaction. The "session-key" is generated at random either by one of the parties or by a trusted third party and distributed using the master-key.

The problem with master-key systems is that if the master-key is successfully attacked, the entire system collapses. Similarly, if any of the parties under a given master-key decides to attack the system, they can forge or intercept all messages throughout the entire system. Many complex private-key systems for reducing some of these problems have been proposed and used for various applications. With the advent of public-key systems, secrecy can be maintained without a common master-key or a large number of keys. Instead, if Bob wants to communicate with Alice, Bob sends Alice a session-key encrypted with Alice's public key. Alice decrypts the session-key and uses that over the period of the transaction.

These are examples of cryptographic protocols, methods for communicating while attaining a particular cryptographic objective. These protocols are used primarily to deal with key management and system misuse problems. Many other protocols are applied to eliminate other attacks on these systems.

Secrecy in Storage

Secrecy in storage is usually maintained by a one-key system where the user provides the key to the computer at the beginning of a session, and the system then takes care of encryption and decryption throughout the course of normal use. As an example, many hardware devices are available for personal computers to automatically encrypt all information stored on disk. When the computer is turned on, the user must supply a key to the encryption hardware. The information cannot be read meaningfully without this key, so even if the disk is stolen, the information on it will not be useable. Secrecy in storage has its problems. If the user forgets a key, all of the information encrypted with it becomes permanently unusable. The information is only encrypted while in storage, not when in use by the user. This leaves a major hole for the attacker. If the encryption and decryption are done in software, or if the key is stored somewhere in the system, the system may be circumvented by an attacker. Backups of encrypted information are often stored in plaintext because the encryption mechanism is only applied to certain devices.

Integrity in Transmission

Many of the users of communication systems are not as much concerned about secrecy as about integrity. In an electronic funds transfer, the amount sent from one account to another is often public knowledge. What the bank cares about is that only proper transfers can take place. If an active tapper could introduce a false transfer, funds would be moved illicitly. An error in a single bit could literally cause millions of dollars to be erroneously credited or debited. Cryptographic techniques are widely used to assure that intentional or accidental modification of transmitted information does not cause erroneous actions to take place.

A typical technique for assuring integrity is to perform a checksum of the information being transmitted and transmit the checksum in encrypted form. Once the information and encrypted checksum are received, the information is again check summed and compared to the transmitted checksum after decryption. If the checksums agree, there is a high probability that the message is unaltered. Unfortunately, this scheme is too simple to be of practical value as it is easily forged. The problem is that the checksum of the original message is immediately apparent and a plaintext message with an identical checksum can be easily forged. Designing strong cryptographic checksums is therefore important to the assurance of integrity in systems of this sort.

The key distribution problem in a one-key system is as before, but an interesting alternative is presented by the use of public keys. If we generate a single public-key for the entire system and throw away the private key that would go with it, we can make the checksum impossible to decrypt. In order to verify the original message, we simply generate a new checksum, encrypt with the public key, and verify that the encrypted checksum matches. This is known as a one-way function because it is hard to invert. Actual systems of this sort use high quality cryptographic checksums and complex key distribution and maintenance protocols, but there is a trend towards the use of public keys for key maintenance.

Integrity in Storage

Integrity against random noise has been the subject of much study in the fields of fault tolerant computing and coding theory, but only recently has the need for integrity of stored information against intentional attack become a matter for cryptography. The major mean of assuring integrity of stored information has historically been access control. Access control includes systems of locks and keys, guards, and other mechanisms of a physical or logical nature. The recent advent of computer viruses has changed this to a significant degree, and the use of cryptographic checksums for assuring the integrity of stored information is now becoming widespread.

As in the case of integrity in transmission, a cryptographic checksum is produced and compared to expectations, but storage media tends to have different properties than transmission media. Transmitted information is typically more widely available over a shorter period of time, used for a relatively low volume of information, and accessed at a slower rate than stored information. These parameters cause different trade-offs in how cryptosystems are used.

Authentication of Identity

Authenticating the identity of individuals or systems to each other has been a problem for a very long time. Simple passwords have been used for thousands of years to prove identity. More complex protocols such as sequences of keywords exchanged between sets of parties are often shown in the movies or on television. Cryptography is closely linked to the theory and practice of using passwords, and modern systems often use strong cryptographic transforms in conjunction with physical properties of individuals and shared secrets to provide highly reliable authentication of identity.

Determining good passwords falls into the field known as key selection. In essence, a password can be thought of as a key to a cryptosystem that allows encryption and decryption of everything that the password allows access to. In fact, password systems have been implemented in exactly this way in some commercial products.

The selection of keys has historically been a cause of cryptosystem failure. Although we know from Shannon that $H(K)$ is maximized for a key chosen with an equal probability of each possible value (i.e. at random), in practice when people choose keys, they choose them to make them easy to remember, and therefore not at random. This is most dramatically demonstrated in the poor selection that people make of passwords.

On many systems, passwords are stored in encrypted form with read access available to all so that programs wishing to check passwords needn't be run by privileged users. A side benefit is that the plaintext passwords don't appear anywhere in the system, so an accidental leak of information doesn't compromise system wide protection. A typical algorithm for transforming any string into an encrypted password is designed so that it takes 10 or more msec/transformation to encode a string. By simple calculation, if only capital letters were allowed in a password, it would take .26 seconds to check all the one letter passwords, 6.76 seconds to check all the 2 letter passwords, 4570 seconds for the 4 letter passwords, and by the time we got to 8 letter passwords, it would take about $2*10**9$ seconds (24169 days, over 66 years).

For passwords allowing lower case letters, numbers, and special symbols, this goes up considerably. Studies over the years have consistently indicated that key selection by those without a knowledge of protection is very poor. In a recent study 21% of the users on a computer system had 1 character passwords, with up to 85% having passwords of 1/2 the maximum allowable length, and 92% having passwords of 4 characters or less. These results are quite typical, and dramatically demonstrate that 92% of all passwords could be guessed on a typical system in just over an hour.

Several suggestions for getting unpredictable uniform random numbers include the use of low order bits of Geiger counter counts, the use of the time between entries at a keyboard, low order bits of the amount of light in a room as measured by a light sensitive diode, noisy diode output, the last digit of the first phone number on a given page of a telephone book, and digits from transcendental numbers such as Pi.

Credentialing Systems

A credential is typically a document that introduces one party to another by referencing a commonly known trusted party. For example, when credit is applied for, references are usually requested. The credit of the references is checked and they are contacted to determine the creditworthiness of the applicant. Credit cards are often used to credential an individual to attain further credit cards. A driver's license is a form of credential, as is a passport. Electronic credentials are designed to allow the credence of a claim to be verified electronically. Although no purely electronic credentialing systems are in widespread use at this time, many such systems are being integrated into the smart-card systems in widespread use in Europe. A smart-card is simply a credit-card shaped computer that performs cryptographic functions and stores secret information. When used in conjunction with other devices and systems, it allows a wide variety of cryptographic applications to be performed with relative ease of use to the consumer.

Electronic Signatures

Electronic signatures, like their physical counterparts, are a means of providing a legally binding transaction between two or more parties. To be as useful as a physical signature, electronic signatures must be at least as hard to forge, at least as easy to use, and accepted in a court of law as binding upon all parties to the transaction.

The need for these electronic signatures is especially acute in business dealings wherein the parties to a contract are not in the same physical vicinity. For example, in an international sale of an airplane, signatures are typically required from two bankers, two companies, two insurance agencies, two attorneys, two governments, and often several other parties. The contracts are hundreds of pages long, and signatures must be attained within a relatively short period of time on the same physical document. Faxcimily signatures are not legally binding in all jurisdictions, and the sheer length of a document precludes all parties reading the current copy as they meet at the table to affix signatures. Under current law, all parties must meet in one location in order to complete the transaction. In a transatlantic sale, $100,000 in costs can easily be incurred in such a meeting. An effort in Europe is currently underway to replace physical signatures with electronic signatures based on the RSA cryptosystem. If this effort succeeds, it will allow many millions of dollars to be saved, and launch the era of digital signatures into full scale motion. It will also create a large savings for those who use the system, and therefore act to force others to participate in order to remain competitive.

Electronic Cash

There are patents under force throughout the world today to allow electronic information to replace cash money for financial transactions between individuals. Such a system involves using cryptography to keep the assets of nations in electronic form. Clearly the ability to forge such a system would allow national economies to be destroyed in an instant. The pressure for integrity in such a system is staggaring.

Threshold Systems

Thresholding systems are systems designed to allow use only if a minimal number of parties agree to said use. For example, in a nuclear arms situation, you might want a system wherein three out of five members of the Joint Chiefs of Staff agree. In a banking situation, a safe might only be openned if 4 out of the authorized 23 people allowed to open the safe were present. Such systems preclude a single individual acting alone, while allowing many of the parties to a transaction to be absent without the transaction being halted. Most threshold systems are based on encryption with keys which are distributed in parts. The most common technique for partitioning a key into parts is to form the key as the solution to N equations in N unknowns. If N independent equations are known, the key can be determined by solving the simultaneous equations. If less than N equations are known, the key can be any value since there is still an independent variable in the equations. Any number can be chosen for N and equations can be held by separate individuals. The same general concept can be used to form arbitrary combinations of key requirements by forming ORs and ANDs of encryptions using different sets of keys for different combinations of key holders. The major difficulties with such a system lie in the key distribution problem and the large number of keys necessary to achieve arbitrary key holder combinations.

Systems Using Changing Keys

Shannon has shown us that given enough reuse of a key, it can eventually be determined. It is thus common practice to regularly change keys to limit the exposure due to successful attack on any given key. A common misconception is that changing a key much more often than the average time required to break the cryptosystem, provides an increased margin of safety.

If we assume the key is chosen at random, and that the attacker can check a given percentage of the keys before a key change is made, it is only a matter of time before one of the keys checked by the attacker happens to correspond to one of the random keys. If the attacker chooses keys to attack at random without replacement over the period of key usage, and begins again at the beginning of each period, it is 50% likely that a currently valid key will be found by the time required to try 50% of the total number of keys, regardless of key changes. Thus if a PC could try all the DES keys in 10 years, it would be 50% likely that a successful attack could be launched in 5 years of effort. The real benefit of key changes is that the time over which a broken key is useful is limited to the time till the next key change. This is called limiting the exposure from a stolen key.

Hardware to Support Cryptography

Historically, cryptography has been carried out through the use of cryptographic devices. The use of these devices derives from the difficulty in performing cryptographic transforms manually, the severe nature of errors that result from the lack of redundancy in many cryptographic systems, and the need to make the breaking of codes computationally difficult.

In WWII, the ENIGMA machine was used by the Germans to encode messages, and one of the first computers ever built was the BOMB, which was designed to break ENIGMA cryptograms. Modern supercomputers are used primarily by the NSA to achieve the computational advantage necessary to break many modern cryptosystems. The CRAY could be easily used to break most password enciphering systems, RSA systems with keys of length under about 80 are seriously threatened by the CRAY, and even the DES can be attacked by using special purpose computer hardware. Many devices have emerged in the marketplace for the use of cryptography to encrypt transmissions, act as cryptographic keys for authentication of identification, protect so called debit cards and smart cards, and implementing electronic cash money systems.

References

- What-is-cryptography: golangprograms.com, Retrieved 22, May 2020

- Introduction-to-cryptanalysis: resources.infosecinstitute.com, Retrieved 02, April 2020

- What-is-a-dictionary-attack: nordpass.com, Retrieved 13, Feb 2020

- Attacks-on-cryptosystems, cryptography: tutorialspoint.com, Retrieved 07, Jan 2020

- Maxim-integrated-cryptographic-implementations-hardware-vs-software, embedded-revolution, technologies-21132412: electronicdesign.com, Retrieved 17, March 2020

Branches of Cryptography

There are many branches of cryptography such as classical cryptography, symmetric-key cryptography, public-key cryptography, multivariate cryptography, post-quantum cryptography, quantum cryptography, etc. This chapter deals with each branch and its specific subject matter in a clear and concise manner for the benefit of the reader.

Classical Cryptography

Classical cryptography is based on the mathematics and it relies on the computational difficulty of factorizing large number. The security of classical cryptography is based on the high complexity of the mathematical problem for the instance factorization of large number.

In the classical cryptography the original data i.e., the plain text is transformed into the encoded format i.e. cipher text so that we can transmit this data through insecure communication channels. A data string which known as key is used to control the transformation of the data from plain text to cipher text. This arrangement helps to keep data safe as it required the key for extracting the original information from the cipher text. Without the key no one can read the data. In this technique it is assumed that the only authorized receiver has the key.

Advantages of Classical Cryptography

- While employing the one-time pad, it is unbreakable.

- It is easy to do manually, no computer required.

- It protects the plain text from casual snooping.

Disadvantages of Classical Cryptography

- While employing the one-time pad, it is cumbersome and requires a personal meet-up to exchange the pads.

- If not employing the OTP, anyone who is even remotely interested in knowing what you wrote and knows about cryptography will be able to break the encryption.

Classical Encryption Techniques

There are two basic building blocks of all encryption techniques: substitution and transposition.

Substitution Techniques

A substitution technique is one in which the letters of plaintext are replaced by other letters or by numbers or symbols. If the plaintext is viewed as a sequence of bits, then substitution involves replacing plaintext bit patterns with cipher text bit patterns.

Caesar Cipher (or) Shift Cipher

The earliest known use of a substitution cipher and the simplest was by Julius Caesar. The Caesar cipher involves replacing each letter of the alphabet with the letter standing 3 places further down the alphabet. e.g., Plain text : pay more Cipher text: SDB PRUH PRQHB.

Note that the alphabet is wrapped around, so that letter following „z" is „a". For each plaintext letter p, substitute the cipher text letter c such that,

$$C = E(p) = (p+3) \bmod 26$$

A shift may be any amount, so that general Caesar algorithm is $C = E(p) = (p+k) \bmod 26$. Where k takes on a value in the range 1 to 25. The decryption algorithm is simply $P = D(C) = (C-k) \bmod 26$.

Playfair Cipher

The best known multiple letter encryption cipher is the playfair, which treats diagrams in the plaintext as single units and translates these units into cipher text diagrams. The playfair algorithm is based on the use of 5x5 matrix of letters constructed using a keyword. Let the keyword be "monarchy". The matrix is constructed by filling in the letters of the keyword (minus duplicates) from left to right and from top to bottom, and then filling in the remainder of the matrix with the remaining letters in alphabetical order.

The letter "I" and "j" count as one letter. Plaintext is encrypted two letters at a time according to the following rules:

Repeating plaintext letters that would fall in the same pair are separated with a filler letter such as "x".

M	O	N	A	R
C	H	Y	B	D
E	F	G	I/J	K
L	P	Q	S	T
U	V	W	X	Z

- Plaintext letters that fall in the same row of the matrix are each replaced by the letter to the right, with the first element of the row following the last.

- Plaintext letters that fall in the same column are replaced by the letter beneath, with the top element of the column following the last.

- Otherwise, each plaintext letter is replaced by the letter that lies in its own row and the column occupied by the other plaintext letter.

- Plaintext = meet me at the school house.

- Splitting two letters as a unit => me et me at th es ch ox ol ho us ex Corresponding cipher text => CL KL CL RS PD IL HY AV MP HF XL IU.

Strength of Playfair Cipher

Playfair cipher is a great advance over simple mono alphabetic ciphers. Since there are 26 letters, 26x26 = 676 diagrams are possible, so identification of individual digram is more difficult. Frequency analysis is much more difficult.

Polyalphabetic Ciphers

Another way to improve on the simple monoalphabetic technique is to use different monoalphabetic substitutions as one proceeds through the plaintext message. The general name for this approach is polyalphabetic cipher. All the techniques have the following features in common.

A set of related monoalphabetic substitution rules are used. A key determines which particular rule is chosen for a given transformation.

Vigenere Cipher

In this scheme, the set of related monoalphabetic substitution rules consisting of 26 caesar ciphers with shifts of 0 through 25. Each cipher is denoted by a key letter. e.g., Caesar cipher with a shift of 3 is denoted by the key value 'd' (since a=0, b=1, c=2 and so on). To aid in understanding the scheme, a matrix known as vigenere tableau is constructed.

Each of the 26 ciphers is laid out horizontally, with the key letter for each cipher to its left. A normal alphabet for the plaintext runs across the top. The process of encryption is simple: Given a key letter X and a plaintext letter y, the cipher text is at the intersection of the row labeled x and the column labeled y; in this case, the ciphertext is V.

To encrypt a message, a key is needed that is as long as the message. Usually, the key is a repeating keyword.

- e.g., key = d e c e p t i v e d e c e p t i v e d e c e p t i v e

- PT   = w e a r e d i s c o v e r e d s a v e y o u r s e l f

- CT   = ZICVTWQNGRZGVTWAVZHCQYGLMGJ

		a	b	c	d	e	f	g	h	i	j	k	...	x	y	z
									PLAIN TEXT							
K	a	A	B	C	D	E	F	G	H	I	J	K	...	X	Y	Z
Y	b	B	C	D	E	F	G	H	I	J	K	L	...	Y	Z	A
	c	C	D	E	F	G	H	I	J	K	L	M	...	Z	A	B
L	d	D	E	F	G	H	I	J	K	L	M	N	...	A	B	C
E	e	E	F	G	H	I	J	K	L	M	N	O	...	B	C	D
T	f	F	G	H	I	J	K	L	M	N	O	P	...	C	D	E
T	g	G	H	I	J	K	L	M	N	O	P	Q	...	D	E	F
E	.	.	.	.	.	.	.	.	.	.	.	.	...	.	.	.
R	:	:	:	:	:	:	:	:	:	:	:	:	...	:	:	:
S	x	X	Y	Z	A	B	C	D	E	F	G	H	...			W
	y	Y	Z	A	B	C	D	E	F	G	H	I	...			X
	z	Z	A	B	C	D	E	F	G	H	I	J	...			Y

Decryption is equally simple. The key letter again identifies the row. The position of the cipher text letter in that row determines the column, and the plaintext letter is at the top of that column.

Strength of Vigenere Cipher

There are multiple ciphertext letters for each plaintext letter. Letter frequency information is obscured.

One Time Pad Cipher

It is an unbreakable cryptosystem. It represents the message as a sequence of 0s and 1s. this can be accomplished by writing all numbers in binary, for example, or by using ASCII. The key is a random sequence of 0"s and 1"s of same length as the message. Once a key is used, it is discarded and never used again. The system can be expressed as follows:

$$C_i = P_i \oplus K_i$$

$C_i = i^{th}$ binary digital of cipher text $\quad$ $P_i - i^{th}$ binary digit of pla int ext

$K_i - i^{th}$ binary digit of Key $\quad$ $\oplus -$ exclusive OR operation

Thus the cipher text is generated by performing the bitwise XOR of the plaintext and the key. Decryption uses the same key. Because of the properties of XOR, decryption simply involves the same bitwise operation:

$$P_i = C_i \oplus K_i$$

e.g,. plaintext $= 0\ 0\ 1\ 0\ 1\ 0\ 0\ 1$

key $= 1\ 0\ 1\ 0\ 1\ 1\ 0\ 0$

....

ciphertext $= 1\ 0\ 0\ 0\ 0\ 1\ 0\ 1$

Advantages:

- Encryption method is completely unbreakable for a ciphertext only attack.

Disadvantages:

- It requires a very long key which is expensive to produce and expensive to transmit.

- Once a key is used, it is dangerous to reuse it for a second message; any knowledge on the first message would give knowledge of the second.

Transposition Techniques

All the techniques examined so far involve the substitution of a cipher text symbol for a plaintext symbol. A very different kind of mapping is achieved by performing some sort of permutation on the plaintext letters. This technique is referred to as a transposition cipher.

Rail fence is simplest of such cipher, in which the plaintext is written down as a sequence of diagonals and then read off as a sequence of rows.

- Plaintext = meet at the school house

- To encipher this message with a rail fence of depth 2, we write the message as follows:

  m e a   t   e   c o l   o   s

  e t t h s   H   o   h   u e

- The encrypted message is:

  MEATECOLOSETTHSHOHUE

Row Transposition Ciphers

A more complex scheme is to write the message in a rectangle, row by row, and read the message off, column by column, but permute the order of the columns. The order of columns then becomes the key of the algorithm.

e.g., plaintext = meet at the school house

Key =	4	3	1	2	5	6	7
PT =	m	e	e	t	a	t	t
	H	e	s	c	h	o	o
	1	h	o	u	s	e	

CT = ESOTCUEEHMHLAHSTOETO

CT = ESOTCUEEHMHLAHSTOETO

A pure transposition cipher is easily recognized because it has the same letter frequencies as the original plaintext. The transposition cipher can be made significantly more secure by performing more than one stage of transposition. The result is more complex permutation that is not easily reconstructed.

Symmetric Key Cryptography

Symmetric Key Cryptography also known as Symmetric Encryption is when a secret key is leveraged for both encryption and decryption functions. Symmetric encryption is a type of encryption that uses the same key to encrypt and decrypt data. Both the sender and the recipient have identical copies of the key, which they keep secret and don't share with anyone. This differs from asymmetric encryption, which uses two keys — a public key (that anyone can access) to encrypt information and a private key to decrypt information. Let's do a quick review of how encryption works in general:

- The sender uses an encryption key (usually a string of letters and numbers) to encrypt their message.

- The encrypted message, called ciphertext, looks like scrambled letters and can't be read by anyone along the way.

- The recipient uses a decryption key to transform the ciphertext back into readable text.

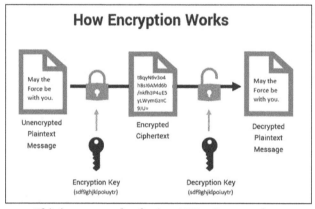

This is an example of using AES 128 encryption.

In the example above, we used the same key for encryption and decryption, which means this is symmetric encryption. Only these two parties (sender and recipient) can read and access the data. This is why it's also sometimes called secret key encryption, secret key cryptography, private key cryptography, symmetric cryptography and symmetric key encryption.

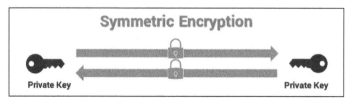

How does symmetric key encryption work? This simplified graphic illustrates the basic concept of how symmetric key encryption works: two identical keys encrypt and decrypt data.

Having only one key to serve both the encryption and decryption functions simplifies the encryption process. After all, you're applying one key to turn plaintext, readable information into unreadable gibberish (ciphertext) and vice versa. One of the advantages of using symmetric encryption is that it provides data privacy and confidentiality without the extra complexity of multiple keys.

Symmetric key encryption does work on its own, for certain use cases. For example, it's useful for encrypting databases and files, where you're not exchanging data publicly between parties. But as with any technical process, there are other advantages and disadvantages of using symmetric key encryption, such as key distribution and management issues, and we'll talk about those a little later.

Symmetric Key Encryption isn't a New Concept

While symmetric key encryption in the sense of encoding digital data through the use of computers is relatively new (it's been around since the mid-1900s), the concept behind isn't. Symmetric cryptography itself is a process that's thought to have been created thousands of years ago.

An early example of symmetric encryption — and probably the best-known symmetric cipher — is attributed to the Roman General Julius Caesar. This particular cipher is aptly known as the Caesar Cipher (more on that in a couple of minutes). However, there have been other types of symmetric ciphers that have existed throughout history, including everything from the Vigenère Cipher — which dates back to the 1500s — to the modern AES algorithm.

Symmetric key encryption is a way for you to encrypt a message so that only you and your intended recipient can read it. It's one type of data encryption, but it's not the only one. There's also another type of encryption that's close in name but is different in terms of what it does: asymmetric encryption. asymmetric encryption is what makes it possible to authenticate and exchange symmetric keys via public channels (such as the internet).

How does Symmetric Encryption Work?

It's time to take a closer look at the symmetric encryption process. To understand how symmetric cryptography works, you need to know what the components are that are involved in the process:

- Your original message that you wish to encrypt (plaintext data).

- A symmetric key encryption algorithm (we'll touch on the different types of algorithms a bit later).

- An identical secret key that only you and your intended recipient have that encrypts and decrypts the data.

- The encrypted message that no one can read (cipher text).

The way that symmetric encryption works is by encrypting and decrypting data through the use of identical keys. The data, once encrypted into ciphertext, can't be read or otherwise understood by anyone who doesn't have the key. This means that you and the party you're communicating with both need to have an identical copy of the key to communicate securely.

To better understand how symmetric encryption works and how all of these components work together, let's consider a basic type of symmetric encryption known as the Caesar cipher.

How a Basic Shift Cipher (Substitution Cipher) Works

An easy way to think of this is to think of this encryption process is through the use of a Caesar cipher, or what known as a substitution or shift ciphers. This was a method by which Caesar was able to secretly communicate with his generals without anyone being able to read the messages (even if the message carriers were intercepted).

In this case, a cipher, also known as an algorithm, is a number or sequence of steps that you'd use to convert plain text information into unreadable ciphertext. With a basic shift cipher, you can encrypt and decrypt a message simply by shifting the message along the alphabet a set number of spaces.

An illustration of how a shift cipher works.

Imagine writing out the entire alphabet in a single long line. And when you use the shift cipher, you'd shift any given letter X number of spaces. So, if you were to shift the letter "G" by nine spaces, it would become "P." The letter "O" would become "X." This means that the message "Good morning, sunshine," for example, then becomes "Pxxm vxawrwp bdwbqrwn" when you shift each letter nine spaces to the right. So, the key in a Caesar cipher is the secret value that only you and your recipient know, which tells you how many letters to shift.

Nowadays, however, we're not passing paper messages back and forth. Today's information exchanges take place through virtual channels via computers, websites, and the internet in general. And while the internet makes things incredibly convenient, banking online or paying for a rideshare over the internet doesn't come without its risks.

The Role of Symmetric Key Encryption in Website Security

Symmetric key encryption is part of the public key infrastructure (PKI) ecosystem, which makes it possible to communicate securely across the insecure internet by converting plain text (readable) data into unrecognizable ciphertext. What this also means is that your browser (client) has already gone through the process of:

- Authenticating our website's server.

- Negotiating with the server on the encryption algorithms to use.

- Generating symmetric session keys.

The way that HTTPS works is that we use asymmetric encryption to first authenticate the website server and to exchange symmetric session keys. This is part of a process known as the TLS handshake — of which there are three versions (TLS 1.0, TLS 1.2 and TLS 1.3). After that, we use symmetric encryption for the actual bulk of the data encryption that takes place during your session.

In general, the TLS handshake:

- Enables our web server to authenticate itself to your browser (web client).

- Establishes parameters to use for secure communication (such deciding which encryption algorithm to use).

- Determines which key exchange protocol to use.

- Generates a session key that only the two communicating parties know using that algorithm and other public and private variables.

The reason for the change to symmetric encryption is that it's faster and less resource-intensive than asymmetric encryption when you're encrypting massive quantities of data. This is particularly important for enterprises who encrypt data at scale. (Think of banks and large companies.)

We won't get into all of the specifics of the handshake here — you'll find a deep dive on that topic in our article on the TLS handshake. But let's explore a few of the encryption algorithms that fall under the symmetric encryption umbrella.

Symmetric Encryption Algorithms

Symmetric algorithms are broken down into two main types: stream and block ciphers. Block ciphers encrypt data in chunks (blocks), whereas stream ciphers encrypt data one bit at a time. So, what are some of the most commonly used or well-known symmetric algorithms?

- Data Encryption Standard (DES): DES is a type of block cipher that encrypts data in 64-bit blocks and using a single key that is one of three sizes (64-bit, 128-bit and 192-bit keys). However, one of every 8 bits is a parity bit, meaning that a single-length key that's 64 bits is really like using a 56-bit key. Although DES is one of the earliest symmetric encryption algorithms, it's viewed as insecure and has been deprecated.

- Triple Data Encryption Standard (TDEA/3DES): Unlike DES, triple DES can use two or three keys, which enables this algorithm to use multiple rounds of encryption (or, more accurate, a round of encryption, round of decryption, and another round of encryption). While 3DES is more secure than its DES predecessor, it's not as secure as its successor, AES.

- Advanced Encryption Standard (AES): This encryption algorithm is what you most commonly will find is use across the internet. The advanced encryption standard is more secure and efficient than DES and 3DES with key options that are 128 bits, 192 bits and 256 bits. However, while it's also a type of block cipher, it operates differently than DES and 3DES because it's based on a substitution-permutation network instead of the Feistel cipher.

- For Symmetric Encryption to Work, the Key Must Stay Secret.

For symmetric encryption to work, however, it means that you and your intended recipient both must know the key and keep it secret. Otherwise, if someone else knows the key, then they can decrypt your data and read it, which makes the entire encryption process pointless. That's why it's vital to keep the secret key secret and away from prying eyes to limit the number of people who have the key.

As such, you should never store secret or private keys in any internet-facing environment. This is true for both asymmetric encryption private keys as well as symmetric keys. You need to keep those keys hidden somewhere where no one is going to be able to find, access, or steal them. Basically, protect those keys like you would a lifetime paid subscription that someone gave you to your favorite gaming service — 'cause I know that *no one's* getting their hands on that.

But the tricky part with symmetric encryption is that there's an assumption that you and your recipient both already have identical copies of the key. But what do you do if you and your recipient have never met, and if you don't already have those identical keys?

Remote Key Distribution

How to Share a Key Securely to Facilitate Symmetric Encryption

Let's say that you want to share secret messages with your friend, Erica, who's in another country but she doesn't have a key to decrypt said messages. This means you'd need to get a shared key to her so that she can securely decrypt the message.

To do this, you'd have to send the secret key across the internet — which you know is anything but secure. After all, your internet connection gets bounced through potentially *dozens* of different touchpoints in its journey. This means that any Tom, Dick or Harry — any cybercriminal, government, or anyone else you don't want reading your messages — could intercept the key en route and decrypt your messages with ease, and you'd be none the wiser. This is known as a man-in-the-middle attack (MitM).

So, sending data (especially keys) across the internet isn't a good idea, which means we need to look at an alternative method. This is where asymmetric tactics — such as asymmetric key exchange (i.e. key generation) methods like RSA and Diffie-Hellman — come into play.

The Role of Key Exchange Protocols

Symmetric encryption algorithms aren't the only algorithms out there that PKI depends upon. There are also asymmetric algorithms and asymmetric key exchange protocols. So, if you're trying to communicate securely with your friend Erica using symmetric key cryptography, you'll use asymmetric encryption tactics to generate and share a secure key that only you and Erica will know.

Historically, symmetric encryption is paired with either RSA or Diffie-Hellman asymmetric algorithms (i.e., key exchange protocols) for the key exchange/generation process. However, these two algorithms have separate roles.

RSA Vs Diffie-Hellman Key Exchanges

The RSA encryption algorithm, which stands for Rivest-Shamir-Adleman (the surnames of the three people who created it), is an authentication and key exchange mechanism that's commonly used in the TLS 1.2 handshake process. In an RSA key exchange, public key encryption facilitates the exchange of a pre-master secret and a randomly generate number from the client that, together, generate a shared session key. With the Diffie-Hellman key exchange, the server and client instead mutually agree upon a value that's used for the session key.

However, the use of RSA for key exchanges is frowned upon (although some systems are still using it) due to vulnerabilities that were discovered by cryptologist Daniel Bleichenbacher. In fact, the RSA key exchange cipher suites (and non-ephemeral Diffie-Hellman groups) were deprecated with the rollout of TLS 1.3 in an effort to mandate perfect forward secrecy (which uses an ephemeral key). So, RSA key exchange was replaced by the exclusive use of ephemeral Diffie-Hellman key exchanges.

The Diffie-Hellman key exchange algorithm is a public key distribution system that uses modular arithmetic to come to an agreed upon secret number (session key). So, as you can see, calling Diffie-Hellman an "encryption" algorithm is actually misleading because it can't be used to encrypt or decrypt anything. And it's not so much a key "exchange" as it is a key *generation* process. Yes, there are variables exchanged, but you're still actually creating the key based on those exchanges.

Diffie-Hellman uses the exchange of public variables (numbers) to generate a shared solution known as a session key. This secret session key is what you'd use to exchange data in a secure channel that's protected by symmetric encryption.

How Secure are Symmetric Keys?

The strength of any cryptographic key depends on a few specific considerations:

- The length of the key.

- The randomness (entropy) of how it was generated.

- How long it takes to reverse it to figure out is individual components.

Now, you may be wondering whether a cybercriminal could just reverse the process to guess the variables to calculate the numbers that were used. It's possible, but the reality of that happening is so remote that it's not practical. I say that because even though cybercriminals understand how these calculations work, it's incredibly difficult to reverse the process to find out the secret number you or your recipient used to generate your matching session keys.

It goes back to the concept that was discussed in the video that shows the uses of mixing of specific colors to create a shared value. While it's easy to combine colors to create the shared value, it's virtually impossible to deconstruct those values to figure out exactly which shades of the colors were used to create them.

Furthermore, since the numbers that are used in these calculations are massive, it would take way longer than any cybercriminal would have during a session to figure them out. Even with the most current supercomputers, an attacker would have to spend hundreds — if not thousands of years — trying to figure out the individual numbers you both used. I don't know about you, but we mortals don't have that much time to spend on such tasks. So, now that we know what symmetric encryption is and how it works, how is it used in the real world?

Examples of where you're Already using Symmetric Encryption

Symmetric encryption is useful in many cases and has implementation opportunities across various industries. For example, symmetric encryption is useful for encrypting banking-related data as well as data storage.

Banking

Ever heard of PCI DSS? The Payment Card Industry Data Security Standards is a set of 12 requirements that businesses or organizations that accept credit card payments must adhere to. Symmetric encryption is a key component of PCI compliance, as it directly correlates to requirement No. 3, which focuses on protecting at-rest cardholder data. This different from requirement No. 4, which focuses on protecting in-transit data. That's all about using asymmetric encryption.

Data at Rest

Data at rest refers to the state of your data while it's sitting on a server or a device. It's not in transit, meaning that it's not being sent across a network or the internet. So, consider the example of a private ledger or a diary. You write either highly valuable or sensitive information in it that you don't want anyone other people to read. So, while you're not sending it anywhere, it doesn't mean that you want someone else to be able to read its contents should they manage to get their hands on it. At rest data encryption is what prevents that type of exposure from happening.

Public-Key Cryptography

Unlike symmetric key cryptography, we do not find historical use of public-key cryptography. It is a relatively new concept. Symmetric cryptography was well suited for organizations such as governments, military, and big financial corporations were involved in the classified communication.

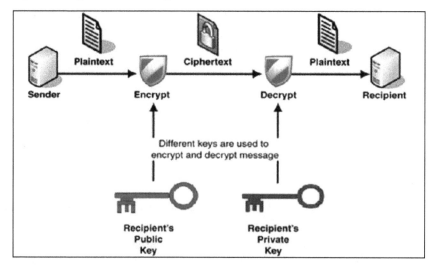

With the spread of more unsecure computer networks in last few decades, a genuine need was felt to use cryptography at larger scale. The symmetric key was found to be non-practical due to challenges it faced for key management. This gave rise to the public key cryptosystems. The process of encryption and decryption is depicted in the following illustration:

The most important properties of public key encryption scheme are:

- Different keys are used for encryption and decryption. This is a property which set this scheme different than symmetric encryption scheme.

- Each receiver possesses a unique decryption key, generally referred to as his private key.

- Receiver needs to publish an encryption key, referred to as his public key.

- Some assurance of the authenticity of a public key is needed in this scheme to avoid spoofing by adversary as the receiver. Generally, this type of cryptosystem involves trusted third party which certifies that a particular public key belongs to a specific person or entity only.

- Encryption algorithm is complex enough to prohibit attacker from deducing the plaintext from the ciphertext and the encryption (public) key.

- Though private and public keys are related mathematically, it is not be feasible to calculate the private key from the public key. In fact, intelligent part of any public-key cryptosystem is in designing a relationship between two keys.

There are three types of Public Key Encryption schemes.

RSA Cryptosystem

This cryptosystem is one the initial system. It remains most employed cryptosystem even today. The system was invented by three scholars Ron Rivest, Adi Shamir, and Len Adleman and hence, it is termed as RSA cryptosystem.

Generation of RSA Key Pair

Each person or a party who desires to participate in communication using encryption needs to generate a pair of keys, namely public key and private key. The process followed in the generation of keys is described below:

- Generate the RSA modulus (n):

  ○ Select two large primes, p and q.

  ○ Calculate n=p*q. For strong unbreakable encryption, let n be a large number, typically a minimum of 512 bits.

- Find Derived Number (e):

  ○ Number e must be greater than 1 and less than $(p - 1)(q - 1)$.

  ○ There must be no common factor for e and $(p - 1)(q - 1)$ except for 1. In other words two numbers e and $(p - 1)(q - 1)$ are coprime.

- Form the public key:

  - The pair of numbers (n, e) form the RSA public key and is made public.

  - Interestingly, though n is part of the public key, difficulty in factorizing a large prime number ensures that attacker cannot find in finite time the two primes (p & q) used to obtain n. This is strength of RSA.

- Generate the private key:

  - Private Key d is calculated from p, q, and e. For given n and e, there is unique number d.

  - Number d is the inverse of e modulo (p - 1)(q − 1). This means that d is the number less than (p - 1)(q - 1) such that when multiplied by e, it is equal to 1 modulo (p - 1)(q - 1).

  - This relationship is written mathematically as follows:

```
ed = 1 mod (p - 1)(q - 1)
```

The Extended Euclidean Algorithm takes p, q, and e as input and gives d as output. Example: An example of generating RSA Key pair is given below. (For ease of understanding, the primes p & q taken here are small values. Practically, these values are very high).

- Let two primes be p = 7 and q = 13. Thus, modulus n = pq = 7 x 13 = 91.

- Select e = 5, which is a valid choice since there is no number that is common factor of 5 and (p − 1)(q − 1) = 6 × 12 = 72, except for 1.

- The pair of numbers (n, e) = (91, 5) forms the public key and can be made available to anyone whom we wish to be able to send us encrypted messages.

- Input p = 7, q = 13, and e = 5 to the Extended Euclidean Algorithm. The output will be d = 29.

- Check that the d calculated is correct by computing:

```
de = 29 × 5 = 145 = 1 mod 72
```

- Hence, public key is (91, 5) and private keys is (91, 29).

Encryption and Decryption

Once the key pair has been generated, the process of encryption and decryption are relatively straightforward and computationally easy. Interestingly, RSA does not directly operate on strings of bits as in case of symmetric key encryption. It operates on numbers modulo n. Hence, it is necessary to represent the plaintext as a series of numbers less than n.

RSA Encryption

- Suppose the sender wish to send some text message to someone whose public key is (n, e).

- The sender then represents the plaintext as a series of numbers less than n.

- To encrypt the first plaintext P, which is a number modulo n. The encryption process is simple mathematical step as:

```
C = Pᵉ mod n
```

- In other words, the ciphertext C is equal to the plaintext P multiplied by itself e times and then reduced modulo n. This means that C is also a number less than n.

- Returning to our Key Generation example with plaintext P = 10, we get ciphertext C:

```
C = 10⁵ mod 91
```

RSA Decryption

- The decryption process for RSA is also very straightforward. Suppose that the receiver of public-key pair (n, e) has received a ciphertext C.

- Receiver raises C to the power of his private key d. The result modulo n will be the plaintext P.

```
Plaintext = Cᵈ mod n
```

Returning again to our numerical example, the ciphertext C = 82 would get decrypted to number 10 using private key 29:

```
Plaintext = 82²⁹ mod 91 = 10
```

RSA Analysis

The security of RSA depends on the strengths of two separate functions. The RSA cryptosystem is most popular public-key cryptosystem strength of which is based on the practical difficulty of factoring the very large numbers.

- Encryption Function: It is considered as a one-way function of converting plaintext into ciphertext and it can be reversed only with the knowledge of private key d.

- Key Generation: The difficulty of determining a private key from an RSA public key is equivalent to factoring the modulus n. An attacker thus cannot use knowledge of an RSA public key to determine an RSA private key unless he can factor n. It is also a one way function, going from p & q values to modulus n is easy but reverse is not possible.

If either of these two functions are proved non one-way, then RSA will be broken. In fact, if a technique for factoring efficiently is developed then RSA will no longer be safe.

The strength of RSA encryption drastically goes down against attacks if the number p and q are not large primes and/ or chosen public key e is a small number.

ElGamal Cryptosystem

Along with RSA, there are other public-key cryptosystems proposed. Many of them are based on different versions of the Discrete Logarithm Problem.

ElGamal cryptosystem, called Elliptic Curve Variant, is based on the Discrete Logarithm Problem. It derives the strength from the assumption that the discrete logarithms cannot be found in practical time frame for a given number, while the inverse operation of the power can be computed efficiently. Let us go through a simple version of ElGamal that works with numbers modulo p. In the case of elliptic curve variants, it is based on quite different number systems.

Generation of ElGamal Key Pair

Each user of ElGamal cryptosystem generates the key pair through as follows:

- Choosing a large prime p. Generally a prime number of 1024 to 2048 bits length is chosen.

- Choosing a generator element g:

  ○ This number must be between 1 and p − 1, but cannot be any number.

  ○ It is a generator of the multiplicative group of integers modulo p. This means for every integer m co-prime to p, there is an integer k such that g^k=a mod n. For example, 3 is generator of group 5 (Z_5 = {1, 2, 3, 4}).

N	3^n	$3^n \bmod 5$
1	3	3
2	9	4
3	27	2
4	81	1

- Choosing the private key. The private key x is any number bigger than 1 and smaller than p−1.

- Computing part of the public key. The value y is computed from the parameters p, g and the private key x as follows:

$y = g^x \bmod p$

- Obtaining Public key. The ElGamal public key consists of the three parameters (p, g, y).

For example, suppose that p = 17 and that g = 6 (It can be confirmed that 6 is a generator of group Z_{17}). The private key x can be any number bigger than 1 and smaller than 71, so we choose x = 5. The value y is then computed as follows:

$y = 6^5 \bmod 17 = 7$

- Thus the private key is 62 and the public key is (17, 6, 7).

Encryption and Decryption

The generation of an ElGamal key pair is comparatively simpler than the equivalent process for RSA. But the encryption and decryption are slightly more complex than RSA.

ElGamal Encryption

Suppose sender wishes to send a plaintext to someone whose ElGamal public key is (p, g, y), then:

- Sender represents the plaintext as a series of numbers modulo p.

- To encrypt the first plaintext P, which is represented as a number modulo p. The encryption process to obtain the ciphertext C is as follows:

  - Randomly generate a number k.

  - Compute two values C1 and C2, where:

```
C1 = gᵏ mod p
C2 = (P*yᵏ) mod p
```

- Send the ciphertext C, consisting of the two separate values (C1, C2), sent together.

- Referring to our ElGamal key generation example given above, the plaintext P = 13 is encrypted as follows:

  - Randomly generate a number, say k = 10.

  - Compute the two values C1 and C2, where:

```
C1 = 6¹⁰ mod 17
C2 = (13*7¹⁰) mod 17 = 9
```

- Send the ciphertext C = (C1, C2) = (15, 9).

ElGamal Decryption

- To decrypt the ciphertext (C1, C2) using private key x, the following two steps are taken:

  - Compute the modular inverse of $(C1)^x$ modulo p, which is $(C1)^{-x}$, generally referred to as decryption factor.

  - Obtain the plaintext by using the following formula:

```
C2 × (C1)⁻ˣ mod p = Plaintext
```

- In our example, to decrypt the ciphertext C = (C1, C2) = (15, 9) using private key x = 5, the decryption factor is:

```
15⁻⁵ mod 17 = 9
```

- Extract plaintext P = (9 × 9) mod 17 = 13.

ElGamal Analysis

In ElGamal system, each user has a private key x. and has three components of public key – prime modulus p, generator g, and public $Y = g^x$ mod p. The strength of the ElGamal is based on the difficulty of discrete logarithm problem.

The secure key size is generally > 1024 bits. Today even 2048 bits long key are used. On the processing speed front, Elgamal is quite slow, it is used mainly for key authentication protocols. Due to higher processing efficiency, Elliptic Curve variants of ElGamal are becoming increasingly popular.

Elliptic Curve Cryptography (ECC)

Elliptic Curve Cryptography (ECC) is a term used to describe a suite of cryptographic tools and protocols whose security is based on special versions of the discrete logarithm problem. It does not use numbers modulo p.

ECC is based on sets of numbers that are associated with mathematical objects called elliptic curves. There are rules for adding and computing multiples of these numbers, just as there are for numbers modulo p. ECC includes variants of many cryptographic schemes that were initially designed for modular numbers such as ElGamal encryption and Digital Signature Algorithm.

It is believed that the discrete logarithm problem is much harder when applied to points on an elliptic curve. This prompts switching from numbers modulo p to points on an elliptic curve. Also an equivalent security level can be obtained with shorter keys if we use elliptic curve-based variants.

The shorter keys result in two benefits:

- Ease of key management.

- Efficient computation.

These benefits make elliptic-curve-based variants of encryption scheme highly attractive for application where computing resources are constrained.

RSA and ElGamal Schemes: A Comparison

Let us briefly compare the RSA and ElGamal schemes on the various aspects.

RSA	ElGamal
It is more efficient for encryption.	It is more efficient for decryption.
It is less efficient for decryption.	It is more efficient for decryption.
For a particular security level, lengthy keys are required in RSA.	For the same level of security, very short keys are required.
It is widely accepted and used.	It is new and not very popular in market.

Multivariate Cryptography

Multivariate cryptography is the generic term for asymmetric cryptographic primitives based on multivariate polynomials over finite fields. The basic objects of multivariate cryptography are systems of nonlinear (usually quadratic) polynomial equations in several variables over a finite field $\mathbb{F} = \mathbb{F}_q$ with q elements.

$$p^{(1)}(x_1,...,x_n)=\sum_{i=1}^{n}\sum_{j=i}^{n}p_{ij}^{(1)} \cdot x_i x_j + \sum_{i=1}^{n}p_i^{(1)} \cdot x_i + p_0^{(1)}$$

$$p^{(2)}(x_1,...,x_n)=\sum_{i=1}^{n}\sum_{j=i}^{n}p_{ij}^{(2)} \cdot x_i x_j + \sum_{i=1}^{n}p_i^{(2)} \cdot x_i + p_0^{(2)}$$

$$\vdots$$

$$p^{(m)}(x_1,...,x_n)=\sum_{i=1}^{n}\sum_{j=i}^{n}p_{ij}^{(m)} \cdot x_i x_j + \sum_{i=1}^{n}p_i^{(m)} \cdot x_i + p_0^{(m)}.$$

The security of multivariate schemes is based on the MQ Problem.

Problem MQ: Given m quadratic polynomials $p^{(1)}(x),...,p^{(m)}(x)$ in the n variables $x_1,...,x_n$ as shown in above equation find a vector $\bar{x}=(\bar{x}_1,...,\bar{x}_n)$ such that $p^{(1)}(\bar{x})=...=p^{(m)}(\bar{x})=0$. The MQ Problem is proven to be NP hard (even for quadratic polynomials over the field GF(2)) and is believed to be hard on average.

The public key of a multivariate cryptosystem is a set of multivariate quadratic polynomials. To build a public key cryptosystem on the basis of the MQ Problem, one starts with an easily invertible quadratic map $\mathcal{F}: \mathbb{F}^n \to \mathbb{F}^m$ (central map). To hide the structure of the central map in the public key, one combines $\mathcal{F}$ with two invertible affine maps $\mathcal{S}: \mathbb{F}^m \to \mathbb{F}^m$ and $\mathcal{T}: \mathbb{F}^n \to \mathbb{F}^n$. The public key of the scheme is the composed map $\mathcal{P}: \mathcal{S} \circ \mathrm{F} \circ \mathcal{T}: \mathrm{Fn} \to \mathrm{Fm}$, the private key consists of the three maps $\mathcal{S}$, $\mathcal{F}$ and $\mathcal{T}$. The standard process of encryption/decryption or signature generation/verification works as shown in Figure.

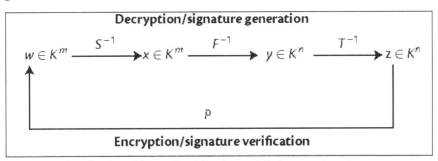

Standard workflow of multivariate public key cryptosystems.

Encryption Schemes (m ≥ n)

An encryption scheme requires that the public key map is injective to ensure that the decryption process outputs a unique plaintext. This is why m ≥ n.

- Encryption: To encrypt a message $z \in \mathbb{F}^n$ one just evaluates the public key to get the ciphertext $w = \mathcal{P}(z) \in \mathbb{F}^m$.

- Decryption: In order to decrypt a ciphertext $w \in \mathrm{Fm}$, one computes recursively $x = \mathcal{S}^{-1}(w) \in \mathbb{F}^m$, $y = \mathcal{F}^{-1}(x) \in \mathbb{F}^n$ and $z = \mathcal{T}^{-1}(y)$. The plaintext corresponding to the ciphertext w is given by $z \in \mathbb{F}^n$. The condition $m \geq n$ guarantees that the pre-image y of x under the central map $\mathcal{F}$ and therefore the decrypted plaintext is unique.

Signature Schemes (m ≤ n)

A signature scheme requires that the public key map is surjective to ensure that one can sign any document. This is why $(m \leq n)$.

- Signature Generation: In order to generate a signature for a message d, one uses a hash function $\mathcal{H} : \{0, 1\}^\star \to \mathbb{F}^m$, to compute the hash value $\mathbf{w} = \mathcal{H}(\mathbf{d}) \in \mathbb{F}^m$. After that, one computes recursively $\mathbf{x} = \mathcal{S}^{-1}(\mathbf{w}) \in \mathbb{F}^m$, $\mathbf{y} = \mathcal{F}^{-1}(\mathbf{x}) \in \mathbb{F}^n$ and $\mathbf{z} = \mathcal{T}^{-1}(\mathbf{y})$. The signature of the message d is given by $z \in \mathbb{F}^n$. Here, $\mathcal{F}^{-1}(\mathbf{x})$ means finding one (of possibly many) pre-image of x under the central map $\mathcal{F}$. The condition $m \leq n$ guarantees that such a pre-image exists. Therefore every message has a signature.

- Signature Verification: To check the authenticity of a signature $\mathbf{z} \in \mathbb{F}^n$ one computes the hash value $\mathbf{w} = \mathcal{H}(\mathbf{d}) \in \mathbb{F}^m$ of the message d and evaluates the public map to obtain $\mathbf{w}' = \mathcal{P}(\mathbf{z}) \mathbf{z} \in \mathbb{F}^m$. If $\mathbf{w}' = \mathbf{w}$ holds, the signature is accepted, otherwise it is rejected.

Standard Attacks

Attacks against multivariate schemes can be divided into two main groups:

Direct Attacks

In this type of attack one tries to solve the public system $\mathcal{P}(\mathbf{z}) = \mathbf{w}$ directly as an instance of the MQ Problem. The most common way to do this is by a Gröbner basis attack such as the F_4 algorithm. The complexity of this algorithm is, for $m \approx n$, exponential in the number of equations. Table shows, for different underlying fields, the minimal number of equations in a determined system $(m = n)$ needed to reach given levels of security.

Table: Minimal number of equations needed to reach given levels of security.

Security level (bit)	Number of equations		
	GF(16)	GF(31)	GF(256)
80	30	28	26
100	39	36	33
128	51	48	43
192	80	75	68
256	110	103	93

Structural Attacks

In a structural attack one tries to utilize the special structure of the central map of a multivariate scheme to recover the private key. Two well-known examples for such an attack are rank and differential attacks.

The *MinRank attack* aims at finding a linear combination of the quadratic forms associated to the public key polynomials of low rank. Such a linear combination corresponds to a central polynomial. By finding linear combinations of low rank it is therefore possible to recover the private key of the multivariate cryptosystem.

A *differential attack* searches for symmetries or invariants of the differential $\mathcal{G}(x, y) = \mathcal{P}(x+y) - \mathcal{P}(x) - \mathcal{P}(y) + \mathcal{P}(0)$ of the public key. These invariants can be used to analyze the structure of the scheme and to recover the central map.

Signature Schemes

UOV

The (unbalanced) Oil and Vinegar signature scheme was proposed by Kipnis and Patarin.

Let $\mathbb{F}$ be a finite field and o and v be integers. We define $n = o + v$, $V = \{1,...,v\}$, and $O = \{v+1,...,n\}$. We call $x_1,...,x_v$ the Vinegar variables and $x_{v+1},...,x_n$ Oil variables. For $o = v$ the scheme is called balanced Oil and Vinegar (OV), for $v > o$ we speak of the unbalanced Oil and Vinegar signature scheme (UOV).

Key Generation: The central map $\mathcal{F}: \mathbb{F}^n \to \mathbb{F}^o$ of the (U)OV signature scheme consists of o quadratic polynomials $f^{(1)},...,f^{(0)}$ of the form,

$$f^{(k)} = \sum_{i,j\in V} \alpha_{ij}^{(k)} \cdot x_i x_j + \sum_{i\in V, j\in O} \beta_{ij}^{(k)} \cdot x_i x_j + \sum_{i\in O\cup V} \gamma_i^{(k)} \cdot x_i + \delta^{(k)} \ (k = 1,....,0\}$$

The polynomials $f^{(1)},..., f^{(o)}$ contain no quadratic terms $x_i x_j$ with both $i, j \in O$. This fact will later be used to invert $\mathcal{F}$. To hide the structure of $\mathcal{F}$ in the public key, one combines $\mathcal{F}$ with one invertible affine map $\mathcal{T}: \mathbb{F}^n \to \mathbb{F}^n$. Therefore, the public key of the scheme has the form $\mathcal{P} = \mathcal{F} \circ \mathcal{T}: \mathbb{F}^n \to \mathbb{F}^o$, the private key consists of $\mathcal{F}$ and $\mathcal{T}$.

Inversion of the Central Map

In order to find a pre-image $\mathbf{x} \in \mathbb{F}^n$ of $\mathbf{y} \in \mathbb{F}^o$ under the central map $\mathcal{F}$, one chooses randomly the values of the Vinegar variables $x_1,...,x_v$ and substitutes them into the polynomials $f^{(1)},...,f^{(0)}$. Due to the special structure of the central polynomials, we obtain by this strategy o linear polynomials $\tilde{f}^{(1)},...,\tilde{f}^{(0)}$ in the o Oil variables $x_{v+1},...,x_n$. We can solve the resulting linear system $\tilde{f}^{(k)}(x_{v+1},...,x_n) = y_k \ (k = 1,....,0)$ by Gaussian elimination. If the system has no solution, we choose other values for the Vinegar variables and try again.

Example: Let $\mathbb{F} = GF(7)$ and $o = v = 2$. Let the central map $\mathcal{F} = (f^{(1)}, f^{(2)})$ of our (balanced) OV instance be given by,

$$f^{(1)}(x_1,...,x_4) = 2x_1^2 + 3x_1 x_2 + 6x_1 x_3 + x_1 x_4 + 4x_2^2 + 5x_2 x_4 + 3x_1 + 2x_2 + 5x_3 + x_4 + 6,$$

$$f^{(2)}(x_1,...,x_4) = 3x_1^2 + 6x_1 x_2 + 5x_1 x_4 + 3x_2^2 + 5x_2 x_3 + x_2 x_4 + 2x_1 + 5x_2 + 4x_3 + 2x_4 + 1.$$

In order to find a pre-image $\mathbf{x} = (x_1, x_2, x_3, x_4)$ of $\mathbf{y} = (3, 4)$ under the central map $\mathcal{F}$, we choose random values for x_1 and x_2, e.g. $(x_1, x_2) = (1, 4)$, and substitute them into $f^{(1)}$ and $f^{(2)}$. By doing so, we obtain,

$$\tilde{f}^{(1)}\left(x_3, x_4\right) = 4x_3 + x_4 + 4,$$
$$\tilde{f}^{(2)}\left(x_3, x_4\right) = 3x_3 + 4x_4.$$

By solving the linear system $\tilde{f}^{(1)} = y_1 = 3$, $\tilde{f}^{(2)} = y_2 = 4$, we obtain $(x3, x4) = (1, 2)$. Therefore, the required pre-image is $\mathbf{x} = (1, 4, 1, 2) \in \mathbb{F}^4$.

Signature Generation: In order to generate a signature $\mathbf{z} \in \mathbb{F}^n$ for a message d, one uses a hash function $\mathcal{H} : \{0, 1\} \to \mathbb{F}^o$, to compute $\mathbf{w} = \mathcal{H}(d) \in \mathbb{F}^o$ and performs the following two steps:

- Compute a pre-image $\mathbf{x} \in \mathbb{F}^n$ of w under the central map $\mathcal{F}$. This is done as described in the previous paragraph.

- Compute the signature $\mathbf{z} \in \mathbb{F}^n$ of the document d by $\mathbf{z} = \mathcal{T}^{-1}(\mathbf{x})$.

Signature Verification: To check the authenticity of a signature $\mathbf{z} \in \mathbb{F}^n$ one uses the hash function $\mathcal{H}$ to compute $\mathbf{w} = \mathcal{H}(d) \in \mathbb{F}^o$ and computes $\mathbf{w}' = \mathcal{P}(\mathbf{z})$. If $\mathbf{w}' = \mathbf{w}$ holds, the signature is accepted, otherwise rejected.

Security: For the security of (U)OV we require $v \geq 2.o$ (unbalanced Oil and Vinegar (UOV)). Besides of that, the UOV scheme resisted (for suitable parameter sets) cryptanalysis for 20 years now and is therefore believed to offer high security.

Rainbow

The Rainbow signature scheme can be seen as a multi-layer version of UOV. By their modifications, Ding and Schmidt were able to reduce key and signature sizes as well as improve the performance of UOV.

Let $\mathbb{F}$ be a finite field and $0 < v1 < v2 < \ldots < vu+1 = n$ be a sequence of integers. We set $V_i = \{1,...,v\}$, $O_i = \{v_i + ,...,v_{i+}\}$ and $O_i = v_{i+1} - v_i (i = 1,...,u)$.

Key Generation: The central map $\mathbb{F}$ of the Rainbow signature scheme consists of $m = n - v1$ quadratic polynomials $f^{(v_i+1)},...,f^{(n)}$ of the form,

$$f^{(k)}\left(\mathbf{x}\right) = \sum_{i, j \in V\ell} \alpha_{ij}^{(k)} x_i x_j + \sum_{i \in V\ell, j \in O_\ell} \beta_{ij}^{(k)} x_i x_j + \sum_{i \in V_\ell \cup O_\ell} \gamma_i^{(k)} x_i + \delta^{(k)},$$

where $\ell \in \{1,...,u\}$ is the only integer such that $k \in O_\ell$.

In every polynomial f(k) with $k \in O_\ell$, there is no quadratic term xixj where both i and j are in O_ℓ. If we therefore substitute the variables $x_i (i \in V_\ell)$ into the equations $f^{(k)}(k \in O_\ell)$, we obtain a system of O_ℓ linear equations in the   variables $x_i (i \in O_\ell)$. This fact will later be used during the signature generation process of the scheme.

To hide the structure of $\mathcal{F}$ in the public key, one composes it with two invertible affine or linear maps $\mathcal{S} : \mathbb{F}^m \to \mathbb{F}^m$ and $\mathcal{T} : \mathbb{F}^n \to \mathbb{F}^n$.

Hence, the public key of Rainbow has the form $\mathcal{P} = \mathcal{S} \circ \mathcal{F} \circ \mathcal{T} : \mathbb{F}^n \rightarrow \mathbb{F}^m$ the private key consists of the three maps $\mathcal{S}$, $\mathcal{F}$ and $\mathcal{T}$.

Inversion of the Central Map

Since the Rainbow central map consists of several layers of UOV, it can be inverted by inverting the single UOV layers recursively. The variables of the ith layer are hereby used as the Vinegar variables of the $i + 1^{th}$ layer.

Algorithm: Inversion of the Rainbow central map.
Input: Rainbow central map $\mathcal{F} = (f^{(v_1+1)},...,f^{(n)})$, vector $\mathbf{y} \in \mathbb{F}^m$.
Output: vector $\mathbf{x} \in \mathbb{F}^n$ with $\mathcal{F}(\mathbf{x}) = \mathbf{y}$.
1: Choose random values for the variables $x_1, \ldots , x v_1$ and substitute these values into the polynomials $f^{(i)}$ ($i = v_1 + 1, \ldots n$).
2: for $\ell = 1 = 1$ to v do.
3: Perform Gaussian Elimination on the polynomials $f^{(i)}(i \in O_\ell)$ to get the values of the variables $x_i(i \in O_\ell)$.
4: Substitute the values of $x_i(i \in O_\ell)$. into the polynomials $f^{(i)}(i = v_{\ell+1} + 1,..., n)$.
5: end for

Example: Let $\mathbb{F} = GF(7)$.We consider a Rainbow instance with 2 layers, $(v_1, o_1, o_2) = (2, 2, 2)$ and central map $\mathcal{F} = (f^{(3)}, \ldots , f^{(6)})$ with,

$$f^{(3)} = x_1^2 + 3x_1x_2 + 5x_1x_3 + 6x_1x_4 + 2x_2^2 + 6x_2x_3 + 4x_2x_4 + 2x_2 + 6x_3 + 2x_4 + 5,$$

$$f^{(4)} = 2x_1^2 + x_1x_2 + x_1x_3 + 3x_1x_4 + 4x_1 + x_2^2 + x_2x_3 + 4x_2x_4 + 6x_2 + x_4,$$

$$f^{(5)} = 2x_1^2 + 3x_1x_2 + 3x_1x_3 + 3x_1x_4 + x_1x_5 + 3x_1x_6 + 6x_1 + 4x_2^2 + x_2x_3 + 4x_2x_4$$
$$+ x_2x_5 + 3x_2x_6 + 3x_2 + 3x_3x_4 + x_3x_5 + 2x_3x_6 + 2x_3 + 3x_4x_5 + x_5 + 6x_6,$$

$$f^{(6)} = 2x_1^2 + 5x_1x_2 + x_1x_3 + 5x_1x_4 + 5x_1x_6 + 6x_1 + 5x_2^2 + 3x_2x_3 + 5x_2x_5 + 4x_2x_6$$
$$+ x_2 + 3x_3^2 + 5x_3x_4 + 4x_3x_5 + 2x_3x_6 + 4x_3 + x_4^2 + 6x_4x_5 + 3x_4x_6 + 4x_4 + 4x_5 + x_6 + 2.$$

Let us assume that we want to find a pre-image $\mathbf{x} \in \mathbb{F}^6$ of $\mathbf{y} = (6, 2, 0, 5)$ under the map $\mathcal{F}$. To do this, we choose random values for the vinegar variables x_1 and x_2, e.g. $(x_1, x_2) = (0, 1)$ and substitute them into the polynomials $f^{(3)}, \ldots , f^{(6)}$. By doing so, we get:

$$\tilde{f}^{(3)} = 5x_3 + 6x_4 + 2,$$

$$\tilde{f}^{(4)} = x_3 + 5x_4,$$

$$\tilde{f}^{(5)} = 3x_3x_4 + x_3x_5 + 2x_3x_6 + 3x_3 + 3x_4x_5 + 4x_4 + 2x_5 + 2x_6,$$

$$\tilde{f}^{(6)} = 3x_3^2 + 5x_3x_4 + 4x_3x_5 + 2x_3x_6 + x_4^2 + 6x_4x_5 + 3x_4x_6 + 4x_4 + 2x_5 + 5x_6 + 1.$$

By setting $\tilde{f}^{(3)} = y_1 = 6$ and $\tilde{f}^{(4)} = y_2 = 2$, we obtain $(x3, x4) = (3, 4)$. Substituting these values into $\tilde{f}^{(5)}$ and $\tilde{f}^{(6)}$ yields,

$$\tilde{\tilde{f}}^{(5)} = 3x_5 + x_6 + 5,$$

$$\tilde{\tilde{f}}^{(6)} = 3x_5 + 2x_6 + 1.$$

By setting $\tilde{\tilde{f}}^{(5)} = y_3 = 0$ and $\tilde{\tilde{f}}^{(6)} = y_4 = 5$, we obtain $(x_5, x_6) = (0, 2)$. Altogether, we get the pre-image $x = (0, 1, 3, 4, 0, 2)$.

Signature Generation: To generate a signature for a message d, one uses a hash function $\mathcal{H} : \{0, 1\}$ $\rightarrow \mathbb{F}^m$ to compute the hash value $\mathbf{w} = \mathcal{H}(d) \in \mathbb{F}^m$ and performs the following three steps:

- Compute $\mathbf{x} = \mathcal{S}^{-1}(\mathbf{w}) \in \mathbb{F}^m$.

- Compute a pre-image $\mathbf{y} \in \mathbb{F}^n$ of x under the central map $\mathcal{F}$. This is done as shown in Algorithm.

- Compute the signature $\mathbf{z} \in \mathbb{F}^n$ by $\mathbf{z} = \mathcal{T}^{-1}(\mathbf{y})$.

Signature Verification: To check if $\mathbf{z} \in \mathbb{F}^n$ is a valid signature for a message d, one computes $\mathbf{w} = \mathcal{H}(d) \in \mathbb{F}^m$ and $\mathbf{w}' = \mathcal{P}(\mathbf{z})$. If If $\mathbf{w}' = \mathbf{w}$ holds the signature is accepted otherwise rejected.

Security: As the Rainbow signature scheme can be seen as an extension of the widely studied UOV signature scheme, major parts of the security analysis of UOV relate to Rainbow, too. However, the additional structure of the Rainbow central map enables a number of new attack strategies, such as the MinRank attack and the Rainbow-Band-Separation attack. This attack aims at finding linear maps which transform the public polynomials into quadratic maps of the form of equation $f^{(k)}(\mathbf{x}) = \sum_{i,j \in V\ell} \alpha_{ij}^{(k)} x_i x_j + \sum_{i \in V\ell, j \in O\ell} \beta_{ij}^{(k)} x_i x_j + \sum_{i \in V\ell \cup O\ell} \gamma_i^{(k)} x_i + \delta^{(k)}$, which then can be used to forge signatures. These linear maps can be computed by solving systems of multivariate nonlinear equations. Due to these additional attack possibilities the parameter selection of Rainbow is a challenging task.

Efficiency and Implementation

Both UOV and Rainbow require only simple operations such as matrix vector multiplication and matrix inversion over small finite fields. Therefore, these schemes are very easy to implement and can also be used on embedded devices. Especially Rainbow is very efficient and is one of the fastest available signature schemes.

Other Schemes

Other important examples for multivariate signature schemes include:

- HFEv-: The HFEv- signature scheme as proposed by Patarin is an example for a multivariate signature scheme of the BigField family, which means that the central map $\mathcal{F}$ is defined over an extension field. HFEv- is one of the best studied multivariate schemes and therefore is believed to offer high security.

- Gui: The Gui signature scheme as proposed is an extension of the HFEv- signature scheme. Due to a specially designed signature generation algorithm, it is possible to create secure signatures of length only 120 bit (80 bit security level), which are the shortest signatures of all existing signature schemes (both classical and post-quantum).

Table: Parameters and Key Sizes of Current Multivariate Signature Schemes.

Security level (bit)	Scheme parameters	Public size (kB)	Private size kB)	Hash size (bit)	Signature size (bit)
80	UOV (GF(2^8), 28, 56)	99.9	95.8	224	672
	Rainbow (GF(2^8), 17, 13, 13)	25.1	19.9	208	344
	HFEv- (GF(7), 62, 8, 2, 2)	47.1	2.9	168	192
	Gui (GF(2), 95, 9, 5, 5)	60.1	3.0	- 1	120
100	UOV (GF(2^8), 35, 70)	193.8	183.2	280	840
	Rainbow (GF(2^8), 26, 17, 16)	59.0	44.4	264	472
	HFEv-(GF(7), 78, 8, 3, 3)	93.5	4.5	210	243
120	Gui(GF(2), 127, 9, 4, 4)	139.1	5.2	-1	163
128	UOV (GF(2^8), 45, 90)	409.4	381.8	360	1,080
	Rainbow (GF(2^8), 36, 22, 21)	136.1	101.3	344	632
	HFEv-(GF(7), 100, 8, 4, 4)	65.2	2.8	264	296

Encryption Schemes

Simple Matrix

The SimpleMatrix (or ABC) encryption scheme was proposed by Tao et al. The scheme can be described as follows:

Let $\mathbb{F}$ be a finite field with q elements and $s \in \mathbb{N}$. We set $n = s^2$ and $m = 2 \cdot n$.

Key Generation: We define three matrices A; B and C of the form,

$$A = \begin{pmatrix} x_1 & \cdots & x_s \\ \vdots & & \vdots \\ x_{(s-1)\cdot s+1} & \cdots & x_n \end{pmatrix}, \; B = \begin{pmatrix} b_1 & \cdots & b_s \\ \vdots & & \vdots \\ b_{(s-1)\cdot s+1} & \cdots & b_n \end{pmatrix}, \; C = \begin{pmatrix} c_1 & \cdots & c_s \\ \vdots & & \vdots \\ c_{(s-1)\cdot s+1} & \cdots & c_n \end{pmatrix}.$$

Here, $x_1, \ldots, x_n$ are the linear monomials of the multivariate polynomial ring $\mathbb{F}[x_1, \ldots, x_n]$, whereas $b_1, \ldots, b_n$ and $c_1, \ldots, c_n$ are randomly chosen linear combinations of $x_1, \ldots, x_n$. One computes two $s \times s$ matrices E_1 and E_2 containing quadratic polynomials by $E_1 = A \cdot B$ and E2 = $A \cdot C$. The central map $\mathcal{F}$ of the scheme consists of the m components of E_1 and E_2.

The public key of the scheme is the composed map $\mathcal{P} = \mathcal{S} \circ \mathcal{F} \circ \mathcal{T} : \mathbb{F}^n \to \mathbb{F}^m$ with two randomly chosen invertible linear maps $\mathcal{S} : \mathbb{F}^m \to \mathbb{F}^m$ and $\mathcal{T} : \mathbb{F}^n \to \mathbb{F}^n$, the private key consists of the matrices B and C and the linear maps $\mathcal{S}$ and $\mathcal{T}$.

- Encryption: To encrypt a message $z \in \mathbb{F}^n$, one simply computes $w = \mathcal{P}(z) \in \mathbb{F}^m$.

- Decryption: To decrypt a ciphertext $w \in \mathbb{F}^m$, one performs the following three steps:

  ○ Compute $x = \mathcal{S}^{-1}(w)$. The elements of the vector $x \in \mathbb{F}^m$ are written into matrices $\bar{E}_1$ and $\bar{E}_2$ as follows,

$$\overline{E}_1 = \begin{pmatrix} x_1 & \cdots & x_s \\ \vdots & & \vdots \\ x_{(s-1)\cdot s+1} & \cdots & x_n \end{pmatrix}, \ \overline{E}_2 = \begin{pmatrix} x_{n+1} & \cdots & x_{n+s} \\ \vdots & & \vdots \\ x_{n+(s-1)\cdot s+1} & \cdots & x_m \end{pmatrix}.$$

○ In the second step one has to find a vector $\mathbf{y} = (\mathbf{y}_1, \ldots, \mathbf{y}_n) \in \mathbb{F}^n$ such that $\mathcal{F}(\mathbf{y}) = \mathbf{x}$. To do this, one assumes that the matrix $\overline{A} = A(\mathbf{y})$ is invertible. One considers the relations fi $\overline{A}^{-1} \cdot \overline{E}_1 - B = 0$ and $\overline{A}^{-1} \cdot \overline{E}_2 - C = 0$. One interprets the elements of $\overline{A}^{-1}$ as new variables $r_1, \ldots, r_n$ and therefore gets m linear equations in the m variables $r_1, \ldots, r_n, y_1, \ldots, y_n$. Hence, the values of $y_1, \ldots, y_n$ can be recovered by Gaussian Elimination.

○ Finally, one computes the plaintext $\mathbf{z} \in \mathbb{F}^n$ by $\mathbf{z} = \mathcal{T}^{-1}(y_1, \ldots, y_n)$.

It might happen that the linear system in the second step has multiple solutions $y^{(1)}, \ldots, y^{(\ell)}$. In this case one has to perform the third step of the decryption process for each of these solutions to get a set of possible plaintexts $\mathbf{z}^{(1)}, \ldots, \mathbf{z}^{(\ell)}$. By encrypting these plaintexts one can test which of them corresponds to the given ciphertext w.

If, in the second step of the decryption process, the matrix $\overline{A} = A(\mathbf{y})$ is not invertible, the plaintext z cannot be recovered (decryption failure). This happens with a probability of about $\frac{1}{q}$. In order to decrease the probability of decryption failures; one therefore uses the SimpleMatrix scheme over large fields $\mathbb{F}$ (e.g. $\mathbb{F} \in \{GF(2^{16}), GF(2^{32})\}$). Furthermore, a number of techniques has been proposed to reduce the probability of decryption failures of the SimpleMatrix scheme. However, a general solution to this problem is still missing. On the other hand, public key encryption schemes are mainly used for the key establishment of symmetric ciphers such as AES. Therefore, if one key cannot be transmitted correctly, it is easy to replace it by another plaintext.

SRP

Another promising candidate for a public key encryption scheme on the basis of multivariate polynomials is the SRP encryption scheme of Yasuda et al. The scheme combines several multivariate schemes into one, which prevents some of the known attacks against multivariate schemes. However, similar to many multivariate schemes, the key sizes are quite large.

Table: Parameters and Key Sizes of Current Multivariate Encryption Schemes.

Security level (bit)	Scheme parameters	Public size (kB)	Private size (kB)	Plaintext size (bit)	Ciphertext size (bit)
80	SimpleMatrix(GF(2^{16}), 7)	244.0	33.3	784	1,568
	SRP(GF(31), 33, 32, 16, 5, 16)	66.9	39.9	245	430
100	SimpleMatrix(GF(2^{16}), 8)	536.3	56.6	1,024	2,048
	SRP(GF(31), 43, 43, 20, 5, 20)	154.3	85.9	330	555
128	SimpleMatrix(GF(2^{16}), 9)	1,076.7	90.5	1,296	2,592
	SRP(GF(31), 59, 59, 28, 5, 28)	385.8	212.4	450	755

Post-Quantum Cryptography

Post-quantum cryptography is centered around the algorithms that are designed to secure data in the age of quantum computing and beyond. It's key that we develop these cryptography algorithms and purpose-built hardware cryptographic engines, as processing these algorithms in software may be too slow for certain high-throughput networking equipment. The new algorithms could be much more computationally intensive than our existing standards, including RSA and ECC, specifically if their implementations need to be protected against side-channel attacks.

Challenges being Faced in Developing Post-Quantum Security Algorithms

These post-quantum cryptography algorithms are more complex than our current algorithms. One of the main challenges is the size of the keys themselves. Current encryption and signature algorithms have keys that are a few hundred or thousand bits long. Some of the proposed post-quantum algorithms have key sizes of several tens of kilobytes up to a megabyte sometimes. This means we need to be able to store these keys efficiently.

When the public keys are used in public key infrastructure certificates (PKIs) and need to be communicated or stored locally on the end device, this will cost more bandwidth and memory, too. And bandwidth requirements will likely increase when using those schemes that have large size ciphertexts. Another major challenge is going to be seen in IoT, where endpoint devices already have limited compute and processing power. As edge computing and the IoT continue to become more ubiquitous, it'll be important that these devices are protected against quantum attacks.

Another major challenge is to be able to assess the security of these new algorithms against both classical and quantum attacks. The underlying new mathematical primitives are not all that well-studied yet, and it's an open problem to know exactly how secure these proposed algorithms are at this time.

Lattice-Based Cryptography

Lattice-based cryptography is the generic term for constructions of cryptographic primitives that involve lattices, either in the construction itself or in the security proof. A lattice can basically be thought of as any regularly spaced grid of points stretching out to infinity. For example, here are 2 different, 2-dimensional lattices.

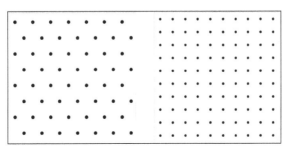

Vector

A vector is nothing more than a fancy name for a point, a tuple of numbers called the coordinates of the vector. So (2,3) is a particular 2-dimensional vector as it has 2 coordinates, and a lattice is a collection of evenly spaced vectors. A special vector of interest is the origin which is the vector with all coordinates set to 0. For example, in 3 dimensions, the origin is (0, 0, 0). We say that a vector is long if it is far away from the origin. Conversely, a vector is short if it is close to the origin.

Basis

Lattices are infinitely large objects but computers only have a finite amount of memory to work with. So we will need a succinct way to represent lattices if we are going to use them in cryptography. For this, we use what is called a basis of a lattice. A basis is a small collection of vectors that can be used to reproduce any point in the grid that forms the lattice.

Let's look at the case of a 2-dimensional lattice, a grid of points on a flat surface like a piece of paper. First, choose two more points that don't happen to lie on a single line going through the origin. For example, we could choose (2,0) and (0,2). Here is how these points can be used to generate the third point:

- First, we choose two whole numbers; say, 3 and -1.

- We multiply the coordinates of the first point by 3 to get the point (6,0) and the coordinates of the second point by -1 to get (0,-2).

- Now we add the results together to get our new point (6,-2).

Using this method, we can use (2,0) and (0,2) to generate an entire grid of evenly spaced points, namely all those with coordinates (x,y) such that both x and y are even numbers where we also count 0 as an even number. In other words, the basis consisting of vectors (2,0) and (0,2) generates the lattice points with even coordinates. The idea is that by choosing a basis we have actually chosen an entire lattice, namely the one whose points are generated by the vectors in the basis. Crucially, in contrast to an infinite grid of points, a basis is a simple finite object which we can represent in a computer's memory.

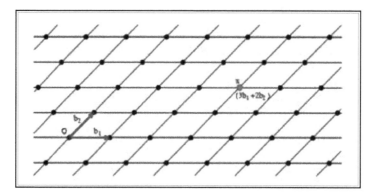

An important thing to notice is that any given lattice doesn't have just one basis. In fact, it has many bases. For example, instead of using (2,0) and (0,2) above we could have just as well chosen (-2,0) and (0, -2) or even (4, 2) and (2, 2). In each case, they end up generating the exact same grid of points.

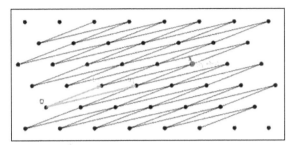

We say that a basis is *short* if it consists of short vectors. Conversely, we say that a basis is *long* if it consists only of long vectors. It turns out that short bases are much more useful than long ones when it comes to solving the types of hard lattice problems cryptographers are interested in.

So what would a *hard* lattice problem look like? It turns out that given what we learned so far, these problems are now very simple to understand. For example, here is the "Short Vector Problem" which is probably the single most important problem in lattice-based crypto. Short vector problem:

- Suppose we are given a long basis for some lattice L.

- Then the short vector problem asks us to find a grid point in L as close as possible (but not equal too) the origin point.

At first glance, this might seem like a relatively easy problem to solve. However, notice that the basis we are given consists of long vectors. So it's not immediately clear how they can be combined to generate a point with only small coordinates, namely a short vector. Moreover, when it comes to cryptography, we're really talking about lattices in much higher dimensions (e.g. 10,000 instead of just 2). That means that our points actually have 10,000 coordinates, not 2 coordinates. So finding a combination of the basis vectors that simultaneously makes all 10,000 generated coordinates small turns out to be quite hard, so much so that we don't know how to solve the problem quickly even with a quantum computer, let alone a conventional one.

Here are two more important and very closely related hard lattice problems used by cryptographers to base security on:

- Short basis problem: Suppose we are given a long basis for some lattice L. The short basis problem asks us to find a short basis for L.

- Closest vector problem: suppose we are given a long basis for lattice L. moreover, we are given a randomly chosen challenge point P. The closest problem asks us to find the closest lattice point in L to challenge P.

It's worth noting that each of these problems is actually quite easy to solve quickly even without a quantum computer if the lattice is described using a short basis instead of a long one.

So why Lattices?

So what is so great about Lattice-based cryptography anyway? Well, out of the various candidate families of hard problems, lattice-based crypto presents several important and very attractive features.

First, it is fair to say that these are the most well understood and widely studied families of hard math problems. Lattices have been studied by mathematicians going back at least as far as the early 1800s when they were considered by Johann Gauß, one of the greatest mathematicians of all time. Of course, Guaß, and others had no concept of a quantum computer and so were hardly trying to develop a quantum algorithm to solve the lattice problems we are interested in today. Yet these older mathematical works still serve as sources of deep understanding and powerful insights into what we can and cannot do when it comes to working with Lattices. After all, although Euclid had no concept of a modern computer, his 2,500-year-old works on number theory still form the core of some very important algorithms we use today (e.g. the aptly named *Euclid's Algorithm*).

Second, Lattice problems are proving to be incredibly versatile in terms of the types of cryptographic schemes they allow us to build. In fact, not only are we able to replace essentially all of our currently endangered schemes, but lattice problems even allow for entirely new classes of *extremely* powerful cryptographic tools for which we simply have no analogs based on factoring or any other hard mathematical problems. And that includes the competing families of hard problems which we believe are still unsolvable with a quantum computer.

Third, Lattice-based cryptographic schemes make up the lion's share of scientific publications in the field of so-called "post-quantum" cryptography. That is the field of cryptography concerned with building schemes secure against attackers armed with powerful quantum computers. Indeed, if you look at the entrants to the "post-quantum" international competition run by the US National Institute for Standards in Technology, which is focused on standardizing new post-quantum secure cryptography, you will notice that the largest family of submissions consist of lattice-based schemes.

Finally, the property of lattice-based problems worth highlighting is somewhat technical in nature. For many cryptographers, it is perhaps the strongest argument in favor of using lattice problems for cryptography.

To understand their property, we must think about different kinds of assumptions. Stating that mathematical problems used by cryptographers are hard to solve is a type of assumption since we have no hard proof of such claims, just a lot of failed attempts at solving them. Moreover, if we are going to base our security on an assumption, then it makes sense to use the weakest, hence most plausible assumption possible. For example, a system that is secure based on the assumption that at least one participant is honest would be preferable to a different system which is secure only if we assume a majority of participants are secure. Assuming there is at least one honest participant is a weaker assumption (i.e. easier to satisfy or more plausible to hold) than assuming a majority of participants are honest.

Normally, in crypto, we assume that our underlying math problems are hard to solve on average. That means that we assume that if you are given a randomly chosen instance of the problem, then it is highly probable that it will be hard to solve. In the case of factoring, for example, the assumption is that it is hard to factor an integer $n = p \times q$ if p and q were chosen at random. This type of average-case hardness stands in contrast to what is called worst-case hardness. A problem is worst-case hard if at least one instance of the problem is hard to solve.

The important point here is that the average-case hardness is a much stricter, thus a more difficult to satisfy, type of hardness than worst-case hardness. For example, it is possible that there are some exceedingly rare corner case instances that are hard to solve, while the vast majority of instances are trivially easy to solve.

Such a problem would still be worst-case hard but not average-case hard because a random instance would almost never end up being one of those corner cases. However, any problem that is average-case hard is most certainly also worst-cast hard. The crux of the matter is that assuming a particular problem is worst-case hard is a much weaker and thus a more plausible assumption to make than to assume that is average-case hard. It turns out that for the type of lattice-based problems we use in crypto, we are usually able to prove the security of our schemes based only on the worst-case hardness of the problems rather than their average-case hardness. In fact, it was exactly this insight by Miklós Ajtai in 1996 that kicked off the entire field of lattice-based cryptography in the first place.

Quantum Cryptography

Rather than depending on the complexity of factoring large numbers, quantum cryptography is based on the fundamental and unchanging principles of quantum mechanics. In fact, quantum cryptography rests on two pillars of 20th century quantum mechanics –the Heisenberg Uncertainty principle and the principle of photon polarization. According the Heisenberg Uncertainty principle, it is not possible to measure the quantum state of any system without disturbing that system. Thus, the polarization of a photon or light particle can only be known at the point when it is measured. This principle plays a critical role in thwarting the attempts of eavesdroppers in a cryptosystem based on quantum cryptography. Secondly, the photon polarization principle describes how light photons can be oriented or polarized in specific directions. Moreover, a photon filter with the correct polarization can only detect a polarized photon or else the photon will be destroyed. It is this "one-way-ness" of photons along with the Heisenberg Uncertainty principle that make quantum cryptography an attractive option for ensuring the privacy of data and defeating eavesdroppers.

Charles H. Bennet and Gilles Brassard developed the concept of quantum cryptography in 1984 as part of a study between physics and information. Bennet and Brassad stated that an encryption key could be created depending on the amount of photons reaching a recipient and how they were received. Their belief corresponds to the fact that light can behave with the characteristics of particles in addition to light waves. These photons can be polarized at various orientations, and these orientations can be used to represent bits encompassing ones and zeros. These bits can be used as a reliable method of forming onetime pads and support systems like PKI by delivering keys in a secure fashion. The representation of bits through polarized photons is the foundation of quantum cryptography that serves as the underlying principle of quantum key distribution. Thus, while the strength of modern digital cryptography is dependent on the computational difficulty of factoring large numbers, quantum cryptography is completely dependent on the rules of physics and is also independent of the processing power of current computing systems. Since the principle of physics will always hold true, quantum cryptography provides an answer to the uncertainty problem that current cryptography suffers from; it is no longer necessary to make assumptions about the computing power of malicious attackers or the development of a theorem to quickly solve the large integer Factorization problem.

A Quantum Key Distribution Example

The following is an example of how quantum cryptography can be used to securely distribute keys. This example includes a sender, "Alice", a receiver, "Bob", and a malicious eavesdropper, "Eve" Alice begins by sending a message to Bob using a photon gun to send a stream of photons randomly chosen in one of four polarizations that correspond to vertical, horizontal or diagonal in opposing directions (0,45,90 or 135 degrees). For each individual photon, Bob will randomly choose a filter and use a photon receiver to count and measure the polarization which is either rectilinear (0 or 90 degrees) or diagonal (45 or 135 degrees), and keep a log of the results based on which measurements were correct vis-à-vis the polarizations that Alice selected. While a portion of the stream of photons will disintegrate over the distance of the link, only a predetermined portion is required to build a key sequence for a onetime pad.

Next, using an out- of-band communication system, Bob will inform Alice to the type of measurement made and which measurements were of the correct type without mentioning the actual results. The photons that were incorrectly measured will be discarded, while the correctly measured photons are translated into bits based on their polarization. These photons are used to form the basis of a onetime pad for sending encrypted information. It is important to point out that neither Alice nor Bob are able to determine what the key will be in advance because the key is the product of both their random choices. Thus, quantum cryptography enables the distribution of a one-time key exchanged securely.

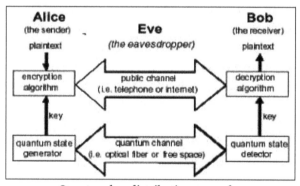

Quantum key distribution example.

Now let us suppose that a malicious attacker attempts to infiltrate the cryptosystem and defeat the quantum key distribution mechanisms. If this malicious attacker, named Eave, tries to eavesdrop, she too must also randomly select either a rectilinear or diagonal filter to measure each of Alice's photons.

Hence, Eve will have an equal chance of selecting the right and wrong filter, and will not be able to confirm with Alice the type of filter used. Even if Eve is able to successfully eavesdrop while Bob confirms with Alice the protons he received, this information will be of little use to Eve unless she knows the correct polarization of each particular photon. As a result, Eve will not correctly interpret the photons that form the final key, and she will not be able to render a meaningful key and thus be thwarted in her endeavors. In sum, there are three significant advantages of this system. First, the Heisenberg Uncertainty principle means that information regarding photons cannot be duplicated because photons will be destroyed once they are measured or tampered with. Since photons are indivisible, once it hits a detector, the photon no longer exists. Secondly, Alice and

Bob must. calculate beforehand the amount of photons needed to form the encryption key so that the length of the one-time pad will correspond to the length of the message. Since mathematically Bob should receive about 25 percent of transmitted photons, if there is a deviation for the predetermined fixed number, Bob can be certain that traffic is being sniffed or something is wrong in the system. This is the result of the fact that if Eve detects a photon, it will no longer exist to be detected by Bob due to Eve's inability to copy an unknown quantum state. If Eve attempts to create and pass on to Bob a photon, she will have to randomly choose its orientation, and on average be incorrect about 50 percent of the time–enough of an error rate to reveal her presence.

Basic quantum key distribution protocol.

- Alice sends a random sequence of photons polarized horizontal (↔), vertical (↕) right circular (↩) and left circular(↪).

- Bob measures the photons' polarization in a random sequence of bases, rectilinear (+) and circular (O).

- Result of bob's measurements (some photons may not be received at all).

- Bob tells alice which besis he used for each photons he received.

- Alice tells him which bases were correct.

- Alice and bob keep only the data from these correctly – measured photons, discarding all the rest.

- This data is interrupted as a binary sequence according to the coding scheme ↔=↪=0and ↕=↩=1.

Desirable QKD Attributes

Broadly stated, QKD offers a technique for coming to agreement upon a shared random sequence of bits within two distinct devices, with a very low probability that other devices (eavesdroppers) will be able to make successful inferences as to those bits' values. In specific practice, such sequences are then used as secret keys for encoding and decoding messages between the two devices.

Confidentiality of Keys

Confidentiality is the main reason for interest in QKD. Public key systems suffer from an on-going uncertainty that decryption is mathematically intractable. Thus key agreement primitives widely used in today's Internet security architecture, e.g., Diffie-Hellman, may perhaps be broken at some point in the future. This would not only hinder future ability to communicate but could reveal past traffic. Classic secret key systems have suffered from different problems, namely, insider threats and the logistical burden of distributing keying material. Assuming that QKD techniques are properly embedded into an overall secure system, they can provide automatic distribution of keys that may offer security superior to that of its competitors.

Authentication

QKD does not in itself provide authentication. Current strategies for authentication in QKD systems include prepositioning of secret keys at pairs of devices, to be used in hash-based authentication schemes, or hybrid QKD-public key techniques. Neither approach is entirely appealing. Prepositioned secret keys require some means of distributing these keys before QKD itself begins, e.g., by human courier, which may be costly and logistically challenging. Furthermore, this approach appears open to denial of service attacks in which an adversary forces a QKD system to exhaust its stockpile of key material, at which point it can no longer perform authentication. On the other hand, hybrid QKD-public key schemes inherit the possible vulnerabilities of public key systems to cracking via quantum computers or unexpected advances in mathematics.

Sufficiently Rapid Key Delivery

Key distribution systems must deliver keys fast enough so that encryption devices do not exhaust their supply of key bits. This is a race between the rate at which keying material is put into place and the rate at which it is consumed for encryption or decryption activities. Today's QKD systems achieve on the order of 1,000 bits/second throughput for keying material, in realistic settings, and often run at much lower rates. This is unacceptably low if one uses these keys in certain ways, e.g., as one-time pads for high speed traffic flows. However it may well be acceptable if the keying material is used as input for less secure (but often secure enough) algorithms such as the Advanced Encryption Standard. Nonetheless, it is both desirable and possible to greatly improve upon the rates provided by today's QKD technology.

Robustness

The QKD community has not traditionally taken this into account. However, since keying material is essential for secure communications, it is extremely important that the flow of keying material not be disrupted, whether by accident or by the deliberate acts of an adversary (i.e. by denial of service). Here QKD has provided a highly fragile service to date since QKD techniques have implicitly been employed along a single point-to-point link. If that link were disrupted, whether by active eavesdropping or indeed by fiber cut, all flow of keying material would cease. In our view a meshed QKD network is inherently far more robust than any single point-to-point link since it offers multiple paths for key distribution.

Distances and Location Independence

In the ideal world, any entity can agree upon keying material with any other (authorized) entity in the world. Rather remarkably, the Internet's security architecture does offer this feature – any Computer on the Internet can form a security association with any other, agreeing upon keys through the Internet IPsec protocols. This feature is notably lacking in QKD, which requires the two entities to have a direct and unencumbered path for photons between them, and which can only operate for a few tens of kilometers through fiber.

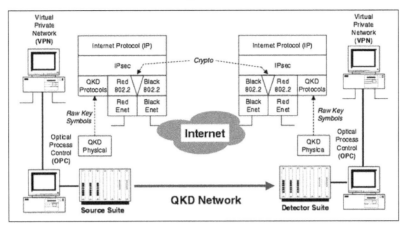

Resistance to Traffic Analysis

Adversaries may be able to perform useful traffic analysis on a key distribution system, e.g., a heavy flow of keying material between two points might reveal that a large volume of confidential information flows, or will flow, between them. It may thus be desirable to impede such analysis. Here QKD in general has had a rather weak approach since most setups have assumed dedicated, point-to point QKD links between communicating entities, which thus clearly lays out the underlying key distribution relationships.

Implementing Quantum Cryptography

The DARPA Quantum Network

The DARPA security model is the cryptographic Virtual Private Network (VPN). Conventional VPNs use both public-key and symmetric cryptography to achieve confidentiality and authentication/integrity. Public-key mechanisms support key exchange or agreement, and authenticate the endpoints. Symmetric mechanisms (e.g. 3DES, SHA1) provide traffic confidentiality and integrity. Thus VPN systems can provide confidentiality and authentication/integrity without trusting the public network interconnecting the VPN sites. In DARPA work, existing VPN key agreement primitives are augmented or completely replaced by keys provided by quantum cryptography. The remainder of the VPN construct is left unchanged; Thus DARPA QKD-secured network is fully compatible with conventional Internet hosts, routers, firewalls, and so forth.

QKD Protocols Implementation

Quantum cryptography involves a surprisingly elaborate suite of specialized protocols, which we term "QKD protocols." Many aspects of these protocols are unusual – both in motivation and in implementation – and may be of interest to specialists in communications protocols.

DARPA have designed this engine so it is easy to "plug in" new protocols, and expect to devote considerable time in coming years to inventing new QKD protocols and trying them in practice. As shown in Figure, these protocols are best described as sub-layers within the QKD protocol suite.

Note, however, that these layers do not correspond in any obvious way to the layers in a communications stack, e.g., the OSI layers. They are in fact closer to being pipeline stages.

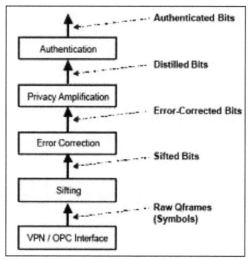

The QKD protocol Stack.

Sifting

Sifting is the process whereby Alice and Bob window away all the obvious "failed q bits" from a series of pulses, these failures include those q bits where Alice's laser never transmitted, Bob's detectors didn't work, photons were lost in transmission, and so forth. They also include those symbols where Alice chose one basis for transmission but Bob chose the other for receiving. At the end of this round of protocol interaction – i.e. after a sift and sift response transaction – Alice and Bob discard all the useless symbols from their internal storage, leaving only those symbols that Bob received and for which Bob's basis matches Alice's.

Error Correction

Error correction allows Alice and Bob to determine all the "error bits" among their shared, sifted bits, and correct them so that Alice and Bob share the same sequence of error-corrected bits. Error bits are ones that Alice transmitted as a 0 but Bob received as a 1, or vice versa. These bit errors can be caused by noise or by eavesdropping. Error correction in quantum cryptography has a very unusual constraint, namely, evidence revealed in error detection and correction (e.g. parity bits) must be assumed to be known to Eve, and thus to reduce the hidden entropy available for key material. As a result, there is very strong motivation to design error detection and correction codes that reveal as little as possible in their public control traffic between Alice and Bob.

Privacy Amplification

Privacy amplification is the process whereby Alice and Bob reduce Eve's knowledge of their shared bits to an acceptable level. This technique is also often called advantage distillation. The side that initiates privacy amplification chooses a linear hash function over the Galois Field GF[2n] where n is the number of bits as input, rounded up to a multiple of 32. He then transmits four things to the other end—the number of bits m of the shortened result, the (sparse) primitive polynomial of the Galois field, a multiplier (n bits long), and an m-bit polynomial to add (i.e. a bit string to exclusive-or) with the product. Each side then performs the corresponding hash and truncates the result to m bits to perform privacy amplification.

Authentication

Authentication allows Alice and Bob to guard against "man in the middle attacks," i.e., allows Alice to ensure that she is communicating with Bob (and not Eve) and vice versa. Authentication must be performed on an on-going basis for all key management traffic, since Eve may insert herself into the conversation between Alice and Bob at any stage in their communication. The original BB84 paper described the authentication problem and sketched a solution to it based on universal families of hash functions, introduced by Wegman and Carter. This approach requires Alice and Bob to already share a small secret key, which is used to select a hash function from the family to generate an authentication hash of the public correspondence between them. By the nature of universal hashing, any party who didn't know the secret key would have an extremely low probability of being able to forge the correspondence, even an adversary with unlimited computational power.

The drawback is that the secret key bits cannot be re-used even once on different data without compromising the security. Fortunately, a complete authenticated conversation can validate a large number of new, shared secret bits from QKD, and a small number of these may be used to replenish the pool. There are many further details in a practical system which we will only mention in passing, including symmetrically authenticating both parties, limiting the opportunities for Eve to force exhaustion of the shared secret key bits, and adapting the system to network asynchrony and retransmissions. Another important point: it is insufficient to authenticate just the QKD protocols; we must also apply these techniques to authenticate the VPN data traffic.

Steganography

Steganography is the practice of hiding information. It has been around for centuries. And in parallel to technological advances, steganography has also evolved and adapted with the advent of computers and the internet. Digital steganography usually involves hiding data inside innocuous files such as images, videos, and audio. Today, digital steganography is one of the important components in the toolboxes of spies and malicious hackers, as well as human rights activists and political dissidents.

Steganography is the use of various methods to hide information from unwanted eyes. In ancient times, steganography was mostly done physically. The oldest documented case of steganography dates to 500 BC, in which Histiaeus, the ruler of Milteus, tattooed a message on the shaved head of one of his slaves and let the hair grow back. He then sent the slave to the Aristagoras, his son-in-law, who shaved the slave's head again and revealed the message. In the centuries that followed, more modern forms of steganography were invented, such as invisible inks. Today, steganography has moved to the digital world. "Steganography by definition is the hiding of one file within another".

How does Steganography Work?

Steganography works by hiding information in a way that doesn't arouse suspicion. One of the most popular techniques is 'least significant bit (LSB) steganography. In this type of steganography, the information hider embeds the secret information in the least significant bits of a media file.

For instance, in an image file each pixel is comprised of three bytes of data corresponding to the colors red, green, and blue (some image formats allocate an additional fourth byte to transparency, or 'alpha'). LSB steganography changes the last bit of each of those bytes to hide one bit of data. So, to hide one megabyte of data using this method, you'll need an eight-megabyte image file.

Since modifying the last bit of the pixel value doesn't result in a visually perceptible change to the picture, a person viewing the original and the steganographically modified images won't be able to tell the difference.

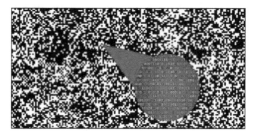

Steganography is the practice of hiding of one file within another.

The same scheme can be applied to other digital media (audio and video), where data is hidden in parts of the file that result in the least change to the audible or visual output. Another less popular steganography technique is the use of word or letter substitution. Here, the sender of the secret message hides the text by distributing it inside a much larger text, placing the words at specific intervals.

While this substitution method is easy to use, it may also make the text look strange and out of place, since the secret words might not fit particularly well into their target sentences. There are other types of steganography, such as hiding an entire partition on a hard drive, or embedding data in the header section of files and network packets. The effectiveness of these methods depends on how much data they can hide and how easy they are to detect.

Who uses Steganography?

Malicious hackers use steganography for a variety of tasks such as hiding malicious payloads and script files. Malware developers often use LSB steganography to hide the code for their malware in images of celebrities and famous songs and execute them with another program after the file is downloaded on the victim's computer.

"The term 'Trojan Horse' is used to describe a dangerous file hidden within a harmless file. Macro attacks are a form of steganography as well," "Steganography will be used by creative hackers whenever there is a need to bypass protections."

Cybercriminals, however, are not the only actors who use steganography on a daily basis. Spies use the technique to communicate with their command center without arousing suspicion among their hosts. Tech-savvy human rights activists and dissidents also use steganography when they want to send sensitive information.

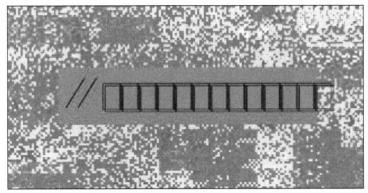

Steganography is used by everyone from human rights activists to cybercriminals.

Visual Cryptography

Visual Cryptography is a cryptographic technique which allows visual information to be encrypted in such a way that decryption becomes a mechanical operation that does not require a computer. In today's computer generation, data security, hiding and all such activities have become probably the most important aspect for most organizations. These organizations spend millions of their currency to just secure their data. This urgency has risen due to increase in cyber theft/ crime. The technology has grown so much that criminals have found multiple ways to perform cybercrime to which the concerned authorities have either less or not sufficient answer to counter. Hence, the method of Cryptography provides the above answers. One of the most major parts of cryptography is Visual cryptography. It has many usage and application areas, mostly using its internal technique called encryption.

Rijndael and RC6 Block Ciphers

Information in different forms such as text, image, multimedia etc. is an important tool in today's day-to-day life. Thus, arise the need to protect this information/data from outside interference which can create a threat at a large scale in many cases.

- Rijndael: The Rijndael block cipher is an iterated block cipher using variable block and key size. It is the only encryption mode using parallel processing. The block cipher algorithm provides mapping of plain text block to cipher text block and consequently, from cipher text block to plain text block using cipher key. Rijndael supports all combinations of block and key sizes of multiple of 32 bits with minimum of 128 bits and maximum of 256 bits.

- RC6: The RC6 block cipher depends mainly on four working registers, each of 32 bits. It is a key having variable parameters such as key and block size, number of rounds. RC6 encrypted algorithm is designated as: -RC6 (w,r,b) where w is the word size, r is the number of rounds, b is the number of bytes.

Study of Rijndael and RC6 with Some Results Visual Encryption

The research was based on a medical image with black area and CS logo with white area. Figure shows the medical image of a brain with black area to be used for encryption.

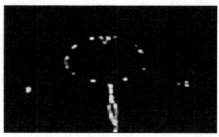

Medical image of a brain with black area.

Figure shows an image consisting of two letters C & S with white area to be used for encryption.

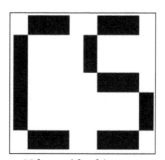

CS logo with white area.

Through the experiments, it was inevitable that Rijndael and RC6 block cipher algorithms work efficiently in ECB Mode using pre- processing. Figures below show the results of the above for both images.

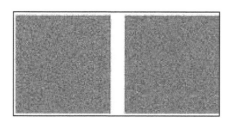   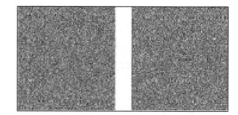

Encrypted medical images with Rijndael and RC6algo-
rithms in ECB mode using pre- processing.

Encrypted CS logo with Rijndael and RC6 algorithms
in ECB mode using pre- processing.

Irregularity of Deviation

It calculates the quality of an image through encryption by finding the minimal deviation in comparison to ideal encryption. Irregular deviation DI is as follows:

$$D_I = \frac{\sum_{i-0}^{255} H_D(i)}{M \times N}$$

Where, M and N give the measurements of the image. Quality of encryption increases with less DI. Irregularity for both algorithms between the encrypted and plain image increases.

Histogram Analysis

The Histogram in this case, uses a bar graph to fix occurrence of one grey level present. X - Axis shows all grey level values and Y - Axis represents a grey level occurrence. Figure shows the original histograms of the brain and logo image, respectively whereas Figures shows the histograms of the encrypted form of both the images, respectively.

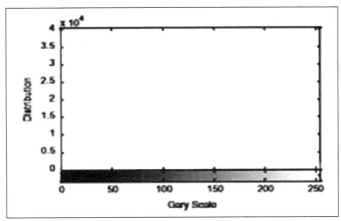

Histogram of the brain image.

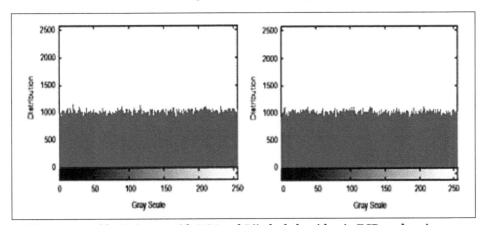

Histogram of the encrypted brain image with RC6 and Rijndael algorithm in ECB mode using pre- processing.

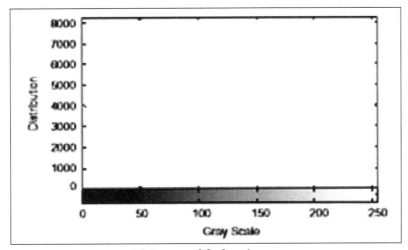

Histogram of the logo image.

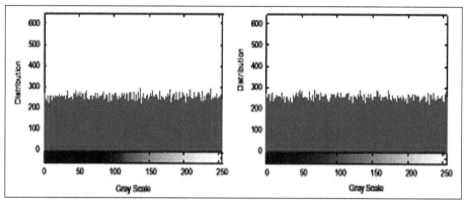

Histogram of the encrypted logo image with RC6 and Rijndael
algorithm in ECB mode using pre- processing.

Encryption Quality Metric

The Quality Metric DP is as follows:

$$D_P = \frac{\sum_{C_I=0}^{255} \left| H\left(C_I - H(C)\right) \right|}{M \times N}$$

Where, $H(C_I)$ is the histogram of the encrypted image. The lower the value of encryption quality metric, better the encryption quality. Pre- processing enhances performances of encryption algorithms. Researchers could have used Steganography to further impact their research of encrypting data in images of black and white backgrounds. The color block cipher algorithms of Rijndael and RC6 would have generated exceptional results using the features of Steganography.

Data Hiding in PDF Files

Portable Document Format (PDF) is a file format developed by Adobe Systems which is unique in nature and independent of any software, hardware or operating system. PDF secures data of all types such as text, images, graphics etc. which makes the data in it very difficult to breach. The first technique looks for trash spaces in the file and replaces those spaces with encrypted version of data. The second technique manages to keep large amount of encrypted data without changing the usefulness of the file. Stego PDF Creator (SPDFC) as well as Secret Data Viewer (SDV) uses these techniques on Windows.

Finding Trash Spaces

The below equations are used to calculate the trash spaces in a PDF file:

$$\left| A_i \right| = \sum_{j=1}^{n} \left| a_j \right|$$

Where, |aj| is the extreme limit of jth element in Ai.

$$\left| X \right| = \sum_{i=1}^{n} \left| A_i \right|$$

The Cardinality of set X calculates complete length of PDF main body as well as the trash spaces. The required steps of finding trash spaces are:

- Assume an array B[], Ascii _ key

- Enter statement" PDF File1"

- Take for loop a=0 to 255

- Assume Ascii_key=a

- Take for loop b=1 to length("PDF File1")

- If statement Ascii_key=ASCII("Character of PDF File1")

- Count the characters, cnt=cnt+1

- Keep all locations in array B[]

- Stop if statement

- Stop second for statement

- Stop first for statement

- Exit

From above technique, illustrated values of trash spaces in response to PDF Version 6 are shown in Figure.

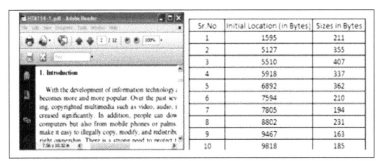

Sr.No	Initial Location (in Bytes)	Sizes in Bytes
1	1595	211
2	5127	355
3	5510	407
4	5918	337
5	6892	362
6	7594	210
7	7805	194
8	8802	231
9	9467	163
10	9818	185

(a) File size 373 KB (b) Trash spaces.

Steps for embedding of data in trash spaces:

- Enter statement" PDF file1"

- Enter statement" Encrypted secret data1"

- Enter statement" S_ key"

- Fetch Trash Space through code

- Take for loop a=1 to length ("Secret data1")

- Take for loop b=1 to length (B[])

- Change to "S_ key"

- Change to "Secret data1"

- Stop second for loop

- Stop first for loop

- Keep the statement" S file"

- Exit

Extraction Algorithm of Trash Spaces

The steps proposed for extraction are:

- Assume an array T[], Ascii_key

- Enter statement" PDF file1"

- Enter S_key

- Take for loop a=1 to length ("PDF file1")

- If statement S_key=String ("Characters of file")

- Keep the String ("Characters of file") in array T[]

- Stop if statement

- Stop for statement

- Exit

Data Appending

The second technique removes some anomalies of the first in the case, when the total size of the trash doesn't equal the data size. So, the steps required for appending secret data using the second technique are:

- Enter statement" PDF file1"

- Enter statement" S_key"

- Enter statement" Encrypted secret data1"

- Go to EOF ("PDF file1")

- Store statement" S_key

- Take for loop a=0 to length ("Secret data1")

- Keep the "Originals"

- Keepthe "Encrypting originals"

- Stop for statement

- Keep the statement" S file"

- Exit

Extraction Algorithm of Data Appending

Steps proposed for finding secret data using the second technique:

- Enter statement" PDF file1"

- Enter statement" S_key"

- Take for loop a=0 to length ("PDF file1")

- If statement S_key=String ("Characters of file")

- Keep the String ("Characters of file") in T[]

- Stop if statement

- Stop for statement

- Reshuffle T []

- Exit

By combining both techniques technique, more data can be stored and hid.

Comparing Performance of Both Techniques with other Known Techniques

On the Basis of Capacity to Handle Data

- Previous Techniques proposed by different researchers: Most of the researchers took a picture as something which can store less data.

- Trash Spaces and Data Appending Techniques: These techniques can handle large amount of data by taking more number of objects as in the case of first technique. In the second technique, more voluminous secret data can be embedded.

On the Basis of Compression to Compress and Decompress Data in Files

- Previous Techniques proposed by different researchers: Here, robustness of files was present but secret data was unchangeable.

- Trash Spaces and Data Appending Techniques: Both these techniques support compression and decompression tests.

On the Basis of Visual Analysis to Visually See Data

- Previous Techniques proposed by different researchers: There were changes which could visually see in those steg files of these techniques.

- Trash Spaces and Data Appending Techniques: No visual changes seen in any of the two techniques. Though, the proposed techniques of the researchers have many advantages as compared to previous traditional techniques but the different extraction algorithms used each for finding trash spaces and data appending have made it a slightly lengthy process. This could have been avoided if the researchers would have used just one algorithm each for both the techniques. The extraction process could have been nested inside the main algorithm and would have sped up the process.

Securing Images through Recursive Visual Cryptography

Security is probably the most challenging and needed property in today's technological era. Many organizations have spent tremendous amount of money just to acquire this property for all their related projects. Without security, the data of any organization or a single unit is under threat of getting misplaced or completely taken out from existence. Such is the case with image authentication. Its security analysis is performed through a special method known as Visual Cryptography Scheme (VCS).

VCS known for its security uses the method of encryption to separate one image into many consecutive images. Advantage of VCS is that it provides the user with decryption of code which does not require any complex computation. The researchers have explained the most widely used Gnanagurupuram- Kak (2, 2)-RVCSwhich is used to authenticate all kinds of images.

The Gnanagurupuram–Kak(2, 2)-RVCS methodmakes the images hidden in 2 places which enhances the images in an effective manner. Some notations required to define the encoding procedure are as follows:

Jj- it is the jth secret image where j is in the range [1, N].

Q (-)- it is the operation of (2,2)-VCS which encrypts I into 2 different pales P1 and P2. For an assumed P1, Q (J, P1) =P2.

Pj, 1(Pj, 2) - 2 places of the jth step in (2, 2)-RVCS which gives Jj=Pj, 2+Pj,2.

R1 (R2)- last of 2 places of (2, 2)-RVCS.

Encoding procedure is as follows:

Enter: Jj where j is in the range [1,N].

Result: For R1 and R2,

1. Take an assumed P1, 1.

2. a) Take for loop a=1 to (N-1)

```
Do loop { Calculate Q(Jj,pj,1)=pj,2;

Pj+1, 1=Pj, 1 concatenate Pj,2 };
```

   b) Calculate Q(PN,PN,1)=PN,2.

3. Result R1=PN, 1 and R2=PN,2.

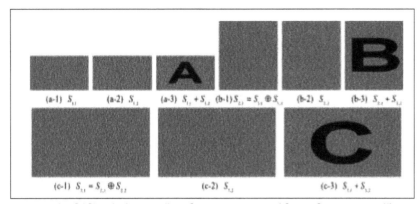

Recursive hiding in images i) 2 places P1,1, P1,2 with result P1,1+ P1,2 ii) 2 places P2,1, P2,2 with result P2,1+ P2,2 iii) 2 places P3,1, P3,2 with result P3,1+ P3,2.

Hence, RVCS has the capability to enhance information in images through recursive hiding. But there are some limitations occurring due to some information present in sub-pixels. Hence, using this method for authentication purpose, the security should be taken under consideration.

Recursive Visual Cryptography is a vast subject inside Visual Cryptography. Though, the researchers have mentioned that they will use the Gnanagurupuram algorithm but still the other techniques need to be mentioned in order to perform a comparative analysis and choose the best security authentication technique.

Cyber Crime through Encryption Techniques

Cybercrime is rapidly gaining momentum in the technology world. It's attracting many such individuals who either have been involved in thefts of any kind in their past or the ones who have a nag for engaging in criminal activities. Criminals use many different means to hide evidence on computers from law enforcement mainly through encryption and other such methods like steganography, digital compression, passwords etc. These techniques are making the law enforcement's tasks more difficult day-by-day so, there is a need to understand how these criminals work and to subsequently find a solution for the same. The researchers have explained the above techniques in detail and how these affect the law enforcement efforts to counter.

Encryption

Real-Time Data Communications

The major effect of using encryption on real-time data communications is on wiretaps. Wiretap provides valuable information about the criminal's intentions, plans and any such rogue activities. Hackers use encryption on real-time data communications to prevent their communication channels to be intercepted by the law enforcement authorities. Internet Relay Chat(IRC) is that channel which enable the hackers to compromise other government machines.

Electronic Mail

The criminals use many different ways to encrypt their data in emails. The most used technique is Pretty Good Privacy (PGP) which provides a key to perform data encryption. This encryption technique is readily available in the Internet for free so, downloading is very easy. Electronic mail is very hard to trace.

Stored Data

This is the most commonly used technique by criminals to encrypt their stolen/confidential data from the law enforcement.

Posts Online

Hackers/criminals create open forums such as Internet web sites to carry message across from one person to another. This type of communication can be accessed by only those individuals who possess the decrypting key to that encrypted message.

Other Cryptographic Technologies Passwords

Passwords

Hackers/criminals keeps their PC's password protected to keep out intruders. This is an easy and most effective way of securing one's identity from the rest of the world. Passwords are used much more often by hackers rather than encryption related techniques.

Compressing Digital Files

Digital compression compresses digital file's size preventing the loss of important details of the file. Criminals use compression for two benefits:

- A decompressed file makes it hard for the law enforcement authorities to seize crucial files.

- Prior to encryption, it can make cracking of system difficult to conduct.

Steganography

Steganography is the method of hiding secret data into another data so that it is even more secured. Criminals use it to trick the concerned authorities into seeing non-existence of files in a hard-disk of computer. A cracker who does not possess the knowledge of the files can be easily mislead and forced to act in a way which can further make their target even more difficult to achieve.

The researchers have stressed a lot on the ways criminals/ hackers use encryption techniques to steal & extract confidential Government and other important organization's data but not so much on the ways to counter such actions. There is a need to talk about both sides of the argument in such cases. The encryption techniques used by criminals can be countered in a similar manner by the law enforcement authorities using decryption (also part of encryption).

Hiding Secret Information in Digital Images

In we are able to see many different ways in which images are secured from interference of hackers and other such outside intruders. The concept of digital watermarking is used to allow the authorization of owner and prevent outside intrusion, random grids used to hide secret images and use of joint encryption techniques to provide the same property.

Mathematical Models to Enhance Visual Cryptography

In various mathematical models are proposed which enhance the cryptographic techniques by making them more reliable during experimentation. The VC schemes based on the equations derived in the models allow the transparencies of the techniques to freely occur and help perform their desired functions. The application of this is seen in.

Preventing Unauthorized Access at Sensitive Application Areas

In the researchers talk about ways in which outside intrusion can be prevented in application areas like bank transactions, fingerprint scanning etc. The cryptographic techniques provide security but not necessarily define how hackers intrude into the system. The term phishing is used which occurs when a second user poses as a trustworthy entity to gather important information about the main user such as passwords, personal information etc.

Visual Cryptography Properties used in Day-to-Day Application Areas

In the researchers have used a new dimension to describe properties of visual cryptography in fields of multimedia and baseball. Cryptography can encrypt audio files more easily than text as audio files are more error tolerant. In baseball, the third- base coach gives visual signals to batters, pitchers etc during the course of the game. The halftone visual cryptography is used to encrypt secret data which is used in multimedia cryptography.

References

- Classical-encryption-technique-8339: brainkart.com, Retrieved 19, Jan 2020

- Classical-cryptography-and-quantum-cryptography: geeksforgeeks.org, Retrieved 22, Feb 2020

- What-is-postquantum-cryptography, embedded-revolution, technologies-21146368: electronicdesign.com, Retrieved 20, April 2020

- What-is-steganography-a-complete-guide-to-the-ancient-art-of-concealing-messages: portswigger.net, Retrieved 11, May 2020

- What-is-lattice-based-cryptography-why-should-you-care: medium.com, Retrieved 25, June 2020

- Current-state-of-multivariate-cryptography-319170467: researchgate.net, Retrieved 05, March 2020

## 3

Elliptic Curves

The algebraic curve whose solutions are restricted to a region of space that is topologically equivalent to a torus is known as the elliptic curve. Elliptic curve cryptography is a key-based technique used for the encryption of the data. This chapter discusses in detail the theories and methodologies related to elliptic curves.

An elliptic curve is defined by an equation in two variables, with coefficients. For cryptography, the variables and coefficients are restricted to elements in a finite field.

Note : Elliptic curves are not ellipses. They are so named because they are described by cubic equations, similar to those used for calculating the circumference of an ellipse.

Definition : Let K be a field of characteristic $\neq 2,3$ and let $x^3 + ax + b$ (where $a, b \in K$) be a cubic polynomial with no multiple roots. An elliptic curve over K is the set of points (x, y) with $x, y \in K$ which satisfy the equation

$$y^2 = x^3 + ax + b$$

together with a single element 0 and called the "point at infinity".

If K is a field of characteristic 2, then an elliptic curve over K is the set of points satisfying an equation of type either

$$y^2 + cy = x^3 + ax + b$$

or else,

$$y^2 + xy = x^3 + ax^2 + b$$

If K is a field of characteristic 3, then an elliptic curve over is the set of points satisfying the equation

$$y^3 = x^3 + ax^2 + bx + c$$

Figure shows two examples of elliptic curves. Now, consider the set of points E (a, b) consisting of all of the points (x, y) that satisfy Equation $y^2 = x^3 + ax + b$ together with the element O. Using a different value of the pair (a, b) results in a different set E (a, b).

Using this terminology, the two curves in Figure depict the sets $E(-1, 0)$ and $E(1, 1)$, respectively.

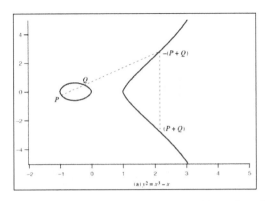 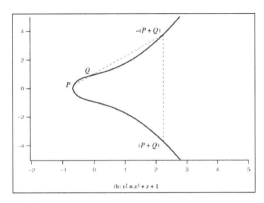

Examples of Elliptic Curves.

Geometric Description of Addition :

A group can be defined based on the set E (a,b) for specific values of a and b in Equation $y^2 = x^3 + ax + b$, provided the following condition is met:

$$4a^3 + 27b^2 \neq 0$$

To define a group, we define an operation, called addition and denoted by +, for the set E (a,b), where a and b satisfy Equation $4a^3 + 27b^2 \neq 0$. In geometric terms, the rules for addition can be stated as follows: If three points on an elliptic curve lie on a straight line, their sum is O.

From this definition, we can define the rules of addition over an elliptic curve:

i. O serves as the additive identity. Thus $O = -O$ and for any point P on the elliptic curve, $P + O = P$. In what follows, assume $P \neq O$ and $Q \neq O$.

ii. The negative of a point P is the point with the same x coordinate but the negative of the y coordinate; that is; if $P = (x, y)$ then $-P = (x, -y)$. Note that these two points can be joined by a vertical line. Note that $P + (-P) = P - P = O$.

iii. To add two points P and Q with different x coordinate, draw a straight line between them and find the third point of intersection R that is the point of intersection (unless the line is tangent to the curve at either P or Q, in which case we take $R = P$ or $R = Q$, respectively). To form a group structure, we need to define addition on these three points as follows: $P + Q = -R$ .That is, we define $P + Q$ to the mirror image (with respect to the axis) of the third points of intersection. Figure illustrates this construction.

iv. The geometric interpretation of the preceding item also applies to two points, P and $-P$, with the same x coordinate. The points are joined by a vertical line, which can be viewed as also intersecting the curve at the infinity point. We therefore have $P + -P = O$.

v. To double a point Q, draw the tangent line and fine the other point of intersection S. Then $Q + Q = 2Q = -S$.

Let $(x_1, y_1), (x_2, y_2)$ and $(x_3, -y_3)$ denote the coordinates of P, Q, and R respectively. We want to express x_3 and y_3 in terms of x_1, y_1, x_2, y_2.

Let $y = \alpha x + \beta$ be the equation of the line passing through P and Q.

$$\therefore \alpha = \frac{y_2 - y_1}{(x_2 - x_1)}$$

The equation of the elliptic curve $y^2 = x^3 + ax + b$ is

$$(\alpha x + \beta)^2 = x^3 + ax + b$$
$$\Rightarrow x^3 - (\alpha x + \beta)^2 + ax + b = 0$$

Roots of the equation are x_1, x_2, x_3.

$$(x - \alpha)(x - \beta)(x - \gamma) = 0$$
$$\Rightarrow x^3 - (\alpha + \beta + \gamma)x^2 + (\alpha\beta + \beta\gamma + \gamma\alpha)x - \alpha\beta\gamma = 0$$

$$Sum\ of\ the\ roots = (\alpha + \beta + \gamma)$$

Addition of two points:

$$x_1 + x_2 + x_3 = \alpha^2$$
$$\therefore x_3 = \alpha^2 - x_1 - x_2$$

$$y_3 = \alpha x_3 + \beta$$
$$y_1 = \alpha x_1 + \beta$$
$$\therefore \beta = y_1 - \alpha x_1$$

$$y_3 = \alpha x_3 + y_1 - \alpha x_1$$
$$\therefore y_3 = \alpha(x_3 - x_1) + y_1$$
$$\therefore -y_3 = \alpha(x_1 - x_3) - y_1$$

$$-R = (x_3, y_3)$$

$$x_3 = \left(\frac{y_2 - y_1}{x_2 - x_1}\right)^2 - x_1 - x_2$$

$$y_3 = \left(\frac{y_2 - y_1}{x_2 - x_1}\right)(x_1 - x_3) - y_1$$

$$y^2 = x^3 + ax + b \qquad P = Q = (x_1, y_1)$$
$$\therefore 2y\frac{dy}{dx} = 3x^2 + a$$

$$\therefore \frac{dy}{dx} = \frac{3x^2 + a}{2y} = \alpha$$

$$x_3 = \left(\frac{3x_1^2 + a}{2y_1}\right)^2 - 2x_1$$

$$y_3 = \left(\frac{3x_1^2 + a}{2y_1}\right)(x_1 - x_3) - y_1$$

$R = (x_3, -y_3)$ is the point of intersection of the tangent at P and the elliptic curve.

Example : On the elliptic curve $y^2 = x^3 - 36x$ let $P = (-3,9)$ and $Q = (-2,8)$. Find $P+Q$ and $2P$.

Solution.

$$P = (-3,9) \qquad Q = (-2,8)$$

For finding $P+Q$,

$$\alpha = \frac{8-9}{-2+3} = \frac{-1}{1} = -1$$
$$x_3 = \alpha^2 - x_1 - x_2$$
$$= 1+3+2$$
$$= 6$$
$$y_3 = \alpha(x_3 - x_1) - y_1$$
$$= -1(-3-6)-9$$
$$= 9-9$$
$$= 0$$

$$\therefore P+Q = (6,0)$$

For finding $2P$,

$$\alpha = \frac{3x_1^2 - 36}{2y_1}$$
$$= \frac{3(9) - 36}{2(9)}$$
$$= -\frac{1}{2}$$
$$x_3 = \alpha^2 - 2x_1$$
$$= \frac{1}{4} - 2(-3)$$
$$= \frac{25}{4}$$

$$y_3 = -y_1 + \alpha(x_1 - x_3)$$

$$= -9 + \left(-\frac{1}{2}\right)\left(-3 - \frac{25}{4}\right)$$

$$= -\frac{35}{8}$$

$$\therefore 2P = \left(\frac{25}{4}, -\frac{35}{8}\right)$$

Elliptic curves over Z_p :

For elliptic curves over Z_p, we have

$$y^2 = (x^3 + ax + b)\bmod p$$

Now consider the set $E_p(a,b)$ consisting of all pairs of integers (x, y) that satisfy above equation , together with a point at infinity O. The coefficients a and b and the variables x and y are all elements of Z_p.

It can be shown that a finite abelian group can be defined based on the set $E_p(a,b)$ provided that $(x^3 + ax + b)\bmod p$ has no repeated factors. This is equivalent to the condition

$$(4a^3 + 27b^2)\bmod p \neq 0 \bmod p$$

For example, let $a = 1, b = 1$ and $p = 23$ that is, the elliptic curve

$E_{23}(1,1): y^2 = x^3 + x + 1 \pmod{23}$. For the set $E_{23}(1,1)$, we are only interested in the nonnegative integers in the quadrant from $(0,0)$ through $(p-1, p-1)$ that satisfy the equation mod p. Table lists the points (other than O) that are part of $E_{23}(1,1)$. Figure plots the points of $E_{23}(1,1)$.

In case of the finite group $E_p(a,b)$, the number of points N is bounded by:

$$p+1-2\sqrt{p} \leq N \leq p+1+2\sqrt{p}$$

Table : Points on the Elliptic curve $E_{23}(1,1)$ other than O

(0, 1)	(6, 4)	(12, 19)
(0.22)	(6.19)	(13.7)
(1, 7)	(7, 11)	(13, 16)
(1, 16)	(7, 12)	(17, 3)
(3, 10)	(9, 7)	(17, 20)
(3, 13)	(9, 16)	(18, 3)
(4, 0)	(11, 3)	(18, 20)
(5, 4)	(11, 20)	(19, 5)
(5, 19)	(12, 4)	(19, 18)

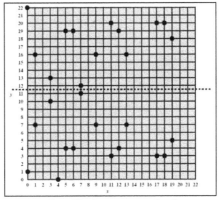

The Elliptic Curve $E_{23}(1, 1)$.

Elliptic Curve Discrete Logarithm Problem

The Elliptic Curve cryptosystem (*ECC*) have the potential to provide relatively small block size, high security public key schemes that can be efficiently implemented. The Elliptic Curve Discrete Logarithm problem (*ECDL P*) is based on the fact that given m.P for some integer m and some point P on the Elliptic Curve where P is known, we have to find v alue of m. The smaller key size of Elliptic Curve Cryptosystem makes possible much more compact implementations for a given level of security , which means faster cryptographic operations, running on smaller chips or more compact software. We mainly concentrate on the Elliptic Curve whose equation is given by $y^2 = x^3 + Ax + B$ defined over a finite field F_p for prime p for A , B in the field. The ECC transforms data into some point representation of the Elliptic Curve. It relies on calculating the multiple of a point P as m.P which is public and it is difficult to find integer m from P and m.P. This is the Elliptic Curve Discrete Logarithm Problem (*ECDL P*). It basically defines a group by the operator addition on the points found on the Elliptic Curve.

Informally a zero-knowledge proof system allows one person to convince another person of some fact without revealing any information about the proof. There are usually two participants, the prover and the verifier. The prover would like to prevent the verifier from gaining any useful information while participating in the protocol.

An Elliptic Curve is defined on a field. The field may be finite or infinite. We will draw our attention towards finite fields. It is denoted by F_q having q elements where $q = p^r$ having p as the characteristic of the field F_q and r as any positive integer. We will mainly consider for the curve where q = p i.e. r = 1. The points on the curve whose x and y values are in the field are taken into account. The ECC transforms the data into some point representation. The points form an Abelian Group w.r.t. the operator addition. There is one point indicated by O called the identity element.

The Order of a point is defined as the number of times the point must be added in order to give the identity element i.e. the point O.

The Generator of the group is a point whose Order is equal to the number of points that are in the group.

The basis of ECC is The Elliptic Curve Discrete Logarithm Problem i.e. the ECDL P.

The Elliptic Curve Discrete Logarithm problem or ECDLP is defined as follows:

Given points P and Q on $E_p($ A, B $)$ such that the equation m.P = Q holds. Compute k given P and Q.

Zero-knowledge Proof

In cryptography, a zero-knowledge proof or zero-knowledge protocol is a method by which one party (the *prover*) can prove to another party (the *verifier*) that a given statement is true, without conveying any information apart from the fact that the statement is indeed true.

If proving the statement requires knowledge of some secret information on the part of the prover, the definition implies that the verifier will not be able to prove the statement in turn to anyone else, since the verifier does not possess the secret information. Notice that the statement being proved must include the assertion that the prover has such knowledge (otherwise, the statement would not be proved in zero-knowledge, since at the end of the protocol the verifier would gain the additional information that the prover has knowledge of the required secret information). If the statement consists *only* of the fact that the prover possesses the secret information, it is a special case known as *zero-knowledge proof of knowledge,* and it nicely illustrates the essence of the notion of zero-knowledge proofs: proving that one has knowledge of certain information is trivial if one is allowed to simply reveal that information; the challenge is proving that one has such knowledge without revealing the secret information or anything else.

For zero-knowledge proofs of knowledge, the protocol must necessarily require interactive input from the verifier, usually in the form of a challenge or challenges such that the responses from the prover will convince the verifier if and only if the statement is true (i.e., if the prover does have the claimed knowledge). This is clearly the case, since otherwise the verifier could record the execution of the protocol and replay it to someone else: if this were accepted by the new party as proof that the replaying party knows the secret information, then the new party's acceptance is either justified—the replayer *does* know the secret information—which means that the protocol leaks knowledge and is not zero-knowledge, or it is spurious—i.e. leads to a party accepting someone's proof of knowledge who does not actually possess it.

Some forms of non-interactive zero-knowledge proofs of knowledge exist, but the validity of the proof relies on computational assumptions (typically the assumptions of an ideal cryptographic hash function).

Abstract Example

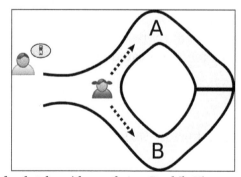

Peggy randomly takes either path A or B, while Victor waits outside.

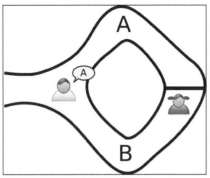

Victor chooses an exit path.

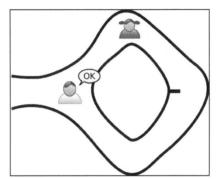

Peggy reliably appears at the exit Victor names.

There is a well-known story presenting the fundamental ideas of zero-knowledge proofs, first published by Jean-Jacques Quisquater and others in their paper "How to Explain Zero-Knowledge Protocols to Your Children". It is common practice to label the two parties in a zero-knowledge proof as Peggy (the prover of the statement) and Victor (the verifier of the statement).

In this story, Peggy has uncovered the secret word used to open a magic door in a cave. The cave is shaped like a ring, with the entrance on one side and the magic door blocking the opposite side. Victor wants to know whether Peggy knows the secret word; but Peggy, being a very private person, does not want to reveal her knowledge (the secret word) to Victor or to reveal the fact of her knowledge to the world in general.

They label the left and right paths from the entrance A and B. First, Victor waits outside the cave as Peggy goes in. Peggy takes either path A or B; Victor is not allowed to see which path she takes. Then, Victor enters the cave and shouts the name of the path he wants her to use to return, either A or B, chosen at random. Providing she really does know the magic word, this is easy: she opens the door, if necessary, and returns along the desired path.

However, suppose she did not know the word. Then, she would only be able to return by the named path if Victor were to give the name of the same path by which she had entered. Since Victor would choose A or B at random, she would have a 50% chance of guessing correctly. If they were to repeat this trick many times, say 20 times in a row, her chance of successfully anticipating all of Victor's requests would become vanishingly small (about one in a million).

Thus, if Peggy repeatedly appears at the exit Victor names, he can conclude that it is very probable—astronomically probable—that Peggy does in fact know the secret word.

One side note with respect to third party observers: Even if Victor is wearing a hidden camera that records the whole transaction, the only thing the camera will record is in one case Victor shouting "A!" and Peggy appearing at A or in the other case Victor shouting "B!" and Peggy appearing at B. A recording of this type would be trivial for any two people to fake (requiring only that Peggy and Victor agree beforehand on the sequence of A's and B's that Victor will shout). Such a recording will certainly never be convincing to anyone but the original participants. In fact, even a person who was present as an observer *at the original experiment* would be unconvinced, since Victor and Peggy might have orchestrated the whole "experiment" from start to finish.

Further notice that if Victor chooses his A's and B's by flipping a coin on-camera, this protocol loses its zero-knowledge property; the on-camera coin flip would probably be convincing to any person watching the recording later. Thus, although this does not reveal the secret word to Victor, it does make it possible for Victor to convince the world in general that Peggy has that knowledge—counter to Peggy's stated wishes. However, digital cryptography generally "flips coins" by relying on a pseudo-random number generator, which is akin to a coin with a fixed pattern of heads and tails known only to the coin's owner. If Victor's coin behaved this way, then again it would be possible for Victor and Peggy to have faked the "experiment", so using a pseudo-random number generator would not reveal Peggy's knowledge to the world in the same way using a flipped coin would.

Definition

A zero-knowledge proof must satisfy three properties:

1. Completeness: if the statement is true, the honest verifier (that is, one following the protocol properly) will be convinced of this fact by an honest prover.

2. Soundness: if the statement is false, no cheating prover can convince the honest verifier that it is true, except with some small probability.

3. Zero-knowledge: if the statement is true, no cheating verifier learns anything other than the fact that the statement is true. In other words, just knowing the statement (not the secret) is sufficient to imagine a scenario showing that the prover knows the secret. This is formalized by showing that every cheating verifier has some *simulator* that, given only the statement to be proved (and no access to the prover), can produce a transcript that "looks like" an interaction between the honest prover and the cheating verifier.

The first two of these are properties of more general interactive proof systems. The third is what makes the proof zero-knowledge.

Zero-knowledge proofs are not proofs in the mathematical sense of the term because there is some small probability, the *soundness error*, that a cheating prover will be able to convince the verifier of a false statement. In other words, zero-knowledge proofs are probabilistic "proofs" rather than deterministic proofs. However, there are techniques to decrease the soundness error to negligibly small values.

A formal definition of zero-knowledge has to use some computational model, the most common one being that of a Turing machine. Let P, V, and S be turing machines. An interactive proof system with (P,V) for a language L is zero-knowledge if for any probabilistic polynomial time (PPT) verifier $\hat{V}$ there exists an expected PPT simulator S such that,

$$\forall x \in L, z \in \{0,1\}^*, \text{View}_{\hat{V}}[P(x) \leftrightarrow \hat{V}(x,z)] = S(x,z)$$

The prover P is modeled as having unlimited computation power (in practice, P usually is a probabilistic Turing machine). Intuitively, the definition states that an interactive proof system (P,V) is zero-knowledge if for any verifier $\hat{V}$ there exists an efficient simulator S that can reproduce the conversation between P and $\hat{V}$ on any given input. The auxiliary string z in the definition plays the role of "prior knowledge". The definition implies that $\hat{V}$ cannot use any prior knowledge string z to mine information out of its conversation with P because we demand that if S is also given this prior knowledge then it can reproduce the conversation between $\hat{V}$ and P just as before.

The definition given is that of perfect zero-knowledge. Computational zero-knowledge is obtained by requiring that the views of the verifier $\hat{V}$ and the simulator are only computationally indistinguishable, given the auxiliary string.

Practical Examples

Discrete Log of a given Value

We can extend these ideas to a more realistic cryptography application. Peggy wants to prove to Victor that she knows the discrete log of a given value in a given group. For example, given a value y, a large prime p and a generator g, she wants to prove that she knows a value x such that $g^x \bmod p = y$, without revealing x. Indeed, revealing x could be used as a proof of identity, in that Peggy could have such knowledge because she chose a random value x that she didn't reveal to anyone, computed $y = g^x \bmod p$ and distributed the value of y to all potential verifiers, such that at a later time, proving knowledge of x is equivalent to proving identity as Peggy.

The protocol proceeds as follows: in each round, Peggy generates a random number r, computes $C = g^r \bmod p$ and discloses this to Victor. After receiving C, Victor randomly issues one of the following two requests: he either requests that Peggy discloses the value of r, or the value of $(x+r) \bmod (p-1)$. With either answer, Peggy is only disclosing a random value, so no information is disclosed by a correct execution of one round of the protocol.

Victor can verify either answer; if he requested r, he can then compute $g^r \bmod p$ and verify that it matches C. If he requested $(x+r) \bmod (p-1)$, he can verify that C is consistent with this, by computing $g^{(x+r) \bmod (p-1)} \bmod p$ and verifying that it matches $C \cdot y \bmod p$. If Peggy indeed knows the value of x, she can respond to either one of Victor's possible challenges.

If Peggy knew or could guess which challenge Victor is going to issue, then she could easily cheat and convince Victor that she knows x when she does not: if she knows that Victor is going to request r, then she proceeds normally: she picks r, computes $C = g^r \bmod p$ and discloses C to Victor; she will be able to respond to Victor's challenge. On the other hand, if she knows that Victor will request $(x+r) \bmod (p-1)$, then she picks a random value r', computes $C' = g^{r'} \cdot (g^x)^{-1} \bmod p$, and disclose C' to Victor as the value of C that he is expecting. When Victor challenges her to reveal $(x+r) \bmod (p-1)$, she reveals r', for which Victor will verify consistency, since he will in turn compute $g^{r'} \bmod p$, which matches $C' \cdot y$, since Peggy multiplied by the inverse of y.

However, if in either one of the above scenarios Victor issues a challenge other than the one she was expecting and for which she manufactured the result, then she will be unable to respond to the challenge under the assumption of infeasibility of solving the discrete log for this group. If she picked r and disclosed $C = g^r \bmod p$, then she will be unable to produce a valid $(x+r) \bmod (p-1)$ that would pass Victor's verification, given that she does not know x. And if she picked a value r' that poses as $(x+r) \bmod (p-1)$, then she would have to respond with the discrete log of the value that she disclosed – a value that she obtained through arithmetic with known values, and not by computing a power with a known exponent.

Thus, a cheating prover has a 0.5 probability of successfully cheating in one round. By executing a large enough number of rounds, the probability of a cheating prover succeeding can be made arbitrarily low.

Hamiltonian Cycle for a Large Graph

The following scheme is due to Manuel Blum.

In this scenario, Peggy knows a Hamiltonian cycle for a large graph G. Victor knows G but not the cycle (e.g., Peggy has generated G and revealed it to him.) Finding a Hamiltonian cycle given a large graph is believed to be computationally infeasible, since its corresponding decision version is known to be NP-complete. Peggy will prove that she knows the cycle without simply revealing it (perhaps Victor is interested in buying it but wants verification first, or maybe Peggy is the only one who knows this information and is proving her identity to Victor).

To show that Peggy knows this Hamiltonian cycle, she and Victor play several rounds of a game.

- At the beginning of each round, Peggy creates H, a graph which is isomorphic to G (i.e. H is just like G except that all the vertices have different names). Since it is trivial to translate a Hamiltonian cycle between isomorphic graphs with known isomorphism, if Peggy knows a Hamiltonian cycle for G she also must know one for H.

- Peggy commits to H. She could do so by using a cryptographic commitment scheme. Alternatively, she could number the vertices of H, then for each edge of H write a small piece of paper containing the two vertices of the edge and then put these pieces of paper upside down on a table. The purpose of this commitment is that Peggy is not able to change H while at the same time Victor has no information about H.

- Victor then randomly chooses one of two questions to ask Peggy. He can either ask her to show the isomorphism between H and G, or he can ask her to show a Hamiltonian cycle in H.

- If Peggy is asked to show that the two graphs are isomorphic, she first uncovers all of H (e.g. by turning all pieces of papers that she put on the table) and then provides the vertex translations that map G to H. Victor can verify that they are indeed isomorphic.

- If Peggy is asked to prove that she knows a Hamiltonian cycle in H, she translates her Hamiltonian cycle in G onto H and only uncovers the edges on the Hamiltonian cycle. This is enough for Victor to check that H does indeed contain a Hamiltonian cycle.

Completeness

If Peggy does know a Hamiltonian cycle in G, she can easily satisfy Victor's demand for either the graph isomorphism producing H from G (which she had committed to in the first step) or a Hamiltonian cycle in H (which she can construct by applying the isomorphism to the cycle in G).

Zero-knowledge

Peggy's answers do not reveal the original Hamiltonian cycle in G. Each round, Victor will learn only H's isomorphism to G or a Hamiltonian cycle in H. He would need both answers for a single H to discover the cycle in G, so the information remains unknown as long as Peggy can generate a distinct H every round. If Peggy does not know of a Hamiltonian Cycle in G, but somehow knew in advance what Victor would ask to see each round then she could cheat. For example, if Peggy knew ahead of time that Victor would ask to see the Hamiltonian Cycle in H then she could generate a Hamiltonian cycle for an unrelated graph. Similarly, if Peggy knew in advance that Victor would ask to see the isomorphism then she could simply generate an isomorphic graph H (in which she also does not know a Hamiltonian Cycle). Victor could simulate the protocol by himself (without Peggy) because he knows what he will ask to see. Therefore, Victor gains no information about the Hamiltonian cycle in G from the information revealed in each round.

Soundness

If Peggy does not know the information, she can guess which question Victor will ask and generate either a graph isomorphic to G or a Hamiltonian cycle for an unrelated graph, but since she does not know a Hamiltonian cycle for G she cannot do both. With this guesswork, her chance of fooling Victor is 2^{-n}, where n is the number of rounds. For all realistic purposes, it is infeasibly difficult to defeat a zero knowledge proof with a reasonable number of rounds in this way.

Variants of Zero-knowledge

Different variants of zero-knowledge can be defined by formalizing the intuitive concept of what is meant by the output of the simulator "looking like" the execution of the real proof protocol in the following ways:

- We speak of *perfect zero-knowledge* if the distributions produced by the simulator and the proof protocol are distributed exactly the same. This is for instance the case in the first example above.

- *Statistical zero-knowledge* means that the distributions are not necessarily exactly the same, but they are statistically close, meaning that their statistical difference is a negligible function.

- We speak of *computational zero-knowledge* if no efficient algorithm can distinguish the two distributions.

Applications

Research in zero-knowledge proofs has been motivated by authentication systems where one party wants to prove its identity to a second party via some secret information (such as a password) but doesn't want the second party to learn anything about this secret. This is called a "zero-knowledge proof of knowledge". However, a password is typically too small or insufficiently random to be used in many schemes for zero-knowledge proofs of knowledge. A zero-knowledge password proof is a special kind of zero-knowledge proof of knowledge that addresses the limited size of passwords.

One of the uses of zero-knowledge proofs within cryptographic protocols is to enforce honest behavior while maintaining privacy. Roughly, the idea is to force a user to prove, using a zero-knowledge proof, that its behavior is correct according to the protocol. Because of soundness, we know that the user must really act honestly in order to be able to provide a valid proof. Because of zero knowledge, we know that the user does not compromise the privacy of its secrets in the process of providing the proof.

In 2016, the Princeton Plasma Physics Laboratory and Princeton University demonstrated a novel technique that may have applicability to future nuclear disarmament talks.

History and Results

Zero-knowledge proofs were first conceived in 1985 by Shafi Goldwasser, Silvio Micali, and Charles Rackoff in their paper "The Knowledge Complexity of Interactive Proof-Systems". This paper introduced the IP hierarchy of interactive proof systems and conceived the concept of *knowledge complexity*, a measurement of the amount of knowledge about the proof transferred from the prover to the verifier. They also gave the first zero-knowledge proof for a concrete problem, that of deciding quadratic nonresidues mod m (this more or less means that there isn't any number x where x^2 is "equivalent" to some given number). Together with a paper by László Babai and Shlomo Moran, this landmark paper invented interactive proof systems, for which all five authors won the first Gödel Prize in 1993.

In their own words, Goldwasser, Micali, and Rackoff say:

Of particular interest is the case where this additional knowledge is essentially 0 and we show that [it] is possible to interactively prove that a number is quadratic non residue mod m releasing 0 additional knowledge. This is surprising as no efficient algorithm for deciding quadratic residuosity mod m is known when m's factorization is not given. Moreover, all known *NP* proofs for this problem exhibit the prime factorization of m. This indicates that adding interaction to the proving process, may decrease the amount of knowledge that must be communicated in order to prove a theorem.

The quadratic nonresidue problem has both an NP and a co-NP algorithm, and so lies in the interj174 of NP and co-NP. This was also true of several other problems for which zero-knowledge proofs were subsequently discovered, such as an unpublished proof system by Oded Goldreich verifying that a two-prime modulus is not a Blum integer.

Oded Goldreich, Silvio Micali, and Avi Wigderson took this one step further, showing that, assuming the existence of unbreakable encryption, one can create a zero-knowledge proof system for the NP-complete graph coloring problem with three colors. Since every problem in NP can be efficiently reduced to this problem, this means that, under this assumption, all problems in NP have zero-knowledge proofs. The reason for the assumption is that, as in the above example, their protocols require encryption. A commonly cited sufficient condition for the existence of unbreakable encryption is the existence of one-way functions, but it is conceivable that some physical means might also achieve it.

On top of this, they also showed that the graph nonisomorphism problem, the complement of the graph isomorphism problem, has a zero-knowledge proof. This problem is in co-NP, but is not currently known to be in either NP or any practical class. More generally, Goldreich, Goldwasser et al. would go on to show that, also assuming unbreakable encryption, there are zero-knowledge proofs for *all* problems in IP = PSPACE, or in other words, anything that can be proved by an interactive proof system can be proved with zero knowledge.

Not liking to make unnecessary assumptions, many theorists sought a way to eliminate the necessity of one way functions. One way this was done was with *multi-prover interactive proof systems*, which have multiple independent provers instead of only one, allowing the verifier to "cross-examine" the provers in isolation to avoid being misled. It can be shown that, without any intractability assumptions, all languages in NP have zero-knowledge proofs in such a system.

It turns out that in an Internet-like setting, where multiple protocols may be executed concurrently, building zero-knowledge proofs is more challenging. The line of research investigating concurrent zero-knowledge proofs was initiated by the work of Dwork, Naor, and Sahai. One particular development along these lines has been the development of witness-indistinguishable proof protocols. The property of witness-indistinguishability is related to that of zero-knowledge, yet witness-indistinguishable protocols do not suffer from the same problems of concurrent execution.

Another variant of zero-knowledge proofs are non-interactive zero-knowledge proofs. Blum, Feldman, and Micali showed that a common random string shared between the prover and the verifier is enough to achieve computational zero-knowledge without requiring interaction.

Definition 2.4. The Zero Knowledge Proof is defined as follows:

There are usually two participants, the prover and the verifier. The prover knows some fact and wishes to prove that to the verifier. The prover and the verifier will be allowed to perform alternatively the following computations:

1. Receive message from the other party.

2. Perform a private computation.

3. Send a message to the other party.

A typical round of the protocol will consist of a challenge by the verifier and a response by the prover. At the end the verifier either accepts or rejects.

Definition 2.5. The Birthday Paradox is defined as follows :

How many people must there be in a room before there is a 50% chance that two of them were born on the same day of the year.

The above problem can be stated in a different way as follows:

Given a random variable that is an integer with uniform distributions between 1 and n and a selection of k instances (k = n) of the random variable, what is the probability p(n, k) that there is at least one duplicate ? The Birthday Paradox is a special case where n = 365 and asks for the value of k such that p(n, k)> 0. 5. The answer to this problem is,

$k \approx O(\sqrt{n})$.

The Modular Linear Equation is stated as $ax = b \pmod{n}$ where a > 0 and n > 0.

Review of Existing Results

Let E be an Elliptic Curve defined over a finite field with F_p having equation $y^2 = x^3 + Ax + B$, where A & B satisfies the inequality $4A^3 + 27B^2 = 0$. We can find the number of points on the curve by checking the Legendre Symbol for y^2 for each value of x. The number of points will be denoted by $\#E(F_p)$.

The Hasses's theorem provides some limit on the number of points on an Elliptic Curve defined over a finite field. It states that $|p +1-\#E(F_p)| \leq 2\sqrt{p}$.

Theorem: The Equation $ax \equiv b \pmod{n}$ is solvable for the unknown x if and only if

$gcd(a, n)|b$.

Theorem: The Equation $ax \equiv b \pmod{n}$ either has d distinct solutions modulo n, where d = gcd (a, n), or it has no solutions.

Theorem: Let d = gcd (a, n), and suppose that $d = ax^f + ny^f$ for some integers x^f and y^f. If d|b, then the equation $ax \equiv b \pmod{n}$ has as one of it's solutions the value x_0, where $x_0 = x^f(b/d) \bmod n$.

Theorem: Suppose that the equation $ax \equiv b \pmod{n}$ is solvable (that is, d|b , where d = gcd (a, n)) and that x_0 is any solution to this equation. Then, this equation has exactly d distinct solutions, modulo n, given by $x_i = x_0 + i(n/d)$ for i = 0 , 1 , 2 , 3 , ..., d - 1.

Corollary: For any n > 1, if gcd (a, n) = 1, then the equation $ax \equiv b \pmod{n}$ has a unique solution, modulo n. In particular if b = 1 then $x = a^{-1} n \in Z^*$.

Theorem: In a coin toss, if the probability of obtaining a head is p then it is expected that after 1 /p tosses the first head is obtained.

Theorem: $\forall n>1$, $\varphi(n)/n = \Omega(\log \log n/ \log n)$.

First we will provide a Zero Knowledge Proof for Elliptic Curve Discrete Logarithm Problem (ECDL P) and explain the properties.

Properties of Zero Knowledge Interactive Proof

A Zero Knowledge Interactive Proof (ZKIP) or Zero Knowledge Protocol is an iterative method for one party to prove to another that a (usually mathematical) statement is true without revealing anything other than the veracity of the statement. A Zero Knowledge Interactive Proof must satisfy three properties :

1. Completeness : If the statement is true, the honest verifier (that is, one following the protocol

property) will be convinced of this fact by an honest prover.

2. Soundness : If the statement is false, no cheating prover can convince the honest verifier that it is true except with small probability.

3. Zero-Knowledge : If the statement is true, no cheating verifier learns anything other than this fact.

Now we will give the Zero Knowledge Proof for Elliptic Curve Discrete Logarithm Prob- lem(EC-DLP) and prove the properties. Let the prover be Alice and the verifier be Bob. Let the Elliptic Curve be denoted by $E_p(A, B)$ and let n be the number of points on the Elliptic Curve. Let $P \in E_p(A, B)$ be a generator of the group. So Alice wants to convince Bob that she knows the value of m where $Q = mP$ without disclosing m. It can be achieved by following steps :

1. Alice picks random integer k with $1 = k = p-1$ where p is the characteristic of the field and sends $R = kP$ to Bob.

2. Bob picks random integer r with $1 = r = p-1$ and sends it to Alice.

3. Alice computes $Y = (k-mr) \mod n$ where n is the number of points on the curve i.e. $\# E(F_p) = n$, and sends it to Alice.

4. Bob verifies if $R == YP + rQ$.

If step 4 is satisfied then Bob accepts else rejects. Now we will verify the three properties stated previously for the protocol as follows :

1. Completeness : Given $Q = mP$. We have to show that if Alice knows value of m , then Bob is convinced that Alice knows it.

   Since Alice knows value of m , all four steps in the protocol can be carried out. At step 3 Alice computes $Y = (k - mr) \mod n$ and sends it to Bob. At step 4, Bob verifies $YP + rQ = R$ or not.Now $YP + rQ = (k - mr) P + rQ = kP - rmP + rQ = kP - rQ + rQ = kP = R$ (verified).

So Bob is convinced that Alice knows m.

2. Soundness : Here we have to show that if Alice does not know value of m then she can't convince Bob that she knows it or succeeds with a very small probability.

   Now suppose Alice doesn't know value of m and wants to convince Bob that she knows it. The only way that Alice can convince Bob is in step 3 of the protocol Alice should send such a value for Y such that Y P should have value R- rQ , so that after adding rQ Bob will get R.

   i.e. $YP = R-rQ$

   i.e. $YP = kP - rmP$

   i.e. $YP = (k - mr)P$

   i.e. $Y = (k -mr) \mod n$

   Now Alice has values of k, r but she doesn't have the value of m. So it can't find value of k-mr. So she can't cheat.

3. Zero-Knowledge : Here we have to show that no information is released in the protocol.

Now in one session of the protocol Bob/Eavesdropper E has the following information:

$P, Q, R = kP, r, Y = (k - mr) \bmod n$.

Now from $Y = (k - mr) \bmod n$, in order to find out value of m it knows value of r. So the only thing left is to know k. But to find k the only way is to solve the ECDLP , $R = kP$ for k. So Bob/Eavesdropper can't know value of m. So the proof is a Perfect Zero-Knowledge.

Attack on the Zero Knowledge Protocol

During the whole protocol the Eavesdropper E has the following information :

point P (known)

point $Q = mP$ (known)

point $R = k\,P$ (known) (k unknown)

number r (known)

number $Y = (k - mr) \bmod n$ (known, m unknown)

From it the Eavsdropper can't find any useful information. But the attack is possible if the attacker uses information from multiple sessions of the challenge-response protocol. Now suppose in one session,

$$Y_1 = (k - mr_1) \bmod n$$

In another session Alice use the same k to compute R and thus,

$$Y_2 = (k - mr_2) \bmod n$$

So from above two euations ? $Y_1 - Y_2 = m(r_2 - r_1) \bmod n$,

$$\Rightarrow m(r_2 - r_1) = (Y_1 - Y_2) \bmod n$$

So $r_2 - r_1$ is known, and $Y_1 - Y_2$ is known. So we can solve form by using Theorem. Here in the Modular Linear Equation $ax \equiv b \bmod n$, $a = (r_2 - r_1)$, $b = (Y_1 - Y_2)$, $x = m$ and the number of solutions = gcd(a, n). The attack proceeds as follows :

In step 1 of the protocol Eavesdropper E gets the value of $R_i = k_iP$(i = 1 , 2 , 3 , ...) where i denotes the session numbers of the challenge-response protocol. Suppose at some session j, E discovers $R_j = R_l$, for some l < j. Thus we have :

$k_jP = k_lP \Rightarrow (k_j - k_l)P = O$. We will assume P is either the generator or a point on the Elliptic Curve with high order. Otherwise ECDLP can be easily solved by any brute force method. Thus we can safely assume without loss of generality $O(P) >> k_j - k_l$. Thus the only way the equality holds if $k_j = k_l$. Thus the entire problem reduces to solving the Modular Linear Equation ($\Rightarrow m(r_2 - r_1) = (Y_1 - Y_2) \bmod n$). From Corollary ($\Rightarrow m(r_2 - r_1) = (Y_1 - Y_2) \bmod n$) of Modular Linear Equation we hence,

$$m = (Y_1 - Y_2)(r_2 - r_1) - 1 \bmod n.$$

As stated in Corollary, $(r_2 - r_1)$-1 would be uniquely defined if gcd $(r_2 - r_1, n) = 1$.

Let $\Delta = r_2 - r_1$. Thus gcd$(\Delta, n) = 1$. W e can adopt the following randomized algorithm

to compute Δ and thus r_2 from r_1.

Algorithm 1 RAND (n)

1: Pick a random number x from (2 , 3 , ..., n - 1).

2: Compute gcd(x, n).

3: if gcd (x, n) = 1 then

4: Set $\Delta \leftarrow$ x.

5: else

6: goto step 1.

7: end if

8: Return Δ.

We know that $|Zn^*| = \Phi (n)$. Thus the tptal number of integers less than n and relatively prime w.r.t n is $\Phi(n)$. Thus the probability that the selected number $x \in Z n^*$ in RAND step 1 is $\Phi (n)/ n$. Thus from Theorem after expected $n / \Phi(n) \in O (\log n / \log\log n)$ iterations we will get $x \in Z n^*$. Thus the expected time complexity of RAND is $O (\log n / \log\log n)$ assuming the time complexity to compute gcd(x, n) is $O (\log n)$. Thus in sessions i and j attacker will use a random number r_1 and $r_2 = r_1 + \Delta$. Now we can clearly see that this attack will fail if Alice chooses different values of k at each session. But in step 1 of the protocol Alice picks up k with $1 \le k \le$ p-1 at random. Thus from Birthday Paradox after O ($\sqrt{p}$) sessions Alice will pick up k used in some earlier session with high probability. Thus after O ($\sqrt{p}$) sessions of the challenge response protocol with high probability an Eavesdropper can compute the value m for ECDLP.

Solution to Overcome the Above Attack

In this section we will provide a solution i.e., a modified Zero Knowledge Proof for the ECDLP that overcomes the above attack and prove the required properties i.e., Completeness, Soundness, and Zero-Knowledge, as explained previously. We also provide an explanation of how it overcomes the above attack.

Let the prover be Alice and the verifier be Bob. Let the Elliptic Curve be denoted by $E_p(A, B)$ and let n be the number of points on the Elliptic Curve. Let $P \in E_p(A, B)$ be a generator of the group. So Alice wants to convince Bob that she knows the value of m where Q = mP without disclosing m. It can be achieved by following steps :

1. Alice picks random integers k_1 and k_2 with $1 \le k_1, k_2 \le$ p - 1 where p is the characteristic of the field and sends $R_1 = k_1 P$ and $R_2 = k_2 Q$ to Bob.

2. Bob picks random integer r with $1 \le r \le$ p - 1 and sends it to Alice.

3. Alice computes $Y = (mrk_2 - k_1) \bmod n$ where n is the number of points on the curve i.e. $\#E(F_p) = n$, and sends it to Alice.

4. Bob verifies if $YP + R_1 == rR_2$.

If step 4 is satisfied then Bob accepts else rejects. Now we will verify the three properties stated previously for the protocol as follows :

1. Completeness : Given $Q = mP$. We have to show that if Alice knows value of m , then Bob is convinced that Alice knows it.

   Since Alice knows value of m , all four steps in the protocol can be carried out. At step 3 Alice computes $Y = (mrk_2 - k_1) \bmod n$ and sends it to Bob. At step 4, Bob verifies $YP + R_1 = rR_2$ or not.

   Now $YP + R_1 = (mrk_2 - k_1)P + k_1P$

   $= mrk_2P - k_1P + k_1P$

   $= mrk_2P$

   $= rk_2Q$ (Replacing mP by Q)

   $= rR_2$ (Replacing k_2Q by R_2) (Verified). So Bob is convinced that Alice knows m.

2. Soundness : Here we have to show that if Alice does not know value of m then she can't convince Bob that she knows it or succeeds with a very small probability.

   Now suppose Alice doesn't know value of m and wants to convince Bob that she knows it. The only way that Alice can convince Bob is in step 3 of the protocol Alice should send such a value for Y such that YP should have value $rR_2 - R_1$, so that after adding R_1 Bob will get rR_2.

   i.e. $YP = rR_2 - R_1$ i.e. $YP = k_2rQ - k_1P$ i.e. $YP = mrk_2P - k_1P$

   i.e. $Y = (mrk_2 - k_1) \bmod n$

   Now Alice has values of r, k_2, k_1 but she doesn't have the value of m. So it can't find value of $(mrk_2 - k_1)$. So she can't cheat.

3. Zero-Knowledge : Here we have to show that no information is released in the protocol.

Now in one session of the protocol Bob/Eavesdropper E has the following information :

$P, Q, R_1 = k_1P, R_2 = k_2Q, Y = (mrk_2 - k_1) \bmod n$.

Now $Y = (mrk_2 - k_1) \bmod n$. From this modular equation to find out value of m the known quantities are r and Y. In this modular linear equation $Y = (mrk_2 - k_1) \bmod n$ we have 3 unknowns m, k_1, and k_2. Thus 2 ECDLPs $R_1 = k_1P$ and $R_2 = k_2Q$ reduces to solving $Y = (mrk_2 - k_1) \bmod n$. Thus in other words if there is an efficient way of obtaining k_1 and k_2 from the modular linear equation $Y = (mrk_2 - k_1) \bmod n$ then there is an efficient solution to 2 ECDLPs $R_1 = k_1P$ and $R_2 = k_2Q$. Hence solving the modular linear equation $Y = (mrk_2 - k_1) \bmod n$ is at least as hard as solving ECDLPs $R_1 = k_1P$ and $R_2 = k_2Q$. So Bob/Eavesdropper can't know value of m. So the proof is a Perfect Zero-Knowledge.

Now we will explain how the attack is avoided. Now suppose as earlier Bob / E gets Y_1 and Y_2 as follows :

$Y_1 = (mr_1k_{12} - k)$ mod n and $Y_2 = (mr_2k_{22} - k)$ mod n i.e., in both sessions R_1 values are same. Here k_{12} and k_{22} indicate the k_2 values in both sessions. Now subtracting as previously we will get $Y_1 - Y_2 = m(r_1k_{12} - r_2k_{22})$ mod n. But as it doesn't know the value of k_{12} and k_{22}, so it can't solve for the Modular Linear Equation. Even if R_2 is same in both cases with $R_2 = k_2Q$ then it will get the final subtraction result as $Y_1 - Y_2 = mk_2(r_1 - r_2)$ mod n. So solving it will give the value of mk_2. Again if we can obtain m efficiently we have an efficient solution to the ECDLP $R_2 = k_2Q$. Thus again we have a reduction from ECDLP to the problem of computing m from mk_2. So this proof system is not susceptible to the previous attack.

The Elliptic Curve cryptosystem (*ECC*) can play an important role in asymmetric cryp- tography. ECC is a stronger option than the RSA and Discrete Logarithm systems for the future. Here we have presented a Zero Knowledge In teractive Proof for *ECDLP* where the elliptic curve is of the form $E_p(A, B)$ where p is a prime. The re- sult can be easily generalized to $E_q(A, B)$ for composite q where $q = p^r$. Given a guess of m for *ECDLP* we can easily verify in polynomial time whether P = m.Q. This shows $ECDLP \in NP \subseteq PSPACE = IP$. This confirms with our result that shows $ECDLP \in IP$. Subsequently we have also presented an attack on the Zero Knowledge Pro-tocol using Birthday Paradox. Lastly we modified the Zero Knowledge Proof to overcome this attack.

Non-interactive Zero-knowledge Proof

Non-interactive zero-knowledge proofs are a variant of zero-knowledge proofs in which no interaction is necessary between prover and verifier. Blum, Feldman, and Micali showed that a common reference string shared between the prover and the verifier is enough to achieve computational zero-knowledge without requiring interaction. Goldreich and Oren gave impossibility results for one shot zero-knowledge protocols in the standard model. In 2003, Goldwasser and Kalai published an instance of an identification scheme for which any hash function will yield an insecure digital signature scheme. These results are not contradictory, as the impossibility result of Goldreich and Oren does not hold in the common reference string model or the random oracle model. Non-interactive zero-knowledge proofs however show a separation between the cryptographic tasks that can be achieved in the standard model and those that can be achieved in 'more powerful' extended models.

The model influences the properties that can be obtained from a zero-knowledge protocol. Pass showed that in the common reference string model non-interactive zero-knowledge protocols do not preserve all of the properties of interactive zero-knowledge protocols; e.g., they do not preserve deniability.

Non-interactive zero-knowledge proofs can also be obtained in the random oracle model using the Fiat–Shamir heuristic.

Definition

Originally, non-interactive zero-knowledge was only defined as a single theorem proof system. In such a system each proof requires its own fresh common reference string. A common reference string in general is not a random string. It may, for instance, consist of randomly chosen group elements that all protocol parties use. Although the group elements are random, the reference string is not as it contains a certain structure (e.g., group elements) that is distinguishable from randomness. Subsequently, Feige, Lapidot, and Shamir introduced multi-theorem zero-knowledge proofs as a more versatile notion for non-interactive zero knowledge proofs.

In this model the prover and the verifier are in possession of a reference string sampled from a distribution, D, by a trusted setup $\sigma \leftarrow \text{Setup}(1^k)$. To prove statement $y \in L$ with witness w, the prover runs $\pi \leftarrow \text{Prove}(\sigma, y, w)$ and sends the proof, π, to the verifier. The verifier accepts if $\text{Verify}(\sigma, y, \pi) = \text{accept}$, and rejects otherwise. To account for the fact that σ may influence the statements that are being proven, the witness relation can be generalized to $(y, w) \in R_\sigma$ parameterized by σ.

Completeness

Verification succeeds for all $\sigma \in \text{Setup}(1^k)$ and every $(y, w) \in R_\sigma$.

More formally, for all k, all $\sigma \in \text{Setup}(1^k)$, and all $(y, w) \in R_\sigma$:

$$\Pr[\pi \leftarrow \text{Prove}(\sigma, y, w) : \text{Verify}(\sigma, y, \pi) = \text{accept}] = 1$$

Soundness

Soundness requires that no prover can make the verifier accept a wrong statement $y \notin L$ except with some small probability. The upper bound of this probability is referred to as the soundness error of a proof system.

More formally, for every malicious prover, $\tilde{P}$, there exists a negligible function, v, such that

$$\Pr\left[\sigma \leftarrow \text{Setup}(1^k), (y, \pi) \leftarrow \tilde{P}(\sigma) : y \notin L \wedge \text{Verify}(\sigma, y, \pi) = \text{accept}\right] = v(k).$$

The above definition requires the soundness error to be negligible in the security parameter, k. By increasing k the soundness error can be made arbitrary small. If the soundness error is o for all k, we speak of *perfect soundness*.

Multi-theorem Zero-knowledge

A non-interactive proof system $(\text{Setup}, \text{Prove}, \text{Verify})$ is multi-theorem zero-knowledge, if there exists a simulator, $\text{Sim} = (\text{Sim}_1, \text{Sim}_2)$, such that for all non-uniform polynomial time adversaries, $\mathcal{A}$,

$$\Pr\left[\sigma \leftarrow \text{Setup}(1^k) : \mathcal{A}^{\text{Prove}(\sigma, \cdot, \cdot)}(\sigma) = 1\right] \equiv \Pr\left[(\sigma, \tau) \leftarrow \text{Sim}_1 : \mathcal{A}^{\text{Sim}(\sigma, \tau, \cdot, \cdot)}(\sigma) = 1\right]$$

Here $\text{Sim}(\sigma, \tau, y, w)$ outputs $\text{Sim}_2(\sigma, \tau, y)$ for $(y, w) \in R_\sigma$ and both oracles output *failure* otherwise.

Pairing-based Non-interactive Proofs

Pairing-based cryptography has led to several cryptographic advancements. One of these advancements is more powerful and more efficient non-interactive zero-knowledge proofs. The seminal idea was to hide the values for the evaluation of the pairing in a commitment. Using different commitment schemes, this idea was used to build zero-knowledge proof systems under the sub-group hiding and under the decisional linear assumption. These proof systems prove circuit satisfiability, and thus by the Cook–Levin theorem allow proving membership for every language in NP. The size of the common reference string and the proofs is relatively small; however, transforming a statement into a boolean circuit incurs considerable overhead.

Proof systems under the sub-group hiding, decisional linear assumption, and external Diffie–Hellman assumption that allow directly proving the pairing product equations that are common in pairing-based cryptography have been proposed.

Under strong knowledge assumptions, it is known how to create sublinear-length computationally sound proof systems for NP-complete languages. More precisely, the proof in such proof systems consists only of a small number of bilinear group elements.

Elliptic Curve Cryptography

Elliptic curve cryptography (ECC) is an approach to public-key cryptography based on the algebraic structure of elliptic curves over finite fields. ECC requires smaller keys compared to non-ECC cryptography (based on plain Galois fields) to provide equivalent security.

Elliptic curves are applicable for key agreement, digital signatures, pseudo-random generators and other tasks. Indirectly, they can be used for encryption by combining the key agreement with a symmetric encryption scheme. They are also used in several integer factorization algorithms based on elliptic curves that have applications in cryptography, such as Lenstra elliptic curve factorization.

Rationale

Public-key cryptography is based on the intractability of certain mathematical problems. Early public-key systems are secure assuming that it is difficult to factor a large integer composed of two or more large prime factors. For elliptic-curve-based protocols, it is assumed that finding the discrete logarithm of a random elliptic curve element with respect to a publicly known base point is infeasible: this is the "elliptic curve discrete logarithm problem" (ECDLP). The security of elliptic curve cryptography depends on the ability to compute a point multiplication and the inability to compute the multiplicand given the original and product points. The size of the elliptic curve determines the difficulty of the problem.

The primary benefit promised by elliptic curve cryptography is a smaller key size, reducing storage and transmission requirements, i.e. that an elliptic curve group could provide the same level of security afforded by an RSA-based system with a large modulus and correspondingly larger key:

for example, a 256-bit elliptic curve public key should provide comparable security to a 3072-bit RSA public key.

The U.S. National Institute of Standards and Technology (NIST) has endorsed elliptic curve cryptography in its Suite B set of recommended algorithms, specifically elliptic curve Diffie–Hellman (ECDH) for key exchange and Elliptic Curve Digital Signature Algorithm (ECDSA) for digital signature. The U.S. National Security Agency (NSA) allows their use for protecting information classified up to top secret with 384-bit keys. However, in August 2015, the NSA announced that it plans to replace Suite B with a new cipher suite due to concerns about quantum computing attacks on ECC.

While the RSA patent expired in 2000, there may be patents in force covering certain aspects of ECC technology. However some argue that the US government elliptic curve digital signature standard (ECDSA; NIST FIPS 186-3) and certain practical ECC-based key exchange schemes (including ECDH) can be implemented without infringing them, including RSA Laboratories and Daniel J. Bernstein .

History

The use of elliptic curves in cryptography was suggested independently by Neal Koblitz and Victor S. Miller in 1985. Elliptic curve cryptography algorithms entered wide use in 2004 to 2005.

Theory

For current cryptographic purposes, an *elliptic curve* is a plane curve over a finite field (rather than the real numbers) which consists of the points satisfying the equation,

$$y^2 = x^3 + ax + b,$$

along with a distinguished point at infinity, denoted ∞. (The coordinates here are to be chosen from a fixed finite field of characteristic not equal to 2 or 3, or the curve equation will be somewhat more complicated.)

This set together with the group operation of elliptic curves is an Abelian group, with the point at infinity as identity element. The structure of the group is inherited from the divisor group of the underlying algebraic variety.

$$\mathrm{Div}^0(E) \to \mathrm{Pic}^0(E) \simeq E,$$

Cryptographic Schemes

Several discrete logarithm-based protocols have been adapted to elliptic curves, replacing the group $(\mathbb{Z}_p)^\times$ with an elliptic curve:

- The elliptic curve Diffie–Hellman (ECDH) key agreement scheme is based on the Diffie–Hellman scheme,

- The Elliptic Curve Integrated Encryption Scheme (ECIES), also known as Elliptic Curve Augmented Encryption Scheme or simply the Elliptic Curve Encryption Scheme,

- The Elliptic Curve Digital Signature Algorithm (ECDSA) is based on the Digital Signature Algorithm,

- The deformation scheme using Harrison's p-adic Manhattan metric,

- The Edwards-curve Digital Signature Algorithm (EdDSA) is based on Schnorr signature and uses twisted Edwards curves,

- The ECMQV key agreement scheme is based on the MQV key agreement scheme,

- The ECQV implicit certificate scheme.

At the RSA Conference 2005, the National Security Agency (NSA) announced Suite B which exclusively uses ECC for digital signature generation and key exchange. The suite is intended to protect both classified and unclassified national security systems and information.

Recently, a large number of cryptographic primitives based on bilinear mappings on various elliptic curve groups, such as the Weil and Tate pairings, have been introduced. Schemes based on these primitives provide efficient identity-based encryption as well as pairing-based signatures, signcryption, key agreement, and proxy re-encryption.

Implementation

Some common implementation considerations include:

Domain Parameters

To use ECC, all parties must agree on all the elements defining the elliptic curve, that is, the *domain parameters* of the scheme. The field is defined by p in the prime case and the pair of m and f in the binary case. The elliptic curve is defined by the constants a and b used in its defining equation. Finally, the cyclic subgroup is defined by its *generator* (a.k.a. *base point*) G. For cryptographic application the order of G, that is the smallest positive number n such that $nG = \infty$, is normally prime. Since n is the size of a subgroup of $E(\mathbb{F}_p)$ it follows from Lagrange's theorem that the number $h = \dfrac{1}{n} | E(\mathbb{F}_p) |$ is an integer. In cryptographic applications this number h, called the *co factor*, must be small ($h \leq 4$) and, preferably, $h = 1$. To summarize: in the prime case, the domain parameters are (p,a,b,G,n,h); in the binary case, they are (m,f,a,b,G,n,h).

Unless there is an assurance that domain parameters were generated by a party trusted with respect to their use, the domain parameters *must* be validated before use.

The generation of domain parameters is not usually done by each participant because this involves computing the number of points on a curve which is time-consuming and troublesome to implement. As a result, several standard bodies published domain parameters of elliptic curves for several common field sizes. Such domain parameters are commonly known as "standard curves" or "named curves"; a named curve can be referenced either by name or by the unique object identifier defined in the standard documents:

- NIST, Recommended Elliptic Curves for Government Use (From Internet Archive Wayback Machine, current link dead)

- SECG, SEC 2: Recommended Elliptic Curve Domain Parameters

- ECC Brainpool (RFC 5639), ECC Brainpool Standard Curves and Curve Generation

SECG test vectors are also available. NIST has approved many SECG curves, so there is a significant overlap between the specifications published by NIST and SECG. EC domain parameters may be either specified by value or by name.

If one (despite the above) wants to construct one's own domain parameters, one should select the underlying field and then use one of the following strategies to find a curve with appropriate (i.e., near prime) number of points using one of the following methods:

- Select a random curve and use a general point-counting algorithm, for example, Schoof's algorithm or Schoof–Elkies–Atkin algorithm,

- Select a random curve from a family which allows easy calculation of the number of points (e.g., Koblitz curves), or

- Select the number of points and generate a curve with this number of points using *complex multiplication* technique.

Several classes of curves are weak and should be avoided:

- Curves over $\mathbb{F}_{2^m}$ with non-prime m are vulnerable to Weil descent attacks.

- Curves such that n divides $p^B - 1$ (where p is the characteristic of the field – q for a prime field, or 2 for a binary field) for sufficiently small B are vulnerable to Menezes–Okamoto–Vanstone (MOV) attack which applies usual Discrete Logarithm Problem (DLP) in a small degree extension field of $\mathbb{F}_p$ to solve ECDLP. The bound B should be chosen so that discrete logarithms in the field $\mathbb{F}_{p^B}$ are at least as difficult to compute as discrete logs on the elliptic curve $E(\mathbb{F}_q)$.

- Curves such that $| E(\mathbb{F}_q) |= q$ are vulnerable to the attack that maps the points on the curve to the additive group of $\mathbb{F}_q$.

Key Sizes

Because all the fastest known algorithms that allow one to solve the ECDLP (baby-step giant-step, Pollard's rho, etc.), need $O(\sqrt{n})$ steps, it follows that the size of the underlying field should be roughly twice the security parameter. For example, for 128-bit security one needs a curve over $\mathbb{F}_q$, where $q \approx 2^{256}$. This can be contrasted with finite-field cryptography (e.g., DSA) which requires 3072-bit public keys and 256-bit private keys, and integer factorization cryptography (e.g., RSA) which requires a 3072-bit value of n, where the private key should be just as large. However the public key may be smaller to accommodate efficient encryption, especially when processing power is limited.

The hardest ECC scheme (publicly) broken to date had a 112-bit key for the prime field case and a 109-bit key for the binary field case. For the prime field case, this was broken in July 2009 using a cluster of over 200 PlayStation 3 game consoles and could have been finished in 3.5 months using this cluster when running continuously. The binary field case was broken in April 2004 using 2600 computers over 17 months.

A current project is aiming at breaking the ECC2K-130 challenge by Certicom, by using a wide range of different hardware: CPUs, GPUs, FPGA.

Projective Coordinates

A close examination of the addition rules shows that in order to add two points, one needs not only several additions and multiplications in $\mathbb{F}_q$ but also an inversion operation. The inversion (for given $x \in \mathbb{F}_q$ find $y \in \mathbb{F}_q$ such that $xy = 1$) is one to two orders of magnitude slower than multiplication. Fortunately, points on a curve can be represented in different coordinate systems which do not require an inversion operation to add two points. Several such systems were proposed: in the *projective* system each point is represented by three coordinates (X, Y, Z) using the following relation: $x = \dfrac{X}{Z}$, $y = \dfrac{Y}{Z}$; in the *Jacobian system* a point is also represented with three coordinates (X, Y, Z), but a different relation is used: $x = \dfrac{X}{Z^2}$, $y = \dfrac{Y}{Z^3}$; in the *López–Dahab system* the relation is $x = \dfrac{X}{Z}$, $y = \dfrac{Y}{Z^2}$; in the *modified Jacobian* system the same relations are used but four coordinates are stored and used for calculations (X, Y, Z, aZ^4); and in the *Chudnovsky Jacobian* system five coordinates are used (X, Y, Z, Z^2, Z^3). Note that there may be different naming conventions, for example, IEEE P1363-2000 standard uses "projective coordinates" to refer to what is commonly called Jacobian coordinates. An additional speed-up is possible if mixed coordinates are used.

Fast Reduction (NIST curves)

Reduction modulo p (which is needed for addition and multiplication) can be executed much faster if the prime p is a pseudo-Mersenne prime, that is $p \approx 2^d$; for example, $p = 2^{521} - 1$ or $p = 2^{256} - 2^{32} - 2^9 - 2^8 - 2^7 - 2^6 - 2^4 - 1$. Compared to Barrett reduction, there can be an order of magnitude speed-up. The speed-up here is a practical rather than theoretical one, and derives from the fact that the moduli of numbers against numbers near powers of two can be performed efficiently by computers operating on binary numbers with bitwise operations.

The curves over $\mathbb{F}_p$ with pseudo-Mersenne p are recommended by NIST. Yet another advantage of the NIST curves is that they use $a = -3$, which improves addition in Jacobian coordinates.

According to Bernstein and Lange, many of the efficiency-related decisions in NIST FIPS 186-2 are sub-optimal. Other curves are more secure and run just as fast.

Applications

Elliptic curves are applicable for encryption, digital signatures, pseudo-random generators and other tasks. They are also used in several integer factorization algorithms that have applications in cryptography, such as Lenstra elliptic curve factorization.

In 1999, NIST recommended 15 elliptic curves. Specifically, FIPS 186-3 has 10 recommended finite fields:

- Five prime fields $\mathbb{F}_p$ for certain primes p of sizes 192, 224, 256, 384, and 521 bits. For each of the prime fields, one elliptic curve is recommended.

- Five binary fields $\mathbb{F}_{2^m}$ for m equal 163, 233, 283, 409, and 571. For each of the binary fields, one elliptic curve and one Koblitz curve was selected.

The NIST recommendation thus contains a total of 5 prime curves and 10 binary curves. The curves were ostensibly chosen for optimal security and implementation efficiency.

In 2013, the *New York Times* stated that Dual Elliptic Curve Deterministic Random Bit Generation (or Dual_EC_DRBG) had been included as a NIST national standard due to the influence of NSA, which had included a deliberate weakness in the algorithm and the recommended elliptic curve. RSA Security in September 2013 issued an advisory recommending that its customers discontinue using any software based on Dual_EC_DRBG. In the wake of the exposure of Dual_EC_DRBG as "an NSA undercover operation", cryptography experts have also expressed concern over the security of the NIST recommended elliptic curves, suggesting a return to encryption based on non-elliptic-curve groups.

Security

Side-channel Attacks

Unlike most other DLP systems (where it is possible to use the same procedure for squaring and multiplication), the EC addition is significantly different for doubling ($P = Q$) and general addition ($P \neq Q$) depending on the coordinate system used. Consequently, it is important to counteract side channel attacks (e.g., timing or simple/differential power analysis attacks) using, for example, fixed pattern window (a.k.a. comb) methods (note that this does not increase computation time). Alternatively one can use an Edwards curve; this is a special family of elliptic curves for which doubling and addition can be done with the same operation. Another concern for ECC-systems is the danger of fault attacks, especially when running on smart cards.

Backdoors

Cryptographic experts have expressed concerns that the National Security Agency has inserted a kleptographic backdoor into at least one elliptic curve-based pseudo random generator. Internal memos leaked by former NSA contractor, Edward Snowden, suggest that the NSA put a backdoor in the Dual_EC_DRBG standard. One analysis of the possible backdoor concluded that an adversary in possession of the algorithm's secret key could obtain encryption keys given only 32 bytes of ciphertext.

The SafeCurves project has been launched in order to catalog curves that are easy to securely implement and are designed in a fully publicly verifiable way to minimize the chance of a backdoor.

Quantum Computing Attacks

In contrast with its current standing over RSA, elliptic curve cryptography is expected to be more vulnerable to an attack based on Shor's algorithm. In theory, making a practical attack feasible many years before an attack on an equivalently secure RSA scheme is possible. This is because smaller elliptic curve keys are needed to match the classical security of RSA. The work of Proos and Zalka show how a quantum computer for breaking 2048-bit RSA requires roughly 4096 qubits, while a quantum computer to break the equivalently secure 224-bit Elliptic Curve Cryptography requires between 1300 and 1600 qubits.

To avoid quantum computing concerns, an elliptic curve-based alternative to Elliptic Curve Diffie Hellman which is not susceptible to Shor's attack is the Supersingular Isogeny Diffie–Hellman Key Exchange of De Feo, Jao and Plut. It uses elliptic curve isogenies to create a drop-in replacement for the quantum attackable Diffie–Hellman and Elliptic curve Diffie–Hellman key exchanges. This key exchange uses the same elliptic curve computational primitives of existing elliptic curve cryptography and requires computational and transmission overhead similar to many currently used public key systems.

In August, 2015, NSA announced that it planned to transition "in the not distant future" to a new cipher suite that is resistant to quantum attacks. "Unfortunately, the growth of elliptic curve use has bumped up against the fact of continued progress in the research on quantum computing, necessitating a re-evaluation of our cryptographic strategy."

Patents

At least one ECC scheme (ECMQV) and some implementation techniques are covered by patents.

Alternative Representations

Alternative representations of elliptic curves include:

- Hessian curves
- Edwards curves
- Twisted curves
- Twisted Hessian curves
- Twisted Edwards curve
- Doubling-oriented Doche–Icart–Kohel curve
- Tripling-oriented Doche–Icart–Kohel curve
- Jacobian curve
- Montgomery curve

Elliptic curve cryptosystem is based Elliptic Curve Discrete Logarithm Problem , i.e., ECDLP. The problem is defined as follows:

Given points P and Q on $E_p(a, b)$ such that the equation kP = Q holds. Compute k given P and Q.

Representing Plaintext Message by a Point on the Elliptic Curve

Suppose the plaintext message is an integer m. We have to represent this by a point on the elliptic curve $y^2 = x^3 + ax + b \pmod{p}$. We choose the x -coordinate of the representative point by m. But it may so happen that m³+am+b (mod p) is not a quadratic residue and thus the ordinate value is undefined.

Let K be the largest integer such that the failure probability $1/2^k$ is acceptable. We also assume that $(m +1)K< p$. the message m will be represented by a point with the abscissa value x = mK + j, where $0 \leq j < K$. Also we assume that p = 3 mod 4. This assumption will help us in computing the square root deterministically. For j=0, 1, 2, ..., K -1 check if z=x³+ax+b (mod p) is a quadratic residue or not. If it,

is a quadratic residue we compute the value of y as $Z^{\frac{P+1}{4}}$ mod p Now we represent the message by P_m= (x, y). If the test fails for all values of j then we fail to map the message to a point. Clearly the failure probability is $1/2^k$.

At the time of decryption we recover the message m from P_m= (x, y) as follows:

$$m = \left\lfloor \frac{x}{K} \right\rfloor.$$

Elliptic Curve Analogue of Diffie- Hellman Key Exchange

Publicly available information: $E_p(a, b)$ and a point G on the curve with high order, i.e., kG = O for large k. Let n be the total number of points on the curve.

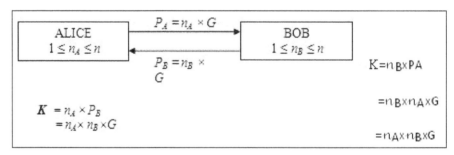

1. Alice chooses her private key n_A such that $1 \leq n_A \leq n$ and computes the public key $P_A = n_A xG$.

2. Bob chooses his private key n_B such that $1 \leq n_B \leq n$ and computes the public key $P_B = n_B xG$.

3. Alice and Bob simultaneously compute the shared key K = $n_A x n_B xG$ after computing $n_A x P_B$ and $n_B x P_A$ respectively.

This key exchange scheme as mentioned earlier is susceptible to intruder-in-the-middle attack. To overcome this all messages should be authenticated by its sender.

Elliptic Curve Analogue of ElGamal Cryptosystem

Bob's Public Key: P_B

Bob's Secret Key: a where P_B =αG.

Other Publicly Available Information: Elliptic Curve $E_p(a, b)$ and a point G of large order on the elliptic curve and the prime p.

Encryption (Sender: Alice)

Let P_m be the point on the elliptic curve corresponding to the plaintext message m.

- Alice chooses a random number k , such that $1 \leq k \leq p-1$.

- She computes the cipher text C $=\{C_1, C_2\}$ = { kG, P_m + kP_B}.

- She sends the cipher text C $=\{C_1, C_2\}$ to Bob.

Decryption (Receiver: Bob)

After receiving the cipher text C $=\{C_1, C_2\}$

- Bob computes $\alpha C_1 = \alpha kG = k\alpha G = kP_B$.

- Then Bob subtracts the result obtained in Step1 from C_2. Thus Bob computes $C_2 - kP_B = P_m$ and recovers the plaintext.

References

- Sahai, Amit; Vadhan, Salil (1 March 2003). "A complete problem for statistical zero knowledge" (PDF). Journal of the ACM. 50 (2): 196–249. doi:10.1145/636865.636868. Archived (PDF) from the original on 2015-06-25

- Chaum, David; Evertse, Jan-Hendrik; van de Graaf, Jeroen. "An Improved Protocol for Demonstrating Possession of Discrete Logarithms and Some Generalizations". Advances in Cryptology – EuroCrypt '87: Proceedings. 304: 127–141. doi:10.1007/3-540-39118-5_13

- Ben-Sasson, Eli; Chiesa, Alessandro; Garman, Christina; Green, Matthew; Miers, Ian; Tromer, Eran; Virza, Madars (18 May 2014). "Zerocash: Decentralized Anonymous Payments from Bitcoin" (PDF). IEEE. Retrieved 07, March 2020

## 4

Digital Signature and Ciphering

Digital signature is a mathematical programme to verify the authenticity of documents or digital messages. Cipher is a series of well-defined steps that are followed for performing the encryption and decryption. In order to completely understand digital signatures and ciphering it is necessary to understand the processes related to it. The following chapter elucidates the varied processes and mechanisms associated with this area of study.

Digital Signature

A digital signature is a mathematical scheme for demonstrating the authenticity of digital messages or documents. A valid digital signature gives a recipient reason to believe that the message was created by a known sender (authentication), that the sender cannot deny having sent the message (non-repudiation), and that the message was not altered in transit (integrity).

Digital signatures are a standard element of most cryptographic protocol suites, and are commonly used for software distribution, financial transactions, contract management software, and in other cases where it is important to detect forgery or tampering.

Explanation

Digital signatures are often used to implement electronic signatures, a broader term that refers to any electronic data that carries the intent of a signature, but not all electronic signatures use digital signatures. In some countries, including the United States, Turkey, India, Brazil, Indonesia, Mexico, Saudi Arabia, Switzerland and the countries of the European Union, electronic signatures have legal significance.

Digital signatures employ asymmetric cryptography. In many instances they provide a layer of validation and security to messages sent through a non-secure channel: Properly implemented, a digital signature gives the receiver reason to believe the message was sent by the claimed sender. Digital seals and signatures are equivalent to handwritten signatures and stamped seals. Digital signatures are equivalent to traditional handwritten signatures in many respects, but properly implemented digital signatures are more difficult to forge than the handwritten type. Digital signature schemes, in the sense used here, are cryptographically based, and must be implemented properly to be effective. Digital signatures can also provide non-repudiation, meaning that the signer cannot successfully claim they did not sign a message, while also claiming their private key remains secret; further, some non-repudiation schemes offer a time stamp for the digital signature, so that even if the private key is exposed, the signature is valid. Digitally signed messages may be anything re-presentable as a bitstring: examples include electronic mail, contracts, or a message sent via some other cryptographic protocol.

Definition of Digital Signature

A digital signature scheme typically consists of three algorithms;

- A *key generation* algorithm that selects a *private key* uniformly at random from a set of possible private keys. The algorithm outputs the private key and a corresponding *public key.*

- A *signing* algorithm that, given a message and a private key, produces a signature.

- A *signature verifying* algorithm that, given the message, public key and signature, either accepts or rejects the message's claim to authenticity.

Two main properties are required. First, the authenticity of a signature generated from a fixed message and fixed private key can be verified by using the corresponding public key. Secondly, it should be computationally infeasible to generate a valid signature for a party without knowing that party's private key. A digital signature is an authentication mechanism that enables the creator of the message to attach a code that acts as a signature. The Digital Signature Algorithm (DSA), developed by the National Institute of Standards and Technology, is one of many examples of a signing algorithm.

In the following discussion, 1^n refers to a unary number.

Formally, a digital signature scheme is a triple of probabilistic polynomial time algorithms, (G, S, V), satisfying:

- G (key-generator) generates a public key, pk, and a corresponding private key, sk, on input 1^n, where n is the security parameter.

- S (signing) returns a tag, t, on the inputs: the private key, sk, and a string, x.

- V (verifying) outputs *accepted* or *rejected* on the inputs: the public key, pk, a string, x, and a tag, t.

For correctness, S and V must satisfy

$$\Pr \left[\, (pk, sk) \leftarrow G(1^n), \, V(\, pk, x, S(sk, x) \,) = accepted \, \right] = 1.$$

A digital signature scheme is secure if for every non-uniform probabilistic polynomial time adversary, A

$$\Pr \left[\, (pk, sk) \leftarrow G(1^n), (x, t) \leftarrow A^{S(sk, \cdot)}(pk, 1^n), x \notin Q, V(pk, x, t) = accepted \right] < \mathrm{negl}(n),$$

where $A^{S(sk, \cdot)}$ denotes that A has access to the oracle, $S(sk, \cdot)$, and Q denotes the set of the queries on S made by A, which knows the public key, pk, and the security parameter, n. Note that we require any adversary cannot directly query the string, x, on S.

History of Digital Signature

In 1976, Whitfield Diffie and Martin Hellman first described the notion of a digital signature scheme, although they only conjectured that such schemes existed. Soon afterwards, Ronald

Rivest, Adi Shamir, and Len Adleman invented the RSA algorithm, which could be used to produce primitive digital signatures (although only as a proof-of-concept – "plain" RSA signatures are not secure). The first widely marketed software package to offer digital signature was Lotus Notes 1.0, released in 1989, which used the RSA algorithm.

Other digital signature schemes were soon developed after RSA, the earliest being Lamport signatures, Merkle signatures (also known as "Merkle trees" or simply "Hash trees"), and Rabin signatures.

In 1988, Shafi Goldwasser, Silvio Micali, and Ronald Rivest became the first to rigorously define the security requirements of digital signature schemes. They described a hierarchy of attack models for signature schemes, and also presented the GMR signature scheme, the first that could be proved to prevent even an existential forgery against a chosen message attack.

How they Work

To create RSA signature keys, generate a RSA key pair containing a modulus, N, that is the product of two large primes, along with integers, e and d, such that $e\,d \equiv 1 \pmod{\phi(N)}$, where ϕ is the Euler phi-function. The signer's public key consists of N and e, and the signer's secret key contains d.

To sign a message, m, the signer computes a signature, σ, such that $\sigma \equiv m^d \pmod{N}$. To verify, the receiver checks that $\sigma^e \equiv m \pmod{N}$.

As noted earlier, this basic scheme is not very secure. To prevent attacks, one can first apply a cryptographic hash function to the message, m, and then apply the RSA algorithm described above to the result. This approach is secure assuming the hash function is a random oracle.

Most early signature schemes were of a similar type: they involve the use of a trapdoor permutation, such as the RSA function, or in the case of the Rabin signature scheme, computing square modulo composite, n. A trapdoor permutation family is a family of permutations, specified by a parameter, that is easy to compute in the forward direction, but is difficult to compute in the reverse direction without already knowing the private key ("trapdoor"). Trapdoor permutations can be used for digital signature schemes, where computing the reverse direction with the secret key is required for signing, and computing the forward direction is used to verify signatures.

Used directly, this type of signature scheme is vulnerable to a key-only existential forgery attack. To create a forgery, the attacker picks a random signature σ and uses the verification procedure to determine the message, m, corresponding to that signature. In practice, however, this type of signature is not used directly, but rather, the message to be signed is first hashed to produce a short digest that is then signed. This forgery attack, then, only produces the hash function output that corresponds to σ, but not a message that leads to that value, which does not lead to an attack. In the random oracle model, this hash-then-sign form of signature is existentially unforgeable, even against a chosen-plaintext attack.

There are several reasons to sign such a hash (or message digest) instead of the whole document.

For efficiency

> The signature will be much shorter and thus save time since hashing is generally much faster than signing in practice.

For compatibility

> Messages are typically bit strings, but some signature schemes operate on other domains (such as, in the case of RSA, numbers modulo a composite number N). A hash function can be used to convert an arbitrary input into the proper format.

For integrity

> Without the hash function, the text "to be signed" may have to be split (separated) in blocks small enough for the signature scheme to act on them directly. However, the receiver of the signed blocks is not able to recognize if all the blocks are present and in the appropriate order.

Notions of Security

In their foundational paper, Goldwasser, Micali, and Rivest lay out a hierarchy of attack models against digital signatures:

1. In a *key-only* attack, the attacker is only given the public verification key.

2. In a *known message* attack, the attacker is given valid signatures for a variety of messages known by the attacker but not chosen by the attacker.

3. In an *adaptive chosen message* attack, the attacker first learns signatures on arbitrary messages of the attacker's choice.

They also describe a hierarchy of attack results:

1. A *total break* results in the recovery of the signing key.

2. A universal forgery attack results in the ability to forge signatures for any message.

3. A selective forgery attack results in a signature on a message of the adversary's choice.

4. An existential forgery merely results in some valid message/signature pair not already known to the adversary.

The strongest notion of security, therefore, is security against existential forgery under an adaptive chosen message attack.

Applications of Digital Signatures

As organizations move away from paper documents with ink signatures or authenticity stamps, digital signatures can provide added assurances of the evidence to provenance, identity, and status of an electronic document as well as acknowledging informed consent and approval by a signatory. The United States Government Printing Office (GPO) publishes electronic versions of the budget, public and private laws, and congressional bills with digital signatures. Universities including Penn State, University of Chicago, and Stanford are publishing electronic student transcripts with digital signatures.

Below are some common reasons for applying a digital signature to communications:

Authentication

Although messages may often include information about the entity sending a message, that information may not be accurate. Digital signatures can be used to authenticate the source of messages. When ownership of a digital signature secret key is bound to a specific user, a valid signature shows that the message was sent by that user. The importance of high confidence in sender authenticity is especially obvious in a financial context. For example, suppose a bank's branch office sends instructions to the central office requesting a change in the balance of an account. If the central office is not convinced that such a message is truly sent from an authorized source, acting on such a request could be a grave mistake.

Integrity

In many scenarios, the sender and receiver of a message may have a need for confidence that the message has not been altered during transmission. Although encryption hides the contents of a message, it may be possible to *change* an encrypted message without understanding it. (Some encryption algorithms, known as nonmalleable ones, prevent this, but others do not.) However, if a message is digitally signed, any change in the message after signature invalidates the signature. Furthermore, there is no efficient way to modify a message and its signature to produce a new message with a valid signature, because this is still considered to be computationally infeasible by most cryptographic hash functions.

Non-repudiation

Non-repudiation, or more specifically *non-repudiation of origin*, is an important aspect of digital signatures. By this property, an entity that has signed some information cannot at a later time deny having signed it. Similarly, access to the public key only does not enable a fraudulent party to fake a valid signature.

Note that these authentication, non-repudiation etc. properties rely on the secret key *not having been revoked* prior to its usage. Public revocation of a key-pair is a required ability, else leaked secret keys would continue to implicate the claimed owner of the key-pair. Checking revocation status requires an "online" check; e.g., checking a certificate revocation list or via the Online Certificate Status Protocol. Very roughly this is analogous to a vendor who receives credit-cards first checking online with the credit-card issuer to find if a given card has been reported lost or stolen. Of course, with stolen key pairs, the theft is often discovered only after the secret key's use, e.g., to sign a bogus certificate for espionage purpose.

Additional Security Precautions

Putting the Private Key on a Smart Card

All public key / private key cryptosystems depend entirely on keeping the private key secret. A private key can be stored on a user's computer, and protected by a local password, but this has two disadvantages:

- the user can only sign documents on that particular computer

- the security of the private key depends entirely on the security of the computer

A more secure alternative is to store the private key on a smart card. Many smart cards are designed to be tamper-resistant (although some designs have been broken, notably by Ross Anderson and his students). In a typical digital signature implementation, the hash calculated from the document is sent to the smart card, whose CPU signs the hash using the stored private key of the user, and then returns the signed hash. Typically, a user must activate his smart card by entering a personal identification number or PIN code (thus providing two-factor authentication). It can be arranged that the private key never leaves the smart card, although this is not always implemented. If the smart card is stolen, the thief will still need the PIN code to generate a digital signature. This reduces the security of the scheme to that of the PIN system, although it still requires an attacker to possess the card. A mitigating factor is that private keys, if generated and stored on smart cards, are usually regarded as difficult to copy, and are assumed to exist in exactly one copy. Thus, the loss of the smart card may be detected by the owner and the corresponding certificate can be immediately revoked. Private keys that are protected by software only may be easier to copy, and such compromises are far more difficult to detect.

Using Smart Card Readers with a Separate Keyboard

Entering a PIN code to activate the smart card commonly requires a numeric keypad. Some card readers have their own numeric keypad. This is safer than using a card reader integrated into a PC, and then entering the PIN using that computer's keyboard. Readers with a numeric keypad are meant to circumvent the eavesdropping threat where the computer might be running a keystroke logger, potentially compromising the PIN code. Specialized card readers are also less vulnerable to tampering with their software or hardware and are often EAL3 certified.

Other Smart Card Designs

Smart card design is an active field, and there are smart card schemes which are intended to avoid these particular problems, though so far with little security proofs.

Using Digital Signatures only with Trusted Applications

One of the main differences between a digital signature and a written signature is that the user does not "see" what he signs. The user application presents a hash code to be signed by the digital signing algorithm using the private key. An attacker who gains control of the user's PC can possibly replace the user application with a foreign substitute, in effect replacing the user's own communications with those of the attacker. This could allow a malicious application to trick a user into signing any document by displaying the user's original on-screen, but presenting the attacker's own documents to the signing application.

To protect against this scenario, an authentication system can be set up between the user's application (word processor, email client, etc.) and the signing application. The general idea is to provide some means for both the user application and signing application to verify each other's integrity. For example, the signing application may require all requests to come from digitally signed binaries.

Using A Network Attached Hardware Security Module

One of the main differences between a cloud based digital signature service and a locally provided one is risk. Many risk averse companies, including governments, financial and medical institutions, and payment processors require more secure standards, like FIPS 140-2 level 3 and FIPS 201 certification, to ensure the signature is validated and secure.

WYSIWYS

Technically speaking, a digital signature applies to a string of bits, whereas humans and applications "believe" that they sign the semantic interpretation of those bits. In order to be semantically interpreted, the bit string must be transformed into a form that is meaningful for humans and applications, and this is done through a combination of hardware and software based processes on a computer system. The problem is that the semantic interpretation of bits can change as a function of the processes used to transform the bits into semantic content. It is relatively easy to change the interpretation of a digital document by implementing changes on the computer system where the document is being processed. From a semantic perspective this creates uncertainty about what exactly has been signed. WYSIWYS (What You See Is What You Sign) means that the semantic interpretation of a signed message cannot be changed. In particular this also means that a message cannot contain hidden information that the signer is unaware of, and that can be revealed after the signature has been applied. WYSIWYS is a necessary requirement for the validity of digital signatures, but this requirement is difficult to guarantee because of the increasing complexity of modern computer systems. The term WYSIWYS was coined by Peter Landrock and Torben Pedersen to describe some of the principles in delivering secure and legally binding digital signatures for Pan-European projects.

Digital Signatures versus Ink on Paper Signatures

An ink signature could be replicated from one document to another by copying the image manually or digitally, but to have credible signature copies that can resist some scrutiny is a significant manual or technical skill, and to produce ink signature copies that resist professional scrutiny is very difficult.

Digital signatures cryptographically bind an electronic identity to an electronic document and the digital signature cannot be copied to another document. Paper contracts sometimes have the ink signature block on the last page, and the previous pages may be replaced after a signature is applied. Digital signatures can be applied to an entire document, such that the digital signature on the last page will indicate tampering if any data on any of the pages have been altered, but this can also be achieved by signing with ink and numbering all pages of the contract.

Some Digital Signature Algorithms

- RSA-based signature schemes, such as RSA-PSS

- DSA and its elliptic curve variant ECDSA

- Edwards-curve Digital Signature Algorithm and its Ed25519 variant

- ElGamal signature scheme as the predecessor to DSA, and variants Schnorr signature and Pointcheval–Stern signature algorithm

- Rabin signature algorithm

- Pairing-based schemes such as BLS

- Undeniable signatures

- Aggregate signature - a signature scheme that supports aggregation: Given n signatures on n messages from n users, it is possible to aggregate all these signatures into a single signature whose size is constant in the number of users. This single signature will convince the verifier that the n users did indeed sign the n original messages

- Signatures with efficient protocols - are signature schemes that facilitate efficient cryptographic protocols such as zero-knowledge proofs or secure computation

The Current State of use – Legal and Practical

All digital signature schemes share the following basic prerequisites regardless of cryptographic theory or legal provision:

1. Quality algorithms

   Some public-key algorithms are known to be insecure, as practical attacks against them having been discovered.

2. Quality implementations

   An implementation of a good algorithm (or protocol) with mistake(s) will not work.

3. Users (and their software) must carry out the signature protocol properly.

4. The private key must remain private

   If the private key becomes known to any other party, that party can produce *perfect* digital signatures of anything whatsoever.

5. The public key owner must be verifiable

   A public key associated with Bob actually came from Bob. This is commonly done using a public key infrastructure (PKI) and the public key↔user association is attested by the operator of the PKI (called a certificate authority). For 'open' PKIs in which anyone can request such an attestation (universally embodied in a cryptographically protected identity certificate), the possibility of mistaken attestation is non-trivial. Commercial PKI operators have suffered several publicly known problems. Such mistakes could lead to falsely signed, and thus wrongly attributed, documents. 'Closed' PKI systems are more expensive, but less easily subverted in this way.

Only if all of these conditions are met will a digital signature actually be any evidence of who sent the message, and therefore of their assent to its contents. Legal enactment cannot change this reality of the existing engineering possibilities, though some such have not reflected this actuality.

Legislatures, being importuned by businesses expecting to profit from operating a PKI, or by the technological avant-garde advocating new solutions to old problems, have enacted statutes and/or regulations in many jurisdictions authorizing, endorsing, encouraging, or permitting digital signatures and providing for (or limiting) their legal effect. The first appears to have been in Utah in the United States, followed closely by the states Massachusetts and California. Other countries have also passed statutes or issued regulations in this area as well and the UN has had an active model law project for some time. These enactments (or proposed enactments) vary from place to place, have typically embodied expectations at variance (optimistically or pessimistically) with the state of the underlying cryptographic engineering, and have had the net effect of confusing potential users and specifiers, nearly all of whom are not cryptographically knowledgeable. Adoption of technical standards for digital signatures have lagged behind much of the legislation, delaying a more or less unified engineering position on interoperability, algorithm choice, key lengths, and so on what the engineering is attempting to provide.

Industry Standards

Some industries have established common interoperability standards for the use of digital signatures between members of the industry and with regulators. These include the Automotive Network Exchange for the automobile industry and the SAFE-BioPharma Association for the healthcare industry.

Using Separate Key Pairs for Signing and Encryption

In several countries, a digital signature has a status somewhat like that of a traditional pen and paper signature, like in the EU digital signature legislation. Generally, these provisions mean that anything digitally signed legally binds the signer of the document to the terms therein. For that reason, it is often thought best to use separate key pairs for encrypting and signing. Using the encryption key pair, a person can engage in an encrypted conversation (e.g., regarding a real estate transaction), but the encryption does not legally sign every message he sends. Only when both parties come to an agreement do they sign a contract with their signing keys, and only then are they legally bound by the terms of a specific document. After signing, the document can be sent over the encrypted link. If a signing key is lost or compromised, it can be revoked to mitigate any future transactions. If an encryption key is lost, a backup or key escrow should be utilized to continue viewing encrypted content. Signing keys should never be backed up or escrowed unless the backup destination is securely encrypted.

Traditionally signature with a message is used to give evidence of identity and intention with regard to that message. For years people have been using various types of signature to associate their identity and intention to the messages. Wax imprint, seal, and handwritten signature are the common examples. But when someone need to sign a digital message, things turn different. In case of signing a digital document one cannot use any classical approach of signing, because it can be forged easily. Forger just need to cut the signature and paste it with any other message. For signing a digital document one uses digital signature.

Therefore, digital signature are required not to be separated from the message and attached to another. That is a digital signature is required to be both message and signer dependent. For validating the signature anyone can verify the signature, so digital signature are suppose to be verified easily.

A digital signature scheme typically consist of three distinct steps:

1. Key generation:- User compute their public key and corresponding private key.

2. Signing:- In this step user sign a given message with his/her private key.

3. Verification:- In this step user verify a signature for given message and public key.

So the functionality provided by digital signature can be stated as follows:

Authentication:- Digital signature provides authentication of the source of the messages as a message is signed by the private key of the sender which is only known to him/her. Authentication is highly desirable in many applications.

Integrity:- Digital signature provides integrity as digital signature uniquely associate with corresponding message. i.e. After signing a message a message cannot be altered if someone do it will invalidate the signature. There is no efficient method to change message and its signature to produce a new message and valid signature without having private key. So both sender and receiver don't have to worry about in transit alteration.

Non- repudiation:- For a valid signature sender of message cannot deny having signed it.

In this report we are going to discuss different variation of digital signature. First we will describe RSA digital signature scheme and Elgamal signature scheme, along with their elliptic curve version. After covering above signature scheme we will talk about digital signature standards, and then we will cover proxy signature scheme, blind signature scheme and then we will finally talk about short signature scheme.

RSA Digital Signature Scheme

Suppose Alice want to send a message(m) to Bob. She can generate digital signature using RSA digital signature scheme as follow:

Key Generation:-

She can generate key for RSA signature scheme:

1. Choose two distinct large prime numbers p and q.

2. Compute n = pq.

3. n is used as the modulus for both the public and private keys.

4. Compute $\varphi(n) = (p - 1)(q - 1)$, where φ is Euler's totient function.

5. Choose an integer e such that $1 < e < \varphi(n)$ and $\gcd(e, \varphi(n)) = 1$.

6. Compute $d = e{-1} \bmod \varphi(n)$.

Then the public key and private key of user will be (e, n) and (d, n) respectively.

Now she have her public and private key. Now she can generate the signature of a message by encrypting it by her private key.

So she can generate signature corresponding to message(m) as follow:

Signing:-

1. Represent the message m as an integer between o and n − 1.

2. Sign message by raising it to the dth power modulo n.

$$S \equiv m^d \pmod{n}$$

So S is the signature corresponding to message m. Now she can send message m along with the signature S to Bob.

Upon receiving the message and signature (m, S), Bob can verify the signature by decrypting it by Alice public key as follow:

Verification:-

1. Verify signature by raising it to the eth power modulo n.

$$m' \equiv S^e \pmod{n}$$

2. If m' = m (mod n) then signature is valid otherwise not.

    For a valid signature both m and m' will be equal because:

$$S \equiv m^d \pmod{n}$$

$$m' \equiv m^{de} \pmod{n}$$

    and

    e is inverse of d, i.e. $ed \equiv 1 \pmod{\Phi(n)}$.

So, by using above algorithm Alice can generate a valid signature S for her message m, but there is a problem in above define scheme that is the length of the signature is equal to the length of the message. This is a disadvantage when message is long.

There is a modification in the above scheme. The signature scheme is applied to the hash of the message, rather than to the message itself. Now Alice have a message signature pair (m, S). So, the signature S is a valid signature for message m. So a forger (lets say Eve) cannot forge Alice signature. i.e. She cannot use signature S with another message lets say m_1, because S^e is not equal to m_1. Even when the signature scheme is applied to the hash of the message it is infeasible to forge the signature, because it is infeasible to produce two message m, m_1 with same hash value.

In practice, the public key in RSA digital signature scheme is much smaller than the private key. This enable a user to verify the message easily. This is a desired because a message may be verified more than once, so the verification process should be faster than signing process.

The RSA Digital Signature Algorithm:-

Additional instructions for RSA signature algorithm is as follows:

An RSA digital signature key pair consists of an RSA private key, which is used to compute a digital signature, and an RSA public key, which is used to verify a digital signature. An RSA digital signature key pair shall not be used for other purposes (e.g. key establishment).

An RSA public key consists of a modulus n, which is the product of two positive prime integers p and q (i.e., n = pq), and a public key exponent e. Thus, the RSA public key is the pair of values (n, e) and is used to verify digital signatures. The size of an RSA key pair is commonly considered to be the length of the modulus n in bits (nlen). The corresponding RSA private key consists of the same modulus n and a private key exponent d that depends on n and the public key exponent e. Thus, the RSA private key is the pair of values (n, d) and is used to generate digital signatures. In order to provide security for the digital signature process, the two integers p and q, and the private key exponent d shall be kept secret. The modulus n and the public key exponent e may be made known to anyone.

The Standard specifies three choices for the length of the modulus (i.e., nlen): 1024, 2048 and 3072 bits.

An approved hash function, shall be used during the generation of key pairs and digital signatures. When used during the generation of an RSA key pair, the length in bits of the hash function output block shall meet or exceed the security strength associated with the bit length of the modulus n. The security strength associated with the RSA digital signature process is no greater than the minimum of the security strength associated with the bit length of the modulus and the security strength of the hash function that is employed. Both the security strength of the hash function used and the security strength associated with the bit length of the modulus n shall meet or exceed the security strength required for the digital signature process.

Elgamal Digital Signature Scheme

Elgamal digital signature scheme was proposed by Elgamal in 1985. This is based on Diffe-Hellman key exchange. This signature scheme is quite different from RSA signature scheme in terms of validity of signatures corresponding to a message. i.e. there are many valid signatures for a message. Suppose Alice want to sign a message using Elgamal digital signature scheme, she can generate signature S corresponding to message m as follow:

Key generation:-

She can generate key for Elgamal signature scheme as follow:

- Choose p be a large prime.

- Choose g be a randomly chosen generator of the multiplicative group of integers Zp.

- Choose a secret key x such that $1 < x < p - 1$.

- Compute $y = g^x \pmod{p}$.

Then the public key and private key of user will be (p, g, y) and (p, g, x) respectively.

Signing:-

Now Alice has her public and private key so she can sign a message m by using following steps:

1. Choose a random number k such that $0 < k < p - 1$ and $gcd(k, p - 1) = 1$.

2. Compute $r \equiv g^k \pmod p$.

3. Compute $s \equiv (H(m) - xr)k^{-1} \pmod{p - 1}$. Where $H(m)$ is hash of message.

Then the pair (r, s) is the signature of the message m.

Verification:-

Bob can verify the signature (r, s) of message m as follow:

1. Download Alice's public key (p, g, y).

2. Compute $v_1 \equiv g^{H(m)} \pmod p$ and $v_2 \equiv y^r r^s \pmod p$.

3. The signature is declared valid if and only if $v_1 \equiv v_2 \pmod p$.

For a valid signature (r, s), $v_1 \equiv v_2 \pmod p$ since

$$s \equiv (H(m) - xr)k^{-1} \pmod{p - 1}$$

$$sk \equiv (H(m) - xr) \pmod{p - 1}$$

$$H(m) \equiv (sk + xr) \pmod{p - 1}$$

$$v_1 \equiv g^{H(m)} \pmod p$$

$$v_1 \equiv g^{(sk + xr)} \pmod p$$

$$v_1 \equiv g^{(sk)} g^{(xr)} \pmod p$$

$$v_1 \equiv (g^k)^s (g^x)^r \pmod p$$

$$v_1 \equiv y^r r^s \pmod p$$

$$v_1 \equiv v_2 \pmod p$$

The security of Elgamal digital signature scheme relies on the difficulty of computing discrete logarithms. The security of the system follows from the fact that since x is kept private for forging Elgamal digital signature one do need to solve discrete logarithm problem.

Suppose Eve want to forge Alice signature for a message m_1 and she doesn't know x (as x kept private by Alice), then she cannot compute s(as $s \equiv (H(m_1) - xr)k^{-1} \pmod{p - 1}$). Now the only option left is to choose s which satisfies the verification. Thus s should satisfy equation $y^r r^s \equiv g^{H(m)} \pmod p$ as Eve knows (p, g, y) so she can compute r. So the equation can be rearrange as $r^s \equiv y^{-r} g^{H(m)} \pmod p$, which is again a discrete logarithm problem. So Elgamal signature scheme is secure, as long as discrete logarithm are difficult to compute.

Digital Signature Standards

Digital signature standards define some standards to be followed. A digital signature scheme includes a signature generation and a signature verification. Each user has a public and private key and is the owner of that key pair.

For both the signature generation and verification processes, the message (i.e., the signed data) is converted to a fixed-length representation of the message by means of an approved hash function. Both the original message and the digital signature are made available to a verifier.

A verifier requires assurance that the public key to be used to verify a signature belongs to the entity that claims to have generated a digital signature (i.e., the claimed signatory). That is, a verifier requires assurance that the signatory is the actual owner of the public/private key pair used to generate and verify a digital signature. A binding of an owners identity and the owners public key shall be effected in order to provide this assurance.

A verifier also requires assurance that the key pair owner actually possesses the private key associated with the public key, and that the public key is a mathematically correct key. By obtaining these assurances, the verifier has assurance that if the digital signature can be correctly verified using the public key, the digital signature is valid (i.e., the key pair owner really signed the message). Digital signature validation includes both the (mathematical) verification of the digital signature and obtaining the appropriate assurances.

Technically, a key pair used by a digital signature algorithm could also be used for purposes other than digital signatures (e.g., for key establishment). However, a key pair used for digital signature generation and verification as specified in this Standard shall not be used for any other purpose. A number of steps are required to enable a digital signature generation or verification capability in accordance with Standards.

Initial Setup:-

Each intended signatory shall obtain a digital signature key pair that is generated as specified for the appropriate digital signature algorithm, either by generating the key pair itself or by obtaining the key pair from a trusted party. The intended signatory is authorized to use the key pair and is the owner of that key pair. Note that if a trusted party generates the key pair, that party needs to be trusted not to masquerade as the owner, even though the trusted party knows the private key.

After obtaining the key pair, the intended signatory (now the key pair owner) shall obtain assurance of the validity of the public key and assurance that he/she actually possesses the associated private key.

Digital Signature Generation:-

Prior to the generation of a digital signature, a message digest shall be generated on the information to be signed using an appropriate approved hash function.

Using the selected digital signature algorithm, the signature private key, the message digest, and any other information required by the digital signature process, a digital signature shall be generated according to the Standard.

The signatory may optionally verify the digital signature using the signature verification process and the associated public key. This optional verification serves as a final check to detect otherwise undetected signature generation computation errors; this verification may be prudent when signing a high-value message, when multiple users are expected to verify the signature, or if the verifier will be verifying the signature at a much later time.

Digital Signature Verification and Validation:-

In order to verify a digital signature, the verifier shall obtain the public key of the claimed signatory, (usually) based on the claimed identity. A message digest shall be generated on the data whose signature is to be verified (i.e., not on the received digital signature) using the same hash function that was used during the digital signature generation process. Using the appropriate digital signature algorithm, the domain parameters (if appropriate), the public key and the newly computed message digest, the received digital signature is verified in accordance with this Standard. If the verification process fails, no inference can be made as to whether the data is correct, only that in using the specified public key and the specified signature format, the digital signature cannot be verified for that data.

Before accepting the verified digital signature as valid, the verifier shall have

1. assurance of the signatory claimed identity,

2. assurance of the validity of the public key,

3. assurance that the claimed signatory actually possessed the private key that was used to generate the digital signature at the time that the signature was generated.

If the verification and assurance processes are successful, the digital signature and signed data shall be considered valid. However, if a verification or assurance process fails, the digital signature should be considered invalid.

Blind & Prony Signature

Suppose Alice want her message to be sign by Bob without letting him know the content of the message, she can got it done using Blind signature scheme. Blind signatures scheme, proposed by Chaum, allow a signer to interactively sign messages for users such that the messages are hidden from the signer. Blind signature typically have two basic security properties: blindness says that a malicious signer cannot decide upon the order in which two messages have been signed in two executions with an honest user, and unforgeability demands that no adversarial user can create more signatures than interactions with the honest signer took place.

Blind signatures are typically employed in privacy-related protocols where the signer and message author are different parties. Blind signature schemes see a great deal of use in applications where sender privacy is important, some of them are:

1. Cryptographic election systems (e-Vote).

2. Digital cash schemes (e-Cash).

Blind signature scheme can be used with RSA signature algorithm. In RSA signature scheme a signature is computed by encrypting the message by the private key. In case of the blind signature there is one additional step Blinding the message. Alice can blind her message and get is signed by Bob, and remove the blinding factor after getting it signed. Suppose (e, N) and (d, N) is the public key and private key of Bob respectively then Alice can blind her message as follows:

Blinding the message:-

1. Alice chooses a random value r, such that r is relatively prime to N (i.e. gcd(r, N) = 1).

2. Calculate blinding factor by raising r to the public key e (mod N) (i.e. blinding factor is equal to r^e(mod N)).

3. Blind the message by computing the product of the message and blinding factor, i.e.

$m' \equiv mr^e$ (mod N)

Now Alice can send blinded message m' to Bob. Now m' does not leak any information about m, as r is private to Alice. Any malicious user need to solve discrete logarithm problem for recovering original m from m'.

Signing:-

When Bob (signing authority) receive a blinded message from Alice (user) he will sign the message by his private key

$S' \equiv (m')^d$(mod N)

S' is the signature corresponding to message m'. Bob send S' to Alice. Alice removes the blinding factor from the signature by dividing it r and revel the original RSA signature S as follow:

$S \equiv S'r^{-1}$ (mod N)

Now Alice message m with signature S, signature can be verified using Bob's public key.

Verification:-

Now signature can be verified as usual RSA signature.

1. Verify signature by raising it to the eth power module N.

$m' \equiv S^e$ (mod N)

2. If m' = m (mod N) then signature is valid otherwise not.

The above scheme will work fine. i.e. (S, m) is a valid signature message tuple corresponding to Bob. Since

$S \equiv S'r^{-1}$ (mod N)

$\equiv (m')^d r^{-1}$ (mod N)

$\equiv (mr^e)^d r^{-1}$ (mod N)

$\equiv m^d r^{ed} r^{-1}$ (mod N)

$\equiv m^d r r^{-1}$ (mod N)

$\equiv m^d$ (mod N)

Proxy Signature:-

In proxy signature scheme a user Alice (original signer) delegates her signing capability to another user, Bob(proxy signer), so that Bob can sign messages on behalf of Alice. Proxy signature can be validate for its correctness and can be distinguished between a normal signature and a proxy signature. So the verifier can be convinced of the original signer's agreement on the signed message. Proxy signature is used in a number of applications, including electronic commerce, mobile agents, distributed shared object systems, and many more. For example, the president of a company delegates a signing right to his/her secretary before a vacation. The secretary can make a signature on behalf of the president, and a verifier can be confident that the signature has been made by the authorized secretary. The verifier can also be convinced of the president's agreement on the signed message. Typically, a proxy signature scheme is as follows. The original signer Alice sends the proxy signer Bob a signature that is associated with a specific message. Bob makes a proxy private key using this information. Bob can then sign on a message with the proxy private key using a normal signature scheme. After the message and signature have been sent to the verifier, he/she recovers a proxy public key using public information and verifies the proxy signature using a normal signature scheme.

Proxy Signature scheme is introduced by Mambo. Proxy signature scheme is based on a discrete logarithm problem. The original signer has the private key x and public key $y \equiv g^x \pmod{p}$. Proxy signature scheme is as follow:

System Parameters:-

The original signer choose k randomly and computes $r = g^k \bmod p$, and $s = x + kr \bmod p$. Now original signer send these system parameters to the proxy signer.

i.e. original signer sends (r, s) to the proxy signer. The proxy signer checks the validity of (r, s) as follows:

$$g^s = yr^r \bmod p$$

If this equality holds, the proxy signer accepts (r, s) as the valid proxy secret key.

Signing

The proxy signer signs a message m, then its signature S_p is generated. After that, the proxy signer sends the message and its signature, which are (m, S_p, r), to the verifier.

Verification

Upon receiving (m, S_p, r), the verifier recovers y' by $y' = yr^r \bmod p$ and substitute y' for y. After that, the verifier proceeds the verification phase of normal signature scheme.

Short Signature Scheme

Short signature scheme give the shortest signature among all discussed signature schemes. This signature scheme use elliptic curve and bilinear pairing. We will discuss this signature scheme starting from the basic signature scheme and then type of bilinear pairing it uses, after that security multiplier and finally types of elliptic curve used in this scheme.

Short signature scheme is in three parts, KeyGen, Sign, and Verify. It makes use of a hash function $h : \{0, 1\}^* \to G^*$. Where G is the base group and g is generator. G, g are system parameters.

1. Key Generation:- Choose a random $x \in Z^*_p$, and compute $v \leftarrow g^x$. x is the secret key and v is the public key.

2. Signing:- For a message $M \in \{0, 1\}^*$, and secret key x, Compute $h \leftarrow h(M)$, and $\sigma \leftarrow h^x$. The signature is $\sigma \in G^*$.

3. Verification:- For a given public key v, a message M, and a signature, compute $h \leftarrow h(M)$ and verify that (g, v, h, σ) is a valid Diffie-Hellman tuple.

So short signature scheme use bilinear pairing in verification of the signature.

Bilinear pairing:-

Let G_1 and G_T be two cyclic groups of prime order q. Let G_2 be a group and each element of G_2 has order dividing q. A bilinear pairing e is $e : G_1 \times G_2 \to G_T$ such that,

$e(g_1, g_2) = 1_{GT}$ for all $g_2 \in G_2$ if and only if $g_1 = 1_{G1}$, and similarly $e(g_1, g_2) = 1_{GT}$ for all $g_1 \in G_1$ if and only if $g_2 = 1_{G2}$.

for all $g_1 \in G_1$ and $g_2 \in G_2$, $e(g_1, g_2) = e(g_1^a, g_2^b)^{ab}$ for all $a, b \in Z$.

Security Multiplier: - Let a finite field F_p^l where p is a prime and l is a positive integer, and an elliptic curve E over F_p^l have m points. Let, point P of elliptic curve has order q, where $q^2!/m$. Then subgroup P has a security multiplier $\alpha > 0$, if order of p^l in F_q^* is α. We will discuss different families of elliptic curve Which are classified by the value of security multiplier.

Type 1

Let p be a prime where $p = 2 \pmod 3$. Let E be the elliptic curve defined over F_p, and equation of the curve is $y^2 = x^3 + b$, Typically $b = \pm 1$. Then $E(F_p)$ is supersingular curve, and number of points, $\#E(F_p) = p + 1$, and $\#E(F_p^2) = (p + 1)^2$. For any odd $j / p + 1$, $G = E(F_p)[j]$ is cyclic and has security multiplier $\alpha = 2$. Let | be the cube root of unity. Consider the following map, sometimes referred to as a distortion map:

$$\Phi(x, y) = (|x, y)$$

Then Φ maps points of $E(F_p)$ to points of $E(F_{p2}) \backslash E(F_p)$. Thus if f denotes the bilinear pairing, then defining $e : G \times G \to F_{q2}$ by $e(P, Q) = f(P, \Phi(Q))$ gives a bilinear non-degenerate map.

Type 2

Unlike above discussed curve this type of curve have low characteristic field. Let F is a finite field defined over 3^l where | is a positive exponent. Let curve $E^+ : y^2 = x^3 + 2x + 1$, and

$E : y^2 = x^3 + 2x-1$, over F_3^l.

when $| = \pm 1 \bmod 12$

$\#E^+(F_3^l) = 3^l + 1 + 3^{(l+1)/2}$

when $| = \pm 5 \bmod 12$

$$\#E^+ (F_3{}^|) = 3^| + 1 - 3^{(|+1)/2}$$

when $| = \pm 1 \bmod 12$

$$\#E^-(F_3{}^|) = 3^| + 1 - 3^{(|+1)/2}$$

when $l = \pm 5 \bmod 12$

$$\#E^- (F_3{}^|) = 3^| + 1 + 3^{(|+1)/2}$$

Type 3

Let p be a prime where $p \equiv 3 \pmod 4$. Let E be the elliptic curve defined over F_p, and equation of the curve is $y^2 = x^3 + ax$, where $a \in Z(\bmod p)$. Then $E(F_q)$ is supersingular curve, and number of point, $\#E(F_p) = p + 1$, and $\#E(F_{p2}) = (p + 1)^2$. For any odd $j | p + 1$, Group $G = E(F_p)[j]$ is cyclic and has security multiplier $\alpha = 2$.

Type 4

Type 4 curves are non-supersingular. By considering cyclotomic polynomials, elliptic curve with security multiplier 12 can be generated. Let $q(x) = 36x^4 + 36x^3 + 24x^2 + 6x + 1$. Let $t(x) = 6x^2 + 1$. If D = 3, then solution of CM equation will always be $V = 6x^2 + 4x + 1$. It turns out $q(x) + 1 - t(x) \mid q(x)12 - 1$. So the value of security multiplier is 12. Following algorithm is used to generate curves:

1. Pick an integer x of a desired magnitude. It may be negative.

2. Check if $q(x)$ is prime.

3. Check if $n = q(x) - t(x) + 1$ has a large prime factor r. (Ideally it should be prime.)

4. Try different values of k until a random point of $y^2 = x^3 + k$ has order n.

Type 5

Type 5 curve are also non-supersingular curve. Type 6 curve are ordinary curves with security multiplier 6. Order of type 6 curves is a prime or a prime multiplied by a small constant. Let a finite field F defined over some p where $p = s*q$. Where s is a small constant and q is a prime. When type 5 curve is defined over field F_{p6}, its order is a multiple of q^2.

Cipher

In cryptography, a cipher (or cypher) is an algorithm for performing encryption or decryption—a series of well-defined steps that can be followed as a procedure. An alternative, less common term is *encipherment*. To encipher or encode is to convert information into cipher or code. In common parlance, 'cipher' is synonymous with 'code', as they are both a set of steps that encrypt a message; however, the concepts are distinct in cryptography, especially classical cryptography.

Edward Larsson's rune cipher resembling that found on the Kensington Runestone.
Also includes runically unrelated blackletter writing style and pigpen cipher.

Codes generally substitute different length strings of characters in the output, while ciphers generally substitute the same number of characters as are input. There are exceptions and some cipher systems may use slightly more, or fewer, characters when output versus the number that were input.

Codes operated by substituting according to a large codebook which linked a random string of characters or numbers to a word or phrase. For example, "UQJHSE" could be the code for "Proceed to the following coordinates." When using a cipher the original information is known as plaintext, and the encrypted form as ciphertext. The ciphertext message contains all the information of the plaintext message, but is not in a format readable by a human or computer without the proper mechanism to decrypt it.

The operation of a cipher usually depends on a piece of auxiliary information, called a key (or, in traditional NSA parlance, a *cryptovariable*). The encrypting procedure is varied depending on the key, which changes the detailed operation of the algorithm. A key must be selected before using a cipher to encrypt a message. Without knowledge of the key, it should be extremely difficult, if not impossible, to decrypt the resulting ciphertext into readable plaintext.

Most modern ciphers can be categorized in several ways:

- By whether they work on blocks of symbols usually of a fixed size (block ciphers), or on a continuous stream of symbols (stream ciphers).

- By whether the same key is used for both encryption and decryption (symmetric key algorithms), or if a different key is used for each (asymmetric key algorithms). If the algorithm is symmetric, the key must be known to the recipient and sender and to no one else. If the algorithm is an asymmetric one, the enciphering key is different from, but closely related to, the deciphering key. If one key cannot be deduced from the other, the asymmetric key algorithm has the public/private key property and one of the keys may be made public without loss of confidentiality.

Etymology

The word "cipher" (minority spelling "cypher") in former times meant "zero" and had the same origin: Middle French as *cifre* and Medieval Latin as *cifra,* from the Arabic *sifr* = zero. "Cipher" was later used for any decimal digit, even any number. There are many theories about how the word "cipher" may have come to mean "encoding". In fact the more ancient source of word "Cypher" is the ancient Hebrew; there are more than 100 verses in the Hebrew Bible - Torah using word "Cepher": means (Book or Story telling), and in some of them the word "Cipher" literally means (Counting)-- (Numerical description)-- Example, Book 2 Samuel 24:10, Isaiah 33:18, and Jeremiah 52:25.

- Encoding often involved numbers.

- The Roman number system was very cumbersome because there was no concept of zero (or empty space). The concept of zero (which was also called "cipher"), which is now common knowledge, was alien to medieval Europe, so confusing and ambiguous to common Europeans that in arguments people would say "talk clearly and not so far fetched as a cipher". Cipher came to mean concealment of clear messages or encryption.

    o The French formed the word "chiffre" and adopted the Italian word "zero".

    o The English used "zero" for "0", and "cipher" from the word "ciphering" as a means of computing.

    o The Germans used the words "Ziffer" (digit) and "Chiffre".

    o The Dutch still use the word "cijfer" to refer to a numerical digit.

    o The Serbians use the word "cifra", which refers to a digit, or in some cases, any number. Besides "cifra", they use word "broj" for a number.

    o The Italians and the Spanish also use the word "cifra" to refer to a number.

    o The Swedes use the word "siffra" which refers to a digit and "nummer" to refer to a combination of "siffror".

Ibrahim Al-Kadi concluded that the Arabic word *sifr,* for the digit zero, developed into the European technical term for encryption.

As the decimal zero and its new mathematics spread from the Arabic world to Europe in the Middle Ages, words derived from *sifr* and *zephyrus* came to refer to calculation, as well as to privileged knowledge and secret codes. According to Ifrah, "in thirteenth-century Paris, a 'worthless fellow' was called a '... cifre en algorisme', i.e., an 'arithmetical nothing'." Cipher was the European pronunciation of sifr, and cipher came to mean a message or communication not easily understood.

Versus Codes

In non-technical usage, a "(secret) code" typically means a "cipher". Within technical discussions, however, the words "code" and "cipher" refer to two different concepts. Codes work at the level of meaning—that is, words or phrases are converted into something else and this chunking generally shortens the message.

An example of this is the Commercial Telegraph Code which was used to shorten long telegraph messages which resulted from entering into commercial contracts using exchanges of Telegrams.

Another example is given by whole words cipher s, which allow the user to replace an entire word with a symbol or character, much like the way Japanese utilize Kanji (Japanese) characters to supplement their language. ex "The quick brown fox jumps over the lazy dog".

Ciphers, on the other hand, work at a lower level: the level of individual letters, small groups of letters, or, in modern schemes, individual bits and blocks of bits. Some systems used both codes and ciphers in one system, using superencipherment to increase the security. In some cases the terms codes and ciphers are also used synonymously to substitution and transposition.

Historically, cryptography was split into a dichotomy of codes and ciphers; and coding had its own terminology, analogous to that for ciphers: "*encoding, codetext, decoding*" and so on.

However, codes have a variety of drawbacks, including susceptibility to cryptanalysis and the difficulty of managing a cumbersome codebook. Because of this, codes have fallen into disuse in modern cryptography, and ciphers are the dominant technique.

Types

There are a variety of different types of encryption. Algorithms used earlier in the history of cryptography are substantially different from modern methods, and modern ciphers can be classified according to how they operate and whether they use one or two keys.

Historical

Historical pen and paper ciphers used in the past are sometimes known as classical ciphers. They include simple substitution ciphers (such as Rot 13) and transposition ciphers (such as a Rail Fence Cipher). For example, "GOOD DOG" can be encrypted as "PLLX XLP" where "L" substitutes for "O", "P" for "G", and "X" for "D" in the message. Transposition of the letters "GOOD DOG" can result in "DGOGDOO". These simple ciphers and examples are easy to crack, even without plaintext-ciphertext pairs.

Simple ciphers were replaced by polyalphabetic substitution ciphers (such as the Vigenère) which changed the substitution alphabet for every letter. For example, "GOOD DOG" can be encrypted as "PLSX TWF" where "L", "S", and "W" substitute for "O". With even a small amount of known or estimated plaintext, simple polyalphabetic substitution ciphers and letter transposition ciphers designed for pen and paper encryption are easy to crack. It is possible to create a secure pen and paper cipher based on a one-time pad though, but the usual disadvantages of one-time pads apply.

During the early twentieth century, electro-mechanical machines were invented to do encryption and decryption using transposition, polyalphabetic substitution, and a kind of "additive" substitution. In rotor machines, several rotor disks provided polyalphabetic substitution, while plug boards provided another substitution. Keys were easily changed by changing the rotor disks and the plugboard wires. Although these encryption methods were more complex than previous schemes and required machines to encrypt and decrypt, other machines such as the British Bombe were invented to crack these encryption methods.

Modern

Modern encryption methods can be divided by two criteria: by type of key used, and by type of input data.

By type of key used ciphers are divided into:

- symmetric key algorithms (Private-key cryptography), where the same key is used for encryption and decryption,

- asymmetric key algorithms (Public-key cryptography), where two different keys are used for encryption and decryption.

In a symmetric key algorithm (e.g., DES and AES), the sender and receiver must have a shared key set up in advance and kept secret from all other parties; the sender uses this key for encryption, and the receiver uses the same key for decryption. The Feistel cipher uses a combination of substitution and transposition techniques. Most block cipher algorithms are based on this structure. In an asymmetric key algorithm (e.g., RSA), there are two separate keys: a *public key* is published and enables any sender to perform encryption, while a *private key* is kept secret by the receiver and enables only him to perform correct decryption.

Ciphers can be distinguished into two types by the type of input data:

- block ciphers, which encrypt block of data of fixed size,

- stream ciphers, which encrypt continuous streams of data.

Key Size and Vulnerability

In a pure mathematical attack, (i.e., lacking any other information to help break a cipher) two factors above all count:

- Computational power available, i.e., the computing power which can be brought to bear on the problem. It is important to note that average performance/capacity of a single computer is not the only factor to consider. An adversary can use multiple computers at once, for instance, to increase the speed of exhaustive search for a key (i.e., "brute force" attack) substantially.

- Key size, i.e., the size of key used to encrypt a message. As the key size increases, so does the complexity of exhaustive search to the point where it becomes impracticable to crack encryption directly.

Since the desired effect is computational difficulty, in theory one would choose an algorithm and desired difficulty level, thus decide the key length accordingly.

An example of this process can be found at Key Length which uses multiple reports to suggest that a symmetric cipher with 128 bits, an asymmetric cipher with 3072 bit keys, and an elliptic curve cipher with 512 bits, all have similar difficulty at present.

Claude Shannon proved, using information theory considerations, that any theoretically unbreakable cipher must have keys which are at least as long as the plaintext, and used only once: one-time pad.

Ciphers:

1. Block Cipher

2. Stream Cipher

Block Cipher: The same function is used to encrypt successive blocks (memory less).

Stream Cipher: This processes plan text as small as single bit. It has memory.

- One – Time – Pad (corresponding cipher is called Vernam cipher)

$$c_i = m_i \oplus k_i$$

m_i : plain text

k_i : keystream

c_i : cipher text

- Decryption :

$$m_i = c_i \oplus k_i$$
$$= m_i \oplus k_i \oplus k_i$$
$$= m_i$$

- Assumption: is truly random.

Synchronous Stream Ciphers:

{There is a clock which is same at both the ends}

Definition: a synchronous stream cipher is one in which the key stream is generated independently of the plain text and cipher text:

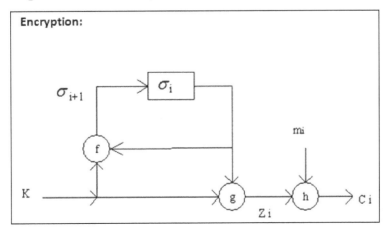

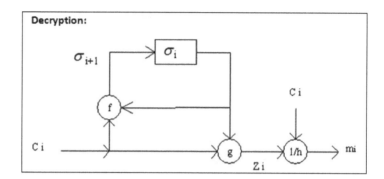

Properties of Synchronous stream cipher:

- Synchronization requirement: In a synchronous stream cipher, both the sender and receiver must be synchronized using the same key. If synchronization is lost due to cipher text digits being inserted or deleted during transmission, then decryption fails and can only be restored through additional techniques for re-synchronization. This involves either re-initialization or placing special marker at regular intervals or redundancy in plain text.

- No error propagation: A cipher text digit that is modified during transmission doesn't effect decryption of other cipher text digits.

Active attacks: As a consequence of properly (i), the insertion, deletion or replay of cipher text digits by an active adversary causes immediate loss of synchronization and hence might possibly be detected by decryptors.

Application: Stream ciphers are used for video data stream.

## 5

Cryptographic Technologies

There are various technologies related to cryptography like rotor machine which is a stream cipher device used for the encryption and decryption of messages. Disk encryption is another technology which is used for the protection of information by converting the information in an unreadable code. Other technologies like cryptosystem, hybrid cryptosystem, onion routing, secure multi-party communication, etc. are also carefully analyzed in this chapter.

Rotor Machine

In cryptography, a rotor machine is an electro-mechanical stream cipher device used for encrypting and decrypting secret messages. Rotor machines were the cryptographic state-of-the-art for a prominent period of history; they were in widespread use in the 1920s–1970s. The most famous example is the German Enigma machine, whose messages were deciphered by the Allies during World War II, producing intelligence code-named *Ultra*.

A series of three rotors from an Enigma machine, used by Germany during World War II.

The primary component is a set of *rotors*, also termed *wheels* or *drums*, which are rotating disks with an array of electrical contacts on either side. The wiring between the contacts implements a fixed substitution of letters, replacing them in some complex fashion. On its own, this would offer little security; however, after encrypting each letter, the rotors advance positions, changing the substitution. By this means, a rotor machine produces a complex polyalphabetic substitution cipher, which changes with every keypress.

Background

In classical cryptography, one of the earliest encryption methods was the simple substitution cipher, where letters in a message were systematically replaced using some secret scheme. *Monoalphabetic* substitution ciphers used only a single replacement scheme — sometimes termed an "alphabet"; this could be easily broken, for example, by using frequency analysis. Somewhat more secure were schemes involving multiple alphabets, polyalphabetic ciphers. Because such schemes were implemented by hand, only a handful of different alphabets could be used; anything more complex would be impractical. However, using only a few alphabets left the ciphers vulnerable to attack. The invention of rotor machines mechanised polyalphabetic encryption, providing a practical way to use a much larger number of alphabets.

40-point rotors from a machine made by Tatjana van Vark.

The earliest cryptanalytic technique was frequency analysis, in which letter patterns unique to every language could be used to discover information about the substitution alphabet(s) in use in a mono-alphabetic substitution cipher. For instance, in English, the plaintext letters E, T, A, O, I, N and S, are usually easy to identify in ciphertext on the basis that since they are very frequent, their corresponding ciphertext letters will also be as frequent. In addition, bigram combinations like NG, ST and others are also very frequent, while others are rare indeed (Q followed by anything other than U for instance). The simplest frequency analysis relies on one ciphertext letter always being substituted for a plaintext letter in the cipher: if this is not the case, deciphering the message is more difficult. For many years, cryptographers attempted to hide the telltale frequencies by using several different substitutions for common letters, but this technique was unable to fully hide patterns in the substitutions for plaintext letters. Such schemes were being widely broken by the 16th century.

In the mid-15th century, a new technique was invented by Alberti, now known generally as polyalphabetic ciphers, which recognised the virtue of using more than a single substitution alphabet; he also invented a simple technique for "creating" a multitude of substitution patterns for use in a message. Two parties exchanged a small amount of information (referred to as the *key*) and used it to create many substitution alphabets, and so many different substitutions for each plaintext letter over the course of a single plaintext. The idea is simple and effective, but proved more difficult to use than might have been expected. Many ciphers were only partial implementations of Alberti's, and so were easier to break than they might have been (e.g. the Vigenère cipher).

Not until the 1840s (Babbage) was any technique known which could reliably break any of the polyalphabetic ciphers. His technique also looked for repeating patterns in the ciphertext, which provide clues about the length of the key. Once this is known, the message essentially becomes a series of messages, each as long as the length of the key, to which normal frequency analysis can be applied. Charles Babbage, Friedrich Kasiski, and William F. Friedman are among those who did most to develop these techniques.

Cipher designers tried to get users to use a different substitution for every letter, but this usually meant a very long key, which was a problem in several ways. A long key takes longer to convey (securely) to the parties who need it, and so mistakes are more likely in key distribution. Also, many users do not have the patience to carry out lengthy, letter perfect evolutions, and certainly not under time pressure or battlefield stress. The 'ultimate' cipher of this type would be one in which such a 'long' key could be generated from a simple pattern (ideally automatically), producing a cipher in which there are so many substitution alphabets that frequency counting and statistical attacks would be effectively impossible. Enigma, and the rotor machines generally, were just what was needed since they were seriously polyalphabetic, using a different substitution alphabet for each letter of plaintext, and automatic, requiring no extraordinary abilities from their users. Their messages were, generally, much harder to break than any previous ciphers.

Mechanization

It is relatively straightforward to create a machine for performing simple substitution. We can consider an electrical system with 26 switches attached to 26 light bulbs; when you turn on any one of the switches, one of the light bulbs is illuminated. If each switch is operated by a key on a typewriter, and the bulbs are labelled with letters, then such a system can be used for encryption by choosing the wiring between the keys and the bulb: for example, typing the letter A would make the bulb labelled Q light up. However, the wiring is fixed, providing little security.

Rotor machines build on this idea by, in effect, changing the wiring with each key stroke. The wiring is placed inside a rotor, and then rotated with a gear every time a letter was pressed. So while pressing A the first time might generate a Q, the next time it might generate a J. Every letter pressed on the keyboard would spin the rotor and get a new substitution, implementing a polyalphabetic substitution cipher.

Depending on the size of the rotor, this may or may not be more secure than hand ciphers. If the rotor has only 26 positions on it, one for each letter, then all messages will have a (repeating) key 26 letters long. Although the key itself (mostly hidden in the wiring of the rotor) might not be known, the methods for attacking these types of ciphers don't need that information. So while such a *single rotor* machine is certainly easy to use, it's no more secure than any other partial polyalphabetic cipher system.

But this is easy to correct. Simply stack more rotors next to each other, and gear them together. After the first rotor spins "all the way", make the rotor beside it spin one position. Now you would have to type $26 \times 26 = 676$ letters (for the Latin alphabet) before the key repeats, and yet it still only requires you to communicate a key of two letters/numbers to set things up. If a key of 676 length is not long enough, another rotor can be added, resulting in a period 17,576 letters long.

In order to be as easy to decipher as encipher, some rotor machines, most notably the Enigma machine, were designed to be *symmetrical*, i.e., encrypting twice with the same settings recovers the original message.

History

Invention

The concept of a rotor machine occurred to a number of inventors independently at a similar time.

In 2003, it emerged that the first inventors were two Dutch naval officers, Theo A. van Hengel (1875 – 1939) and R. P. C. Spengler (1875 – 1955) in 1915 (De Leeuw, 2003). Previously, the invention had been ascribed to four inventors working independently and at much the same time: Edward Hebern, Arvid Damm, Hugo Koch and Arthur Scherbius.

In the United States Edward Hugh Hebern built a rotor machine using a single rotor in 1917. He became convinced he would get rich selling such a system to the military, the Hebern Rotor Machine, and produced a series of different machines with one to five rotors. His success was limited, however, and he went bankrupt in the 1920s. He sold a small number of machines to the US Navy in 1931.

In Hebern's machines the rotors could be opened up and the wiring changed in a few minutes, so a single mass-produced system could be sold to a number of users who would then produce their own rotor keying. Decryption consisted of taking out the rotor(s) and turning them around to reverse the circuitry. Unknown to Hebern, William F. Friedman of the US Army's SIS promptly demonstrated a flaw in the system that allowed the ciphers from it, and from any machine with similar design features, to be cracked with enough work.

Another early rotor machine inventor was Dutchman Hugo Koch, who filed a patent on a rotor machine in 1919. At about the same time in Sweden, Arvid Gerhard Damm invented and patented another rotor design. However, the rotor machine was ultimately made famous by Arthur Scherbius, who filed a rotor machine patent in 1918. Scherbius later went on to design and market the Enigma machine.

The Enigma Machine

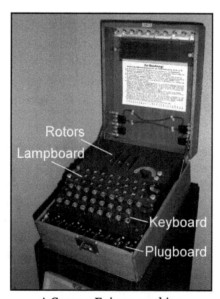

A German Enigma machine.

The most widely known rotor cipher device is the German Enigma machine used during World War II, of which there were a number of variants.

The standard Enigma model, Enigma I, used three rotors. At the end of the stack of rotors was an additional, non-rotating disk, the "reflector," wired such that the input was connected electrically back out to another contact on the same side and thus was "reflected" back through the three-rotor stack to produce the ciphertext.

When current was sent into most other rotor cipher machines, it would travel through the rotors and out the other side to the lamps. In the Enigma, however, it was "reflected" back through the disks before going to the lamps. The advantage of this was that there was nothing that had to be done to the setup in order to decipher a message; the machine was "symmetrical" at all times.

The Enigma's reflector guaranteed that no letter could be enciphered as itself, so an *A* could never turn back into an *A*. This helped Polish and, later, British efforts to break the cipher.

Scherbius joined forces with a mechanical engineer named Ritter and formed Chiffriermaschinen AG in Berlin before demonstrating Enigma to the public in Bern in 1923, and then in 1924 at the World Postal Congress in Stockholm. In 1927 Scherbius bought Koch's patents, and in 1928 they added a *plugboard*, essentially a non-rotating manually rewireable fourth rotor, on the front of the machine. After the death of Scherbius in 1929, Willi Korn was in charge of further technical development of Enigma.

As with other early rotor machine efforts, Scherbius had limited commercial success. However, the German armed forces, responding in part to revelations that their codes had been broken during World War I, adopted the Enigma to secure their communications. The *Reichsmarine* adopted Enigma in 1926, and the German Army began to use a different variant around 1928.

The Enigma (in several variants) was the rotor machine that Scherbius's company and its successor, Heimsoth & Reinke, supplied to the German military and to such agencies as the Nazi party security organization, the *SD*.

The Poles broke the German Army Enigma beginning in December 1932, not long after it had been put into service. On July 25, 1939, just five weeks before Hitler's invasion of Poland, the Polish General Staff's Cipher Bureau shared its Enigma-decryption methods and equipment with the French and British as the Poles' contribution to the common defense against Nazi Germany. Dilly Knox had already broken Spanish Nationalist messages on a commercial Enigma machine in 1937 during the Spanish Civil War.

A few months later, using the Polish techniques, the British began reading Enigma ciphers in collaboration with Polish Cipher Bureau cryptologists who had escaped Poland, overrun by the Germans, to reach Paris. The Poles continued breaking German Army Enigma — along with Luftwaffe Enigma traffic — until work at Station *PC Bruno* in France was shut down by the German invasion of May–June 1940.

The British continued breaking Enigma and, assisted eventually by the United States, extended the work to German Naval Enigma traffic (which the Poles had been reading before the war), most especially to and from U-boats during the Battle of the Atlantic.

Various Machines

The rotor stack from an Enigma rotor machine. The rotors of this machine contain 26 contacts.

During World War II (WWII), both the Germans and Allies developed additional rotor machines. The Germans used the Lorenz SZ 40/42 and Siemens and Halske T52 machines to encipher tele-printer traffic which used the Baudot code; this traffic was known as Fish to the Allies. The Allies developed the Typex (British) and the SIGABA (American). During the War the Swiss began devel-opment on an Enigma improvement which became the NEMA machine which was put into service after WWII. There was even a Japanese developed variant of the Enigma in which the rotors sat horizontally; it was apparently never put into service. The Japanese PURPLE machine was not a rotor machine, being built around electrical stepping switches, but was conceptually similar.

Rotor machines continued to be used even in the computer age. The KL-7 (ADONIS), an encryp-tion machine with 8 rotors, was widely used by the U.S. and its allies from the 1950s until the 1980s. The last Canadian message encrypted with a KL-7 was sent on June 30, 1983. The Soviet Union and its allies used a 10-rotor machine called Fialka well into the 1970s.

Typex was a printing rotor machine used by the United Kingdom and its Commonwealth,
and was based on the Enigma patents.

A unique rotor machine was constructed in 2002 by Netherlands-based Tatjana van Vark. This unusual device is inspired by Enigma, but makes use of 40-point rotors, allowing letters, numbers and some punctuation; each rotor contains 509 parts.

A software implementation of a rotor machine was used in the crypt command that was part of early UNIX operating systems. It was among the first software programs to run afoul of U.S. export regulations which classified cryptographic implementations as munitions.

List of Rotor Machines

- Combined Cipher Machine
- Enigma machine
- Lorenz SZ 40/42
- Siemens and Halske T52
- Fialka
- Hebern rotor machine
- HX-63
- KL-7
- Lacida
- M-325
- Mercury
- NEMA
- OMI cryptograph
- Portex
- RED
- SIGABA
- SIGCUM
- Hagelin's family of machines including the C-36, the C-52 the CD-57 and the M-209
- BID/60 (Singlet)
- Typex

Cryptographically Secure Pseudorandom Number Generator

A cryptographically secure pseudo-random number generator (CSPRNG) or cryptographic pseudo-random number generator (CPRNG) is a pseudo-random number generator (PRNG) with properties that make it suitable for use in cryptography.

Many aspects of cryptography require random numbers, for example:

- key generation

- nonces

- one-time pads

- salts in certain signature schemes, including ECDSA, RSASSA-PSS

The "quality" of the randomness required for these applications varies. For example, creating a nonce in some protocols needs only uniqueness. On the other hand, generation of a master key requires a higher quality, such as more entropy. And in the case of one-time pads, the information-theoretic guarantee of perfect secrecy only holds if the key material comes from a true random source with high entropy.

Ideally, the generation of random numbers in CSPRNGs uses entropy obtained from a high-quality source, generally the operating system's randomness API. However, unexpected correlations have been found in several such ostensibly independent processes. From an information-theoretic point of view, the amount of randomness, the entropy that can be generated, is equal to the entropy provided by the system. But sometimes, in practical situations, more random numbers are needed than there is entropy available. Also the processes to extract randomness from a running system are slow in actual practice. In such instances, a CSPRNG can sometimes be used. A CSPRNG can "stretch" the available entropy over more bits.

Requirements

The requirements of an ordinary PRNG are also satisfied by a cryptographically secure PRNG, but the reverse is not true. CSPRNG requirements fall into two groups: first, that they pass statistical randomness tests; and secondly, that they hold up well under serious attack, even when part of their initial or running state becomes available to an attacker.

- Every CSPRNG should satisfy the next-bit test. That is, given the first k bits of a random sequence, there is no polynomial-time algorithm that can predict the $(k+1)$th bit with probability of success better than 50%. Andrew Yao proved in 1982 that a generator passing the next-bit test will pass all other polynomial-time statistical tests for randomness.

- Every CSPRNG should withstand "state compromise extensions". In the event that part or all of its state has been revealed (or guessed correctly), it should be impossible to reconstruct the stream of random numbers prior to the revelation. Additionally, if there is an entropy input while running, it should be infeasible to use knowledge of the input's state to predict future conditions of the CSPRNG state.

  Example: If the CSPRNG under consideration produces output by computing bits of π in sequence, starting from some unknown point in the binary expansion, it may well satisfy the next-bit test and thus be statistically random, as π appears to be a random sequence. (This would be guaranteed if π is a normal number, for example.) However, this algorithm is not cryptographically secure; an attacker who determines which bit of pi (i.e. the state of the algorithm) is currently in use will be able to calculate all preceding bits as well.

Most PRNGs are not suitable for use as CSPRNGs and will fail on both counts. First, while most

PRNGs outputs appear random to assorted statistical tests, they do not resist determined reverse engineering. Specialized statistical tests may be found specially tuned to such a PRNG that shows the random numbers not to be truly random. Second, for most PRNGs, when their state has been revealed, all past random numbers can be retrodicted, allowing an attacker to read all past messages, as well as future ones.

CSPRNGs are designed explicitly to resist this type of cryptanalysis.

Definitions

In the asymptotic setting, a family of deterministic polynomial time computable functions $G_k : \{0, 1\}^k \to \{0, 1\}^{p(k)}$ for some polynomial p, is a pseudorandom number generator (PRG), if it stretches the length of its input ($p(k) > k$ for any k), and if its output is computationally indistinguishable from true randomess, i.e. for any probabilistic polynomial time algorithm A, which outputs 1 or 0 as a distinguisher,

$$| \Pr_{x \leftarrow \{0,1\}^k}[A(G(x)) = 1] - \Pr_{r \leftarrow \{0,1\}^{p(k)}}[A(r) = 1] | < \quad (k)$$

for some negligible function μ. (The notation $x \leftarrow X$ means that x is chosen uniformly at random from the set X.)

There is an equivalent characterization: For any function family $G_k : \{0, 1\}^k \to \{0, 1\}^{p(k)}$, G is a PRG if and only if the next output bit of G cannot be predicted by a polynomial time algorithm.

A forward-secure PRG with block length $t(k)$ is a PRG $G_k : \{0, 1\}^k \to \{0, 1\}^k \times \{0, 1\}^{t(k)}$ polynomial time computable function, where the input string s_i with length k is the current state at period i, and the output (s_{i+1}, y_i) consists of the next state s_{i+1} and the pseudorandom output block y_i of period i. Such a PRG is called forward secure if it withstands state compromise extensions in the following sense. If the initial state s_1 is chosen at uniformly random from $\{0, 1\}^k$, for any i, $(y_1 y_2 \cdots y_i, s_{i+1})$ must be computationally indistinguishable from $(r_{i \cdot t(k)}, s_{i+1})$, in which $r_{i \cdot t(k)}$ is chosen at uniformly random from $\{0, 1\}^{i \cdot t(k)}$.

Any PRG $G : \{0, 1\}^k \to \{0, 1\}^{p(k)}$ can be turned into a forward secure PRG with block length $p(k)$ - k by splitting its output into the next state and the actual output. This is done by setting $G(s) = (G_0(s), G_1(s))$, in which $|G_0(s)| = |s| = k$ and $|G_1(s)| = p(k)$ - k; then G is a forward secure PRG with G_0 as the next state and G_1 as the pseudorandom output block of the current period.

Entropy Extraction

Santha and Vazirani proved that several bit streams with weak randomness can be combined to produce a higher-quality quasi-random bit stream. Even earlier, John von Neumann proved that a simple algorithm can remove a considerable amount of the bias in any bit stream which should be applied to each bit stream before using any variation of the Santha-Vazirani design.

Designs

In the discussion below, CSPRNG designs are divided into three classes:

1. those based on cryptographic primitives such as ciphers and cryptographic hashes,

2. those based upon mathematical problems thought to be hard,

3. special-purpose designs.

The last often introduce additional entropy when available and, strictly speaking, are not "pure" pseudorandom number generators, as their output is not completely determined by their initial state. This addition can prevent attacks even if the initial state is compromised.

Designs based on Cryptographic Primitives

- A secure block cipher can be converted into a CSPRNG by running it in counter mode. This is done by choosing a random key and encrypting a 0, then encrypting a 1, then encrypting a 2, etc. The counter can also be started at an arbitrary number other than zero. Assuming an n-bit block cipher the output can be distinguished from random data after around $2^{n/2}$ blocks since, following the birthday problem, colliding blocks should become likely at that point, whereas a block cipher in CTR mode will never output identical blocks. For 64 bit block ciphers this limits the safe output size to a few gigabytes, with 128 bit blocks the limitation is large enough not to impact typical applications.

- A cryptographically secure hash of a counter might also act as a good CSPRNG in some cases. In this case, it is also necessary that the initial value of this counter is random and secret. However, there has been little study of these algorithms for use in this manner, and at least some authors warn against this use.

- Most stream ciphers work by generating a pseudorandom stream of bits that are combined (almost always XORed) with the plaintext; running the cipher on a counter will return a new pseudorandom stream, possibly with a longer period. The cipher can only be secure if the original stream is a good CSPRNG, although this is not necessarily the case. Again, the initial state must be kept secret.

Number Theoretic Designs

- The Blum Blum Shub algorithm has a security proof based on the difficulty of the quadratic residuosity problem. Since the only known way to solve that problem is to factor the modulus, it is generally regarded that the difficulty of integer factorization provides a conditional security proof for the Blum Blum Shub algorithm. However the algorithm is very inefficient and therefore impractical unless extreme security is needed.

- The Blum-Micali algorithm has an unconditional security proof based on the difficulty of the discrete logarithm problem but is also very inefficient.

- Daniel Brown of Certicom has written a 2006 security proof for Dual_EC_DRBG, based on the assumed hardness of the *Decisional Diffie–Hellman assumption*, the *x-logarithm problem*, and the *truncated point problem*. The 2006 proof explicitly assumes a lower *outlen* than in the Dual_EC_DRBG standard, and that the P and Q in the Dual_EC_DRBG standard (which were revealed in 2013 to be probably backdoored by NSA) are replaced with non-backdoored values.

Special Designs

There are a number of practical PRNGs that have been designed to be cryptographically secure, including:

- the Yarrow algorithm which attempts to evaluate the entropic quality of its inputs. Yarrow is used in FreeBSD, OpenBSD and Mac OS X (also as /dev/random).

- the Fortuna algorithm, the successor to Yarrow, which does not attempt to evaluate the entropic quality of its inputs.

- the function CryptGenRandom provided in Microsoft's Cryptographic Application Programming Interface.

- ISAAC based on a variant of the RC4 cipher.

- Evolutionary algorithm based on NIST Statistical Test Suite.

- arc4random.

- AES-CTR DRBG is often used as a random number generator in systems that use AES encryption.

- ANSI X9.17 standard (*Financial Institution Key Management (wholesale)*), which has been adopted as a FIPS standard as well. It takes as input a TDEA (keying option 2) key bundle k and (the initial value of) a 64 bit random seed s. Each time a random number is required it:

  o Obtains the current date/time D to the maximum resolution possible.

  o Computes a temporary value $t = \text{TDEA}_k(D)$.

  o Computes the random value $x = \text{TDEA}_k(s \oplus t)$, where $\oplus$ denotes bitwise exclusive or.

  o Updates the seed $s = \text{TDEA}_k(x \oplus t)$.

  Obviously, the technique is easily generalized to any block cipher; AES has been suggested (Young and Yung, op cit, sect 3.5.1).

Standards

Several CSPRNGs have been standardized. For example,

- FIPS 186-4

- NIST SP 800-90A: This standard has three uncontroversial CSPRNGs named Hash_DRBG, HMAC_DRBG, and CTR_DRBG; and a PRNG named Dual_EC_DRBG which has been shown to not be cryptographically secure and probably has a kleptographic NSA backdoor

- ANSI X9.17-1985 Appendix C

- ANSI X9.31-1998 Appendix A.2.4

- ANSI X9.62-1998 Annex A.4, obsoleted by ANSI X9.62-2005, Annex D (HMAC_DRBG)

A good reference is maintained by NIST.

There are also standards for statistical testing of new CSPRNG designs:

- *A Statistical Test Suite for Random and Pseudorandom Number Generators*, NIST Special Publication 800-22.

NSA Kleptographic Backdoor in the Dual_EC_DRBG PRNG

The Guardian and *The New York Times* have reported that the National Security Agency (NSA) inserted a PRNG into NIST SP 800-90A that had a backdoor which allows the NSA to readily decrypt material that was encrypted with the aid of Dual_EC_DRBG. Both papers report that, as independent security experts long suspected, the NSA has been introducing weaknesses into CSPRNG standard 800-90; this being confirmed for the first time by one of the top secret documents leaked to the Guardian by Edward Snowden. The NSA worked covertly to get its own version of the NIST draft security standard approved for worldwide use in 2006. The leaked document states that "eventually, NSA became the sole editor." In spite of the known potential for a kleptographic backdoor and other known significant deficiencies with Dual_EC_DRBG, several companies such as RSA Security continued using Dual_EC_DRBG until the backdoor was confirmed in 2013. RSA Security received a $10 million payment from the NSA to do so.

Disk Encryption

Disk encryption is a technology which protects information by converting it into unreadable code that cannot be deciphered easily by unauthorized people. Disk encryption uses disk encryption software or hardware to encrypt every bit of data that goes on a disk or disk volume. Disk encryption prevents unauthorized access to data storage.

Expressions *full disk encryption (FDE)* or *whole disk encryption* often signify that everything on disk is encrypted – including the programs that can encrypt bootable operating system partitions – when part of the disk is necessarily not encrypted. On systems that use a master boot record (MBR), that part of the disk remains non encrypted. Some hardware-based full disk encryption systems can truly encrypt an entire boot disk, including the MBR.

Transparent Encryption

Transparent encryption, also known as real-time encryption and on-the-fly encryption (OTFE), is a method used by some disk encryption software. "Transparent" refers to the fact that data is automatically encrypted or decrypted as it is loaded or saved.

With transparent encryption, the files are accessible immediately after the key is provided, and the entire volume is typically mounted as if it were a physical drive, making the files just as accessible as any unencrypted ones. No data stored on an encrypted volume can be read (decrypted) without using the correct password/keyfile(s) or correct encryption keys. The entire file system within the volume is encrypted (including file names, folder names, file contents, and other meta-data).

To be transparent to the end user, transparent encryption usually requires the use of device drivers to enable the encryption process. Although administrator access rights are normally required to install such drivers, encrypted volumes can typically be used by normal users without these rights .

In general, every method in which data is transparently encrypted on write and decrypted on read can be called transparent encryption.

Disk Encryption vs. Filesystem-level Encryption

Disk encryption does not replace file encryption in all situations. Disk encryption is sometimes used in conjunction with filesystem-level encryption with the intention of providing a more secure implementation. Since disk encryption generally uses the same key for encrypting the whole volume, all data is decryptable when the system runs. However, some disk encryption solutions use multiple keys for encrypting different partitions. If an attacker gains access to the computer at run-time, the attacker has access to all files. Conventional file and folder encryption instead allows different keys for different portions of the disk. Thus an attacker cannot extract information from still-encrypted files and folders.

Unlike disk encryption, filesystem-level encryption does not typically encrypt filesystem metadata, such as the directory structure, file names, modification timestamps or sizes.

Disk Encryption and Trusted Platform Module

Trusted Platform Module (TPM) is a secure cryptoprocessor embedded in the motherboard that can be used to authenticate a hardware device. Since each TPM chip is unique to a particular device, it is capable of performing platform authentication. It can be used to verify that the system seeking the access is the expected system.

A limited number of disk encryption solutions have support for TPM. These implementations can wrap the decryption key using the TPM, thus tying the hard disk drive (HDD) to a particular device. If the HDD is removed from that particular device and placed in another, the decryption process will fail. Recovery is possible with the decryption password or token.

Although this has the advantage that the disk cannot be removed from the device, it might create a single point of failure in the encryption. For example, if something happens to the TPM or the motherboard, a user would not be able to access the data by connecting the hard drive to another computer, unless that user has a separate recovery key.

Implementations

There are multiple tools available in the market that allow for disk encryption. However, they vary greatly in features and security. They are divided into three main categories: software-based, hardware-based within the storage device, and hardware-based elsewhere (such as CPU or host bus adaptor). Hardware-based full disk encryption within the storage device are called self-encrypting drives and have no impact on performance whatsoever. Furthermore, the media-encryption key never leaves the device itself and is therefore not available to any virus in the operating system.

The Trusted Computing Group Opal drive provides industry accepted standardization for self-encrypting drives. External hardware is considerably faster than the software-based solutions although CPU versions may still have a performance impact, and the media encryption keys are not as well protected.

All solutions for the boot drive require a Pre-Boot Authentication component which is available for all types of solutions from a number of vendors. It is important in all cases that the authentication credentials are usually a major potential weakness since the symmetric cryptography is usually strong.

Password/Data Recovery Mechanism

Secure and safe recovery mechanisms are essential to the large-scale deployment of any disk encryption solutions in an enterprise. The solution must provide an easy but secure way to recover passwords (most importantly data) in case the user leaves the company without notice or forgets the password.

Challenge/Response Password Recovery Mechanism

Challenge/Response password recovery mechanism allows the password to be recovered in a secure manner. It is offered by a limited number of disk encryption solutions.

Some benefits of challenge/response password recovery:

1. No need for the user to carry a disc with recovery encryption key.

2. No secret data is exchanged during the recovery process.

3. No information can be sniffed.

4. Does not require a network connection, i.e. it works for users that are at a remote location.

Emergency Recovery Information (ERI) File Password Recovery Mechanism

An Emergency Recovery Information (ERI) file provides an alternative for recovery if a challenge response mechanism is unfeasible due to the cost of helpdesk operatives for small companies or implementation challenges.

Some benefits of ERI file recovery:

1. Small companies can use it without implementation difficulties.

2. No secret data is exchanged during the recovery process.

3. No information can be sniffed.

4. Does not require a network connection, i.e. it works for users that are at a remote location.

Security Concerns

Most full disk encryption schemes are vulnerable to a cold boot attack, whereby encryption keys can be stolen by cold-booting a machine already running an operating system, then dumping the contents of memory before the data disappears. The attack relies on the data remanence property of computer memory, whereby data bits can take up to several minutes to degrade after power has been removed. Even a Trusted Platform Module (TPM) is not effective against the attack, as the operating system needs to hold the decryption keys in memory in order to access the disk.

Full disk encryption is also vulnerable when a computer is stolen when suspended. As wake-up does not involve a BIOS boot sequence, it typically does not ask for the FDE password. Hibernation, in contrast goes via a BIOS boot sequence, and is safe.

All software-based encryption systems are vulnerable to various side channel attacks such as acoustic cryptanalysis and hardware keyloggers. In contrast, self-encrypting drives are not vulnerable to these attacks since the hardware encryption key never leaves the disk controller.

Full Disk Encryption

Benefits

Full disk encryption has several benefits compared to regular file or folder encryption, or encrypted vaults. The following are some benefits of disk encryption:

1. Nearly everything including the swap space and the temporary files is encrypted. Encrypting these files is important, as they can reveal important confidential data. With a software implementation, the bootstrapping code cannot be encrypted however. (For example, Bit-Locker Drive Encryption leaves an unencrypted volume to boot from, while the volume containing the operating system is fully encrypted.)

2. With full disk encryption, the decision of which individual files to encrypt is not left up to users' discretion. This is important for situations in which users might not want or might forget to encrypt sensitive files.

3. Immediate data destruction, such as simply destroying the cryptographic keys, renders the contained data useless. However, if security towards future attacks is a concern, purging or physical destruction is advised.

The Boot Key Problem

One issue to address in full disk encryption is that the blocks where the operating system is stored must be decrypted before the OS can boot, meaning that the key has to be available before there is a user interface to ask for a password. Most Full Disk Encryption solutions utilize Pre-Boot Authentication by loading a small, highly secure operating system which is strictly locked down and hashed versus system variables to check for the integrity of the Pre-Boot kernel. Some implementations such as BitLocker Drive Encryption can make use of hardware such as a Trusted Platform Module to ensure the integrity of the boot environment, and thereby frustrate attacks that target the boot loader by replacing it with a modified version. This ensures that authentication can take place in a controlled environment without the possibility of a bootkit being used to subvert the pre-boot decryption.

With a Pre-Boot Authentication environment, the key used to encrypt the data is not decrypted until an external key is input into the system.

Solutions for storing the external key include:

- Username / password

- Using a smartcard in combination with a PIN

- Using a biometric authentication method such as a fingerprint

- Using a dongle to store the key, assuming that the user will not allow the dongle to be stolen with the laptop or that the dongle is encrypted as well

- Using a boot-time driver that can ask for a password from the user

- Using a network interchange to recover the key, for instance as part of a PXE boot

- Using a TPM to store the decryption key, preventing unauthorized access of the decryption key or subversion of the boot loader

- Use a combination of the above

All these possibilities have varying degrees of security; however, most are better than an unencrypted disk.

Cryptosystem

In cryptography, a cryptosystem is a suite of cryptographic algorithms needed to implement a particular security service, most commonly for achieving confidentiality (encryption).

Typically, a cryptosystem consists of three algorithms: one for key generation, one for encryption, and one for decryption. The term *cipher* (sometimes *cypher*) is often used to refer to a pair of algorithms, one for encryption and one for decryption. Therefore, the term *cryptosystem* is most often used when the key generation algorithm is important. For this reason, the term *cryptosystem* is commonly used to refer to public key techniques; however both "cipher" and "cryptosystem" are used for symmetric key techniques.

Formal Definition

Mathematically, a cryptosystem or encryption scheme can be defined as a tuple $(\mathcal{P}, \mathcal{C}, \mathcal{K}, \mathcal{E}, \mathcal{D})$ with the following properties.

1. $\mathcal{P}$ is a set called the "plaintext space". Its elements are called plaintexts.

2. $\mathcal{C}$ is a set called the "ciphertext space". Its elements are called ciphertexts.

3. $\mathcal{K}$ is a set called the "key space". Its elements are called keys.

4. $\mathcal{E} = \{E_k : k \in \mathcal{K}\}$ is a set of functions $E_k : \mathcal{P} \to \mathcal{C}..$ Its elements are called "encryption functions".

5. $\mathcal{D} = \{D_k : k \in \mathcal{K}\}$ is a set of functions $D_k : \mathcal{C} \to \mathcal{P}.$ Its elements are called "decryption functions".

For each $e \in \mathcal{K}$, there is $d \in \mathcal{K}$ such that $D_d(E_e(p)) = p$ for all $p \in \mathcal{P}$.

Note; typically this definition is modified in order to distinguish an encryption scheme as being either a symmetric-key or public-key type of cryptosystem.

Examples

A classical example of a cryptosystem is the Caesar cipher. A more contemporary example is the RSA cryptosystem.

Hybrid Cryptosystem

In cryptography, a hybrid cryptosystem is one which combines the convenience of a public-key cryptosystem with the efficiency of a symmetric-key cryptosystem. Public-key cryptosystems are convenient in that they do not require the sender and receiver to share a common secret in order to communicate securely (among other useful properties). However, they often rely on complicated mathematical computations and are thus generally much more inefficient than comparable symmetric-key cryptosystems. In many applications, the high cost of encrypting long messages in a public-key cryptosystem can be prohibitive. This is addressed by hybrid systems by using a combination of both.

A hybrid cryptosystem can be constructed using any two separate cryptosystems:

- a key encapsulation scheme, which is a public-key cryptosystem,

- a data encapsulation scheme, which is a symmetric-key cryptosystem.

The hybrid cryptosystem is itself a public-key system, whose public and private keys are the same as in the key encapsulation scheme.

Note that for very long messages the bulk of the work in encryption/decryption is done by the more efficient symmetric-key scheme, while the inefficient public-key scheme is used only to encrypt/decrypt a short key value.

All practical implementations of public key cryptography today employ the use of a hybrid system. Examples include the TLS protocol which uses a public-key mechanism for key exchange (such as Diffie-Hellman) and a symmetric-key mechanism for data encapsulation (such as AES). The OpenPGP (RFC 4880) file format and the PKCS #7 (RFC 2315) file format are other examples.

Example

To encrypt a message addressed to Alice in a hybrid cryptosystem, Bob does the following:

1. Obtains Alice's public key.

2. Generates a fresh symmetric key for the data encapsulation scheme.

3. Encrypts the message under the data encapsulation scheme, using the symmetric key just generated.

4. Encrypt the symmetric key under the key encapsulation scheme, using Alice's public key.

5. Send both of these encryptions to Alice.

To decrypt this hybrid ciphertext, Alice does the following:

1. Uses her private key to decrypt the symmetric key contained in the key encapsulation segment.

2. Uses this symmetric key to decrypt the message contained in the data encapsulation segment.

Security

If both the key encapsulation and data encapsulation schemes are secure against adaptive chosen ciphertext attacks, then the hybrid scheme inherits that property as well. However, it is possible to construct a hybrid scheme secure against adaptive chosen ciphertext attack even if the key encapsulation has a slightly weakened security definition (though the security of the data encapsulation must be slightly stronger).

Onion Routing

Onion routing is a technique for anonymous communication over a computer network. In an onion network, messages are encapsulated in layers of encryption, analogous to layers of an onion. The encrypted data is transmitted through a series of network nodes called onion routers, each of which "peels" away a single layer, uncovering the data's next destination. When the final layer is decrypted, the message arrives at its destination. The sender remains anonymous because each intermediary knows only the location of the immediately preceding and following nodes.

Development and Implementation

Onion routing was developed in the mid-1990s at the U.S. Naval Research Laboratory by employees Paul Syverson, Michael G. Reed, and David Goldschlag to protect U.S. intelligence communications online. It was further developed by the Defense Advanced Research Projects Agency (DARPA) and patented by the Navy in 1998.

Computer scientists Roger Dingledine and Nick Mathewson joined Syverson in 2002 to develop what would become the largest and best known implementation of onion routing, Tor, then called The Onion Routing project or TOR project. After the Naval Research Laboratory released the code for Tor under a free license, Dingledine, Mathewson and five others founded The Tor Project as a non-profit organization in 2006, with the financial support of the Electronic Frontier Foundation and several other organizations.

Data Structure

In this example onion, the source of the data sends the onion to Router A, which removes a layer of encryption to learn only where to send it next and where it came from (though it does not know if the sender is the origin or just another node). Router A sends it to Router B, which decrypts another layer to learn its next destination. Router B sends it to Router C, which removes the final layer of encryption and transmits the original message to its destination.

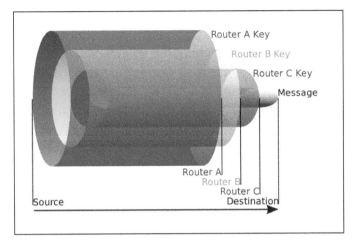

An onion is the data structure formed by "wrapping" a message with successive layers of encryption to be decrypted ("peeled" or "unwrapped") by as many intermediary computers as there are layers before arriving at its destination. The original message remains hidden as it is transferred from one node to the next, and no intermediary knows both the origin and final destination of the data, allowing the sender to remain anonymous.

Onion Creation and Transmission

To create and transmit an onion, the originator selects a set of nodes from a list provided by a "directory node". The chosen nodes are arranged into a path, called a "chain" or "circuit", through which the message will be transmitted. To preserve the anonymity of the sender, no node in the circuit is able to tell whether the node before it is the originator or another intermediary like itself. Likewise, no node in the circuit is able to tell how many other nodes are in the circuit and only the final node, the "exit node", is able to determine its own location in the chain.

Using asymmetric key cryptography, the originator obtains a public key from the directory node to send an encrypted message to the first ("entry") node, establishing a connection and a shared secret ("session key"). Using the established encrypted link to the entry node, the originator can then relay a message through the first node to a second node in the chain using encryption that only the second node, and not the first, can decrypt. When the second node receives the message, it establishes a connection with the first node. While this extends the encrypted link from the originator, the second node cannot determine whether the first node is the originator or just another node in the circuit. The originator can then send a message through the first and second nodes to a third node, encrypted such that only the third node is able to decrypt it. The third, as with the second, becomes linked to the originator but connects only with the second. This process can be repeated to build larger and larger chains, but is typically limited to preserve performance.

When the chain is complete, the originator can send data over the Internet anonymously. When the final recipient of the data sends data back, the intermediary nodes maintain the same link back to the originator, with data again layered, but in reverse such that the final node this time removes the first layer of encryption and the first node removes the last layer of encryption before sending the data, for example a web page, to the originator.

Weaknesses

Timing Analysis

One of the reasons typical Internet connections are not considered anonymous is the ability of Internet service providers to trace and log connections between computers. For example, when a person accesses a particular website, the data itself may be secured through a connection like HTTPS such that your password, emails, or other content is not visible to an outside party, but there is a record of the connection itself, what time it occurred, and the amount of data transferred. Onion routing creates and obscures a path between two computers such that there's no discernible connection directly from a person to a website, but there still exist records of connections between computers. Traffic analysis searches those records of connections made by a potential originator and tries to match timing and data transfers to connections made to a potential recipient. For example, a person may be seen to have transferred exactly 51 kilobytes of data to an unknown computer just three seconds before a different unknown computer transferred exactly 51 kilobytes of data to a particular website. Factors that may facilitate traffic analysis include nodes failing or leaving the network and a compromised node keeping track of a session as it occurs when chains are periodically rebuilt.

Garlic routing is a variant of onion routing associated with the I2P network that encrypts multiple messages together to make it more difficult for attackers to perform traffic analysis.

Exit Node Vulnerability

Although the message being sent is transmitted inside several layers of encryption, the job of the exit node, as the final node in the chain, is to decrypt the final layer and deliver the message to the recipient. A compromised exit node is thus able to acquire the raw data being transmitted, potentially including passwords, private messages, bank account numbers, and other forms of personal information. Dan Egerstad, a Swedish researcher, used such an attack to collect the passwords of over 100 email accounts related to foreign embassies.

Exit node vulnerabilities are similar to those on unsecured wireless networks, where the data being transmitted by a user on the network may be intercepted by another user or by the router operator. Both issues are solved by using a secure end-to-end connection like SSL or secure HTTP (S-HTTP). If there is end-to-end encryption between the sender and the recipient, then not even the last intermediary can view the original message.

Secure Multi-Party Computation

Secure multi-party computation (also known as secure computation or multi-party computation/ MPC) is a subfield of cryptography with the goal of creating methods for parties to jointly compute a function over their inputs while keeping those inputs private.

Definition and Overview

In an MPC, a given number of participants, p_1, p_2, ..., p_N, each have private data, respectively d_1, d_2, ..., d_N. Participants want to compute the value of a public function on that private data: $F(d_1, d_2, ..., d_N)$ while keeping their own inputs secret.

For example, suppose we have three parties Alice, Bob and Charlie, with respective inputs x, y and z denoting their salaries. They want to find out the highest of the three salaries, without revealing to each other how much each of them makes. Mathematically, this translates to them computing:

$$F(x,y,z) = max(x,y,z)$$

If there were some trusted outside party (say, they had a mutual friend Tony who they knew could keep a secret), they could each tell their salary to Tony, he could compute the maximum, and tell that number to all of them. The goal of MPC is to design a protocol, where, by exchanging messages only with each other, Alice, Bob, and Charlie can still learn F(x, y, z) without revealing who makes what and without having to rely on Tony. They should learn no more by engaging in their protocol than they would learn by interacting with an incorruptible, perfectly trustworthy Tony.

In particular, all that the parties can learn is what they can learn from the output and their own input. So in the above example, if the output is z, then Charlie learns that his z is the maximum value, whereas Alice and Bob learn (if x, y and z are distinct), that their input is not equal to the maximum, and that the maximum held is equal to z. The basic scenario can be easily generalised to where the parties have several inputs and outputs, and the function outputs different values to different parties.

Informally speaking, the most basic properties that a multi-party computation protocol aims to ensure are:

- Input privacy: No information about the private data held by the parties can be inferred from the messages sent during the execution of the protocol. The only information that can be inferred about the private data is whatever could be inferred from seeing the output of the function alone.

- Correctness: Any proper subset of adversarial colluding parties willing to share information or deviate from the instructions during the protocol execution should not be able to force honest parties to output an incorrect result. This correctness goal comes in two flavours: either the honest parties are guaranteed to compute the correct output (a "robust" protocol), or they abort if they find an error (an MPC protocol "with abort").

There are a wide range of practical applications, varying from simple tasks such as coin tossing to more complex ones like electronic auctions (e.g. compute the market clearing price), electronic voting, or privacy-preserving data mining. A classical example is the Millionaire's Problem: two millionaires want to know who is richer, in such a way that neither of them learns the net worth of the other. A solution to this situation is essentially to securely evaluate the comparison function.

Security Definitions

A key question to ask is; when is such a multiparty computation protocol secure? In modern cryptography, a protocol can only be deemed to be secure if it comes equipped with a "security proof". This is a mathematical proof that the security of the protocol reduces to that of the security of the underlying primitives. But this means we need a definition of what it means for a protocol to be secure. This is hard to formalize, in the case of MPC, since we cannot say that the parties should "learn nothing" since they need to learn the output and this depends on the inputs. In addition, we cannot just say that the output must be "correct" since the correct output depends on the parties' inputs, and we do not know what inputs corrupted parties will use. A formal mathematical definition of security for MPC protocols follows the ideal-real-world paradigm, described below.

The ideal-real-world paradigm imagines two worlds. In the ideal world, there exists an incorruptible trusted party to whom each protocol participant sends its input. This trusted party computes the function on its own and sends back the appropriate output to each party. (In the Alice, Bob, and Charlie example above, Tony performed the role of trusted outside party.) In contrast, in the real-world model, there is no trusted party and all the parties can do is to exchange messages with each other. We say a protocol is secure if one can learn no more about each party's private inputs in the real world than one could learn in the ideal world. Since no messages between the parties are exchanged in the ideal world, this security definition implies that the real-world messages that were exchanged cannot have revealed any secret information.

We stress that the ideal-real-world paradigm provides a simple abstraction of the complexities of MPC that is of great use to anyone using an MPC protocol. Namely, it suffices to construct an application under the pretense that the MPC protocol at its core is actually an ideal execution. If the application is secure in this case, then it is also secure when a real protocol is run instead.

The security requirements on an MPC protocol are so stringent that it may seem that it is rarely possible to actually achieve. Surprisingly, in the late 1980s it was already shown that any function can be securely computed, with security for malicious adversaries. This is encouraging news, but it took a long time until MPC became efficient enough to be used in practice. Unconditionally or information-theoretically secure MPC is closely related to the problem of secret sharing, and more specifically verifiable secret sharing (VSS), which many secure MPC protocols that protect against active adversaries use.

Unlike in traditional cryptographic applications, such as encryption or signatures, the adversary in an MPC protocol can be one of the players engaged in the protocol. In fact, in MPC we assume that corrupted parties may collude in order to breach the security of the protocol. If the number of parties in the protocol is n, then the number of parties who can be adversarial is usually denoted by t. The protocols and solutions for the case of t < n/2 (i.e., when an honest majority is assumed) are very different to those where no such assumption is made. This latter case includes the important case of two-party computation where one of the participants may be corrupted, and the general case where an unlimited number of participants are corrupted and collude to attack the honest participants.

Different protocols can deal with different adversarial powers. We can categorize adversaries according to how willing they are to deviate from the protocol. There are essentially two types of adversaries, each giving rise to different forms of security:

- Semi-Honest (Passive) Security: In this case, we assume that corrupted parties merely cooperate to gather information out of the protocol, but do not deviate from the protocol specification. This is a naive adversary model, yielding weak security in real situations. However, protocols achieving this level of security prevent inadvertent leakage of information between parties, and are thus useful if this is the only concern. In addition, protocols in the semi-honest model are very efficient, and are often an important first step for achieving higher levels of security.

- Malicious (Active) Security: In this case, the adversary may arbitrarily deviate from the protocol execution in its attempt to cheat. Protocols that achieve security in this model provide a very high security guarantee. The only thing that an adversary can do in the case of dishonest majority is to cause the honest parties to "abort" having detected cheating. If the honest parties do obtain output, then they are guaranteed that it is correct. Of course, their privacy is always preserved.

Since security against active adversaries is often only possible at the cost of reducing efficiency one is led to consider a relaxed form of active security called covert security, proposed by Aumann and Lindell. Covert security captures more realistic situations, where active adversaries are willing to cheat but only if they are not caught. For example, their reputation could be damaged, preventing future collaboration with other honest parties. Thus, protocols that are covertly secure provide mechanisms to ensure that, if some of the parties do not follow the instructions, then it will be noticed with high probability, say 75% or 90%. In a way, covert adversaries are active ones forced to act passively due to external non-cryptographic (e.g. business) concerns. This sets a bridge between the two models in the hope of finding protocols, which are efficient yet secure enough for practice.

Like many cryptographic protocols, the security of an MPC protocol can rely on different assumptions:

- It can be computational (i.e. based on some mathematical problem, like factoring) or unconditional (usually with some probability of error which can be made arbitrarily small).

- The model might assume that participants use a synchronized network, where a message sent at a "tick" always arrives at the next "tick", or that a secure and reliable broadcast channel exists, or that a secure communication channel exists between every pair of participants where an adversary cannot read, modify or generate messages in the channel, etc.

The set of honest parties that can execute a computational task is related to the concept of access structure. "Adversary structures" can be static, i.e. the adversary chooses its victims before the start of the multi-party computation, or dynamic, i.e. it chooses its victims during the course of execution of the multiparty computation. Attaining security against a dynamic adversary is often much harder than security against a static adversary. An adversary structure can be defined as a "threshold structure" meaning that it can corrupt or simply read the memory of a number of participants up to some threshold, or be defined as a more complex structure, where it can affect certain predefined subsets of participants, modeling different possible collusions.

History

Secure computation was formally introduced as secure two-party computation (2PC) in 1982 by

Andrew Yao, the first recipient of the Knuth Prize. It is also referred to as Secure function evaluation (SFE), and is concerned with the question: 'Can two party computation be achieved more efficiently and under weaker security assumptions than general MPC?'. The millionaire problem solution gave way to a generalization to multi-party protocols.

Increasingly efficient protocols for MPC have been proposed, and MPC can be now used as a practical solution to various real-life problems such as distributed voting, private bidding and auctions, sharing of signature or decryption functions and private information retrieval. The first large-scale and practical application of multiparty computation took place in Denmark in January 2008.

Protocols used

There are major differences between the protocols proposed for two party computation (2PC) and multiparty computation (MPC).

Two-party Computation

The two party setting is particularly interesting, not only from an applications perspective but also because special techniques can be applied in the two party setting which do not apply in the multi-party case. Indeed, secure multi-party computation (in fact the restricted case of secure function evaluation, where only a single function is evaluated) was first presented in the two-party setting. The original work is often cited as being from one of the two papers of Yao; although the papers do not actually contain what is now known as Yao's protocol.

Yao's basic protocol is secure against semi-honest adversaries and is extremely efficient in terms of number of rounds, which is constant, and independent of the target function being evaluated. The function is viewed as a Boolean circuit, with inputs in binary of fixed length. A Boolean circuit is a collection of gates connected with three different types of wires: circuit-input wires, circuit-output wires and intermediate wires. Each gate receives two input wires and it has a single output wire which might be fan-out (i.e. be passed to multiple gates at the next level). Plain evaluation of the circuit is done by evaluating each gate in turn; assuming the gates have been lexicographically ordered. The gate is represented as a truth table such that for each possible pair of bits (those coming from the input wires' gate) the table assigns a unique output bit; which is the value of the output wire of the gate. The results of the evaluation are the bits obtained in the circuit-output wires.

Yao explained how to garble a circuit (hide its structure) so that two parties, sender and receiver, can learn the output of the circuit and nothing else. At a high level, the sender prepares the garbled circuit and sends it to the receiver, who obliviously evaluates the circuit, learning the encodings corresponding to both his and the senders output. He then just sends back the senders encodings, allowing the sender to compute his part of the output. The sender sends the mapping from the receivers output encodings to bits to the receiver, allowing the receiver to obtain their output.

In more detail, the garbled circuit is computed as follows. The main ingredient is a double-keyed symmetric encryption scheme. Given a gate of the circuit, each possible value of its input wires (either 0 or 1) is encoded with a random number (label). The values resulting from the evaluation of the gate at each of the four possible pair of input bits are also replaced with random labels. The garbled truth table of the gate consists of encryptions of each output label using its inputs labels as keys. The position of these four encryptions in the truth table is randomized so no information on the gate is leaked.

To correctly evaluate each garbled gate the encryption scheme has the following two properties. Firstly, the ranges of the encryption function under any two distinct keys are disjoint (with overwhelming probability). The second property says that it can be checked efficiently whether a given ciphertext has been encrypted under a given key. With these two properties the receiver, after obtaining the labels for all circuit-input wires, can evaluate each gate by first finding out which of the four ciphertexts has been encrypted with his label keys, and then decrypting to obtain the label of the output wire. This is done obliviously as all the receiver learns during the evaluation are encodings of the bits.

The sender's (i.e. circuit creators) input bits can be just sent as encodings to the evaluator; whereas the receiver's (i.e. circuit evaluators) encodings corresponding to his input bits are obtained via a 1-out-of-2 Oblivious Transfer (OT) protocol. A 1-out-of-2 OT protocol, enables the sender, in possession of two values C1 and C2, to send the one requested by the receiver (b a value in {1,2}) in such a way that the sender does not know what value has been transferred, and the receiver only learns the queried value.

If one is considering malicious adversaries, further mechanisms to ensure correct behaviour of both parties need to be provided. By construction it is easy to show security for the sender, as all the receiver can do is to evaluate a garbled circuit that would fail to reach the circuit-output wires if he deviated from the instructions. The situation is very different on the sender's side. For example, he may send an incorrect garbled circuit that computes a function revealing the receiver's input. This would mean that privacy no longer holds, but since the circuit is garbled the receiver would not be able to detect this.

Multiparty Protocols

Most MPC protocols, as opposed to 2PC protocols, make use of secret sharing. In the secret sharing based methods, the parties do not play special roles (as in Yao, of creator and evaluator). Instead the data associated to each wire is shared amongst the parties; and a protocol is then used to evaluate each gate. The function is now defined as a "circuit" over GF(p), as opposed to the binary circuits used for Yao. Such a circuit is called an arithmetic circuit in the literature, and it consists of addition and multiplication "gates" where the values operated on are defined over GF(p).

Secret sharing allows one to distribute a secret among a number of parties by distributing shares to each party. Three types of secret sharing schemes are commonly used; Shamir Secret Sharing, Replicated Secret Sharing and Additive Secret Sharing. In all three cases the shares are random elements of GF(p) that add up to the secret in GF(p); intuitively, security steams because any non-qualifying set shares looks randomly distributed. All three secret sharing schemes are linear, so the sum of two shared secrets, or multiplication a secret by a public constant, can be done locally. Thus linear functions can be evaluated for free.

Replicated Secret Sharing schemes are usually associated with passively secure MPC systems consisting of three parties, of which at most one can be adversarial; such as used in the Sharemind system. MPC systems based on Shamir Secret Sharing are generally associated with systems which can tolerate up to t adversaries out of n, so called threshold systems. In the case of information theoretic protocols actively secure protocols can be realised with Shamir Secret Sharing sharing if $t<n/3$, whilst passively secure ones are available if $t<n/2$. In the case of computationally secure protocols one can tolerate a threshold of $t<n/2$ for actively secure protocols. A practical system adopting this approach is the VIFF framework. Additive secret sharing is used when one wants to tolerate a dishonest majority, i.e. $t<n$, in which case we can only obtain MPC protocols "with abort", this later type is typified by the SPDZ and (multi-party variant) of the TinyOT protocol.

Other Protocols

Virtual Party Protocol is a protocol which uses virtual parties and complex mathematics to hide the identity of the parties.

Secure sum protocols allow multiple cooperating parties to compute sum function of their individual data without revealing the data to one another.

In 2014 a "model of fairness in secure computation in which an adversarial party that aborts on receiving output is forced to pay a mutually predefined monetary penalty" has been described for the Bitcoin network or for fair lottery.

Scalable MPC

Recently, several multi-party computation techniques have been proposed targeting resource-efficiency (in terms of bandwidth, computation, and latency) for large networks. Although much theoretical progress has been made to achieve scalability, practical progress is slower. In particular, most known schemes suffer from either poor or unknown communication and computation costs in practice.

Practical MPC Systems

Many advances have been made on 2PC and MPC systems in recent years.

Yao-based Protocols

One of the main issues when working with Yao-based protocols is that the function to be securely evaluated (which could be an arbitrary program) must be represented as a circuit, usually consisting of XOR and AND gates. Since most real-world programs contain loops and complex data structures, this is a highly non-trivial task. The Fairplay system was the first tool designed to tackle this problem. Fairplay comprises two main components. The first of these is a compiler enabling users to write programs in a simple high-level language, and output these programs in a Boolean circuit representation. The second component can then garble the circuit and execute a protocol to securely evaluate the garbled circuit. As well as two-party computation based on Yao's protocol, Fairplay can also carry out multi-party protocols. This is done using the BMR protocol, which extends Yao's passively secure protocol to the active case.

In the years following the introduction of Fairplay, many improvements to Yao's basic protocol have been created, in the form of both efficiency improvements and techniques for active security. These include techniques such as the free XOR method, which allows for much simpler evaluation of XOR gates, and garbled row reduction, reducing the size of garbled tables with two inputs by 25%.

The approach that so far seems to be the most fruitful in obtaining active security comes from a combination of the garbling technique and the "cut-and-choose" paradigm. This combination seems to render more efficient constructions. To avoid the aforementioned problems with respect to dishonest behaviour, many garblings of the same circuit are sent from the constructor to the evaluator. Then around half of them (depending on the specific protocol) are opened to check consistency, and if so a vast majority of the unopened ones are correct with high probability. The output is the majority vote of all the evaluations. Note that here the majority output is needed. If there is disagreement on the outputs the receiver knows the sender is cheating, but he cannot complain as otherwise this would leak information on his input.

This approach for active security was initiated by Lindell and Pinkas. This technique was implemented by Pinkas et al. in 2009, This provided the first actively secure two-party evaluation of the Advanced Encryption Standard (AES) circuit, regarded as a highly complex (consisting of around 30,000 AND and XOR gates), non-trivial function (also with some potential applications), taking around 20 minutes to compute and requiring 160 circuits to obtain a 2-40 cheating probability.

As many circuits are evaluated, the parties (including the receiver) need to commit to their inputs to ensure that in all the iterations the same values are used. The experiments of Pinkas et al. reported show that the bottleneck of the protocol lies in the consistency checks. They had to send over the net about 6,553,600 commitments to various values to evaluate the AES circuit. In recent results the efficiency of actively secure Yao-based implementations was improved even further, requiring only 40 circuits, and much less commitments, to obtain 2-40 cheating probability. The improvements come from new methodologies for performing cut-and-choose on the transmitted circuits.

More recently, there has been a focus on highly parallel implementations based on garbled circuits, designed to be run on CPUs with many cores. Kreuter, et al. describe an implementation running on 512 cores of a powerful cluster computer. Using these resources they could evaluate the 4095-bit edit distance function, whose circuit comprises almost 6 billion gates. To accomplish this they developed a custom, better optimized circuit compiler than Fairplay and several new optimizations such as pipelining, whereby transmission of the garbled circuit across the network begins while the rest of the circuit is still being generated. The time to compute AES was reduced to 1.4 seconds per block in the active case, using a 512-node cluster machine, and 115 seconds using one node. shelat and Shen improve this, using commodity hardware, to 0.52 seconds per block. The same paper reports on a throughput of 21 blocks per second, but with a latency of 48 seconds per block.

Meanwhile, another group of researchers has investigated using consumer-grade GPUs to achieve similar levels of parallelism. They utilize OT extensions and some other novel techniques to design their GPU-specific protocol. This approach seems to achieve comparable efficiency to the cluster computing implementation, using a similar number of cores. However, the authors only report on an implementation of the AES circuit, which has around 50,000 gates. On the other hand, the hardware required here is far more accessible, as similar devices may already be found in many people's desktop computers or games consoles. The authors obtain a timing of 2.7 seconds per AES block on a standard desktop, with a standard GPU. If they allow security to decrease to something akin to covert security, they obtain a run time of 0.30 seconds per AES block.It should be noted that in the passive security case there are reports of processing of circuits with 250 million gates, and at a rate of 75 million gates per second.

References

- David A. King, The ciphers of the monks - A forgotten number notation of the Middle Ages, Stuttgart: Franz Steiner, 2001 (ISBN 3-515-07640-9)

- Leigh, David; Harding, Luke (2011-02-08). WikiLeaks: Inside Julian Assange's War on Secrecy. PublicAffairs. ISBN 1610390628. Retrieved 01, April 2020

- Pathak Rohit, Joshi Satyadhar, Advances in Information Security and Assurance, Springer Berlin / Heidelberg, ISSN 0302-9743 (Print) 1611-3349 (Online), ISBN 978-3-642-02616-4

- Jared Saia and Mahdi Zamani. Recent Results in Scalable Multi-Party Computation. SOFSEM 2015: Theory and Practice of Computer Science. Springer Berlin Heidelberg. Volume 8939. pp 24–44. 2015. ISBN 978-3-662-46078-8

- Fagoyinbo, Joseph Babatunde (2013-05-24). The Armed Forces: Instrument of Peace, Strength, Development and Prosperity. AuthorHouse. ISBN 9781477226476. Retrieved 25, July 2020

- Cusick, Thomas W. & Stanica, Pantelimon (2009). Cryptographic Boolean functions and applications. Academic Press. p. 164. ISBN 9780123748904

- Chakraborty, D. & Rodriguez-Henriquez F. (2008). "Block Cipher Modes of Operation from a Hardware Implementation Perspective". In Koç, Çetin K. Cryptographic Engineering. Springer. p. 321. ISBN 9780387718163

- Junod, Pascal & Canteaut, Anne (2011). Advanced Linear Cryptanalysis of Block and Stream Ciphers. IOS Press. p. 2. ISBN 9781607508441

- Keliher, Liam et al. (2000). "Modeling Linear Characteristics of Substitution-Permutation Networks". In Hays, Howard & Carlisle, Adam. Selected areas in cryptography: 6th annual international workshop, SAC'99, Kingston, Ontario, Canada, August 9-10, 1999 : proceedings. Springer. p. 79. ISBN 9783540671855

- Baigneres, Thomas & Finiasz, Matthieu (2007). "Dial 'C' for Cipher". In Biham, Eli & Yousseff, Amr. Selected areas in cryptography: 13th international workshop, SAC 2006, Montreal, Canada, August 17-18, 2006 : revised selected papers. Springer. p. 77. ISBN 9783540744610

- van Tilborg, Henk C. A.; Jajodia, Sushil, eds. (2011). Encyclopedia of Cryptography and Security. Springer. ISBN 978-1-4419-5905-8. , p. 455

- Martin, Keith M. (2012). Everyday Cryptography: Fundamental Principles and Applications. Oxford University Press. p. 114. ISBN 9780199695591

- Menezes, Alfred J.; Oorschot, Paul C. van; Vanstone, Scott A. (2001). Handbook of Applied Cryptography (Fifth ed.). p. 251. ISBN 0849385237

- Mark Bando (2007). 101st Airborne: The Screaming Eagles in World War II. Mbi Publishing Company. ISBN 978-0-7603-2984-9. Retrieved 16, May 2020

- "Modern Cryptography: Theory & Practice", Wenbo Mao, Prentice Hall Professional Technical Reference, New Jersey, 2004, pg. 308. ISBN 0-13-066943-1

- Lund, Paul (2009). The Book of Codes. Berkeley and Los Angeles, California: University of California Press. pp. 106–107. ISBN 9780520260139

Diverse Aspects of Cryptography

Encryption is the process in which the original representation of the information is converted into an alternative form known as ciphertext. There is a desirable property of any encryption algorithm and a slight change in key or plain-text results in a significant change in the ciphertext. This property is known as avalanche effect. This chapter closely examines the various aspects of cryptography.

Encryption

In cryptography, encryption is the process of encoding messages or information in such a way that only authorized parties can read it. Encryption does not of itself prevent interception, but denies the message content to the interceptor. In an encryption scheme, the intended communication information or message, referred to as plaintext, is encrypted using an encryption algorithm, generating ciphertext that can only be read if decrypted. For technical reasons, an encryption scheme usually uses a pseudo-random encryption key generated by an algorithm. It is in principle possible to decrypt the message without possessing the key, but, for a well-designed encryption scheme, large computational resources and skill are required. An authorized recipient can easily decrypt the message with the key provided by the originator to recipients, but not to unauthorized interceptors.

Purpose

The purpose of encryption is to ensure that only somebody who is authorized to access data (e.g. a text message or a file), will be able to read it, using the decryption key. Somebody who is not authorized can be excluded, because he or she does not have the required key, without which it is impossible to read the encrypted information.

Types

Symmetric Key

In symmetric-key schemes, the encryption and decryption keys are the same. Communicating parties must have the same key before they can achieve secure communication.

Public Key

In public-key encryption schemes, the encryption key is published for anyone to use and encrypt messages. However, only the receiving party has access to the decryption key that enables messages to be read. Public-key encryption was first described in a secret document in 1973; before then all encryption schemes were symmetric-key (also called private-key).

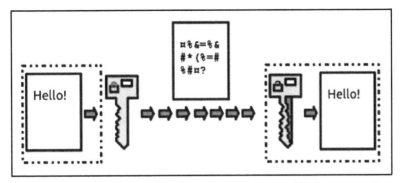

Illustration of how encryption is used within servers Public key encryption.

A publicly available public key encryption application called Pretty Good Privacy (PGP) was written in 1991 by Phil Zimmermann, and distributed free of charge with source code; it was purchased by Symantec in 2010 and is regularly updated.

Uses

Encryption has long been used by military and governments to facilitate secret communication. It is now commonly used in protecting information within many kinds of civilian systems. For example, the Computer Security Institute reported that in 2007, 71% of companies surveyed utilized encryption for some of their data in transit, and 53% utilized encryption for some of their data in storage. Encryption can be used to protect data "at rest", such as information stored on computers and storage devices (e.g. USB flash drives). In recent years there have been numerous reports of confidential data such as customers' personal records being exposed through loss or theft of laptops or backup drives. Encrypting such files at rest helps protect them should physical security measures fail. Digital rights management systems, which prevent unauthorized use or reproduction of copyrighted material and protect software against reverse engineering, is another somewhat different example of using encryption on data at rest.

Encryption is also used to protect data in transit, for example data being transferred via networks (e.g. the Internet, e-commerce), mobile telephones, wireless microphones, wireless intercom systems, Bluetooth devices and bank automatic teller machines. There have been numerous reports of data in transit being intercepted in recent years. Data should also be encrypted when transmitted across networks in order to protect against eavesdropping of network traffic by unauthorized users.

Message Verification

Encryption, by itself, can protect the confidentiality of messages, but other techniques are still needed to protect the integrity and authenticity of a message; for example, verification of a message authentication code (MAC) or a digital signature. Standards for cryptographic software and hardware to perform encryption are widely available, but successfully using encryption to ensure security may be a challenging problem. A single error in system design or execution can allow successful attacks. Sometimes an adversary can obtain unencrypted information without directly undoing the encryption.

Digital signature and encryption must be applied to the ciphertext when it is created (typically on the same device used to compose the message) to avoid tampering; otherwise any node between the sender and the encryption agent could potentially tamper with it. Encrypting at the time of creation is only secure if the encryption device itself has not been tampered with.

Plaintext

In cryptography, plaintext is information a sender wishes to transmit to a receiver. *Cleartext* is often used as a synonym. Plaintext has reference to the operation of cryptographic algorithms, usually encryption algorithms, and is the input upon which they operate. *Cleartext*, by contrast, refers to data that is transmitted or stored unencrypted (that is, 'in the clear').

Overview

With the advent of computing the definition of plaintext expanded to include any data, including binary files, in addition to simple messages and human-readable documents, in a form that can be interpreted or used without needing to be processed using information not generally available (a key). The information, which would normally be called a message, document, file, etc., if to be communicated or stored in encrypted form is referred to as plaintext.

Plaintext is used as input to an encryption algorithm; the output is usually termed ciphertext, particularly when the algorithm is a cipher. Codetext is less often used, and almost always only when the algorithm involved is actually a code. In some systems multiple layers of encryption are used, with the output of one encryption algorithm become the "plaintext" input for the next.

Secure Handling of Plaintext

Weaknesses can be introduced into a cryptosystem through insecure handling of plaintext, allowing an attacker to bypass the cryptography altogether. Plaintext is vulnerable in use and in storage, whether in electronic or paper format. Physical security deals with methods of securing information and its storage media from local, physical, attacks, for instance by entering a building and gaining access to papers, storage media, or computers. Discarded material, if not disposed of securely, may be a security risk; even shredded documents and erased magnetic media can often be reconstructed with sufficient effort.

If plaintext is stored in a computer file , the storage media, the computer and its components, and all backups must be secure. Sensitive data is sometimes processed on computers whose mass storage is removable, in which case physical security of the removed disk is separately vital. In the case of securing a computer, useful (as opposed to handwaving) security must be physical (e.g., against burglary, brazen removal under cover of supposed repair, installation of covert monitoring devices, etc.), as well as virtual (e.g., operating system modification, illicit network access, Trojan programs, ...). The wide availability of keydrives, which can plug into most modern computers and store large quantities of data, poses another severe security headache. A spy (perhaps posing as a cleaning person) could easily conceal one and even swallow it, if necessary.

Discarded computers, disk drives and media are also a potential source of plaintexts. Most operating systems do not actually erase anything — they simply mark the disk space occupied by a deleted file as 'available for use', and remove its entry from the file system directory. The information in a file deleted in this way remains fully present until overwritten at some later time when the operating system reuses the disk space. With even low-end computers commonly sold with many gigabytes of disk space and rising monthly, this 'later time' may be months later, or never. Even overwriting the portion of a disk surface occupied by a deleted file is insufficient in many cases. Peter Gutmann of the University of Auckland wrote a celebrated 1996 paper on the recovery of overwritten information from magnetic disks; areal storage densities have gotten much higher since then, so this sort of recovery is likely to be more difficult than it was when Gutmann wrote.

Also, independently, modern hard drives automatically remap sectors that are starting to fail; those sectors no longer in use will contain information that is entirely invisible to the file system (and all software which uses it for access to disk data), but is nonetheless still present on the physical drive platter. It may, of course, be sensitive plaintext. Some government agencies (e.g., US NSA) require that all disk drives be physically pulverized when they are discarded, and in some cases, chemically treated with corrosives before or after. This practice is not widespread outside of the government, however. For example, Garfinkel and Shelat (2003) analyzed 158 second-hand hard drives acquired at garage sales and the like and found that less than 10% had been sufficiently sanitized. A wide variety of personal and confidential information was found readable from the others.

Laptop computers are a special problem. Laptops containing secret information, some perhaps in plaintext form, belonging to the US State Department, Department of Defense, and the British Secret Service have been stolen or lost. Announcements of similar losses are becoming a common item in news reports. Appropriate disk encryption techniques can safeguard data on misappropriated computers or media.

On occasion, even when the data on the host systems is itself encrypted, the media used to transfer data between such systems is nevertheless plaintext due to poorly designed data policy. An incident in October 2007 in which HM Revenue and Customs lost CDs containing the records of 25 million child benefit recipients in the United Kingdom — the data apparently being entirely unencrypted — is a case in point.

Modern cryptographic systems are designed to resist known plaintext or even chosen plaintext attacks and so may not be entirely compromised when plaintext is lost or stolen. Older systems used techniques such as padding and Russian copulation to obscure information in plaintext that could be easily guessed, and to resist the effects of loss of plaintext on the security of the cryptosystem.

Web Browser Saved Password Security Controversy

Several popular web browsers which offer to store a user's passwords do so in plaintext form. Even though most of them initially hide the saved passwords, it is possible for anyone to view all passwords in cleartext with a few clicks of the mouse, by going into the browsers' security settings options menus. In 2010, it emerged that this is the case with Firefox (still the case as of end-2014), and in Aug 2013 it emerged that Google Chrome does so as well. When a software developer raised the issue with the Chrome security team, a company representative responded that Google would not change the feature, and justified the refusal by saying that hiding the passwords would "provide users with a false sense of security" and "that's just not how we approach security on Chrome".

RSA Problem

In cryptography, the RSA problem summarizes the task of performing an RSA private-key operation given only the public key. The RSA algorithm raises a *message* to an *exponent*, modulo a composite number N whose factors are not known. Thus, the task can be neatly described as finding the eth roots of an arbitrary number, modulo N. For large RSA key sizes (in excess of 1024 bits), no efficient method for solving this problem is known; if an efficient method is ever developed, it would threaten the current or eventual security of RSA-based cryptosystems—both for public-key encryption and digital signatures.

More specifically, the RSA problem is to efficiently compute P given an RSA public key (N, e) and a ciphertext $C \equiv P^e \pmod{N}$. The structure of the RSA public key requires that N be a large semiprime (i.e., a product of two large prime numbers), that $2 < e < N$, that e be coprime to $\varphi(N)$, and that $0 \leq C < N$. C is chosen randomly within that range; to specify the problem with complete precision, one must also specify how N and e are generated, which will depend on the precise means of RSA random keypair generation in use.

The most efficient method known to solve the RSA problem is by first factoring the modulus N. A task believed to be impractical, if N is sufficiently large. The RSA key setup routine already turns the public exponent e, with this prime factorization, into the private exponent d, and so exactly the same algorithm allows anyone who factors N to obtain the *private key*. Any C can then be decrypted with the private key.

Just as there are no proofs that integer factorization is computationally difficult, there are also no proofs that the RSA problem is similarly difficult. By the above method, the RSA problem is at least as easy as factoring, but it might well be easier. Indeed, there is strong evidence pointing to this conclusion: that a method to break the RSA method cannot be converted necessarily into a method for factoring large semiprimes. This is perhaps easiest to see by the sheer overkill of the factoring approach: the RSA problem asks us to decrypt *one* arbitrary ciphertext, whereas the factoring method reveals the private key: thus decrypting *all* arbitrary ciphertexts, and it also allows one to perform arbitrary RSA private-key encryptions. Along these same lines, finding the decryption exponent d indeed *is* computationally equivalent to factoring N, even though the RSA problem does not ask for d.

In addition to the RSA problem, RSA also has a particular mathematical structure that can potentially be exploited *without* solving the RSA problem directly. To achieve the full strength of the RSA problem, an RSA-based cryptosystem must also use a padding scheme like OAEP, to protect against such structural problems in RSA.

Key Schedule

In cryptography, the so-called product ciphers are a certain kind of ciphers, where the (de-)ciphering of data is done in "rounds". The general setup of each round is the same, except for some hard-coded parameters and a part of the cipher key, called a subkey. A key schedule is an algorithm that, given the key, calculates the subkeys for these rounds.

The key schedule of DES ("<<<" denotes a left rotation).

Some Types of Key Schedules

- Some ciphers have simple key schedules. For example, the block cipher TEA simply splits the 128-bit key into four 32-bit pieces and uses them repeatedly in successive rounds.

- DES uses a key schedule where the 56 bit key is divided into two 28-bit halves; each half is thereafter treated separately. In successive rounds, both halves are rotated left by one or two bits (specified for each round), and then 48 subkey bits are selected by Permuted Choice 2 (PC-2) — 24 bits from the left half, and 24 from the right. The rotations mean that a different set of bits is used in each subkey; each bit is used in approximately 14 out of the 16 subkeys.

- In an effort to avoid simple relationships between the cipher key and the subkeys, to resist such forms of cryptanalysis as related-key attacks and slide attacks, many modern ciphers use much more elaborate key schedules, algorithms that use a one-way function to generate an "expanded key" from which subkeys are drawn. Some ciphers, such as Rijndael (AES) and Blowfish, use parts of the cipher algorithm itself for this key expansion, sometimes initialized with some "nothing up my sleeve numbers". Other ciphers, such as RC5, expand keys with functions that are somewhat or completely different from the encryption functions.

Block Size

In modern cryptography, symmetric key ciphers are generally divided into stream ciphers and block ciphers. Block ciphers operate on a fixed length string of bits. The length of this bit string is the block size. Both the input (plaintext) and output (ciphertext) are the same length; the output cannot be shorter than the input — this follows logically from the Pigeonhole principle and the fact that the cipher must be reversible — and it is undesirable for the output to be longer than the input.

Until the announcement of NIST's AES contest, the majority of block ciphers followed the example of the DES in using a block size of 64 bits (8 bytes). However the Birthday paradox tells us that after accumulating a number of blocks equal to the square root of the total number possible, there will be an approximately 50% chance of two or more being the same, which would start to leak information about the message contents. Thus even when used with a proper encryption mode (e.g. CBC or OFB), only 2^{32} x 8 B = 32 GB of data can be safely sent under one key. In practice a greater margin of security is desired, restricting a single key to the encryption of much less data - say a few hundred megabytes. Once that seemed like a fair amount of data, but today it is easily exceeded. If the cipher mode does not properly randomise the input, the limit is even lower.

Consequently, AES candidates were required to support a block length of 128 bits (16 bytes). This should be acceptable for up to 2^{64} x 16 B = 256 Exabytes of data, and should suffice for quite a few years to come. The winner of the AES contest, Rijndael, supports block and key sizes of 128, 192, and 256 bits, but in AES the block size is always 128 bits. The extra block sizes were not adopted by the AES standard.

Many block ciphers, such as RC5, support a variable block size. The Luby-Rackoff construction and the Outerbridge construction can both increase the effective block size of a cipher.

Joan Daemen's 3-Way and BaseKing have unusual block sizes of 96 and 192 bits, respectively.

Avalanche Effect

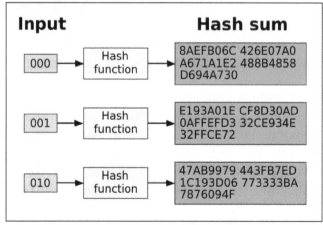

The SHA-1 hash function exhibits good avalanche effect. When a single bit is changed the hash sum becomes completely different.

In cryptography, the avalanche effect refers to a desirable property of cryptographic algorithms, typically block ciphers and cryptographic hash functions. The avalanche effect is evident if, when an input is changed slightly (for example, flipping a single bit) the output changes significantly (e.g., half the output bits flip). In the case of high-quality block ciphers, such a small change in either the key or the plaintext should cause a drastic change in the ciphertext. The actual term was first used by Horst Feistel, although the concept dates back to at least Shannon's *diffusion*.

If a block cipher or cryptographic hash function does not exhibit the avalanche effect to a significant degree, then it has poor randomization, and thus a cryptanalyst can make predictions about the input, being given only the output. This may be sufficient to partially or completely break the algorithm. Thus, the avalanche effect is a desirable condition from the point of view of the designer of the cryptographic algorithm or device.

Constructing a cipher or hash to exhibit a substantial avalanche effect is one of the primary design objectives. This is why most block ciphers are product ciphers. It is also why hash functions have large data blocks. Both of these features allow small changes to propagate rapidly through iterations of the algorithm, such that every bit of the output should depend on every bit of the input before the algorithm terminates.

Strict Avalanche Criterion

The strict avalanche criterion (SAC) is a formalization of the avalanche effect. It is satisfied if, whenever a single input bit is complemented, each of the output bits changes with a 50% probability. The SAC builds on the concepts of completeness and avalanche and was introduced by Webster and Tavares in 1985.

Higher-order generalizations of SAC involve multiple input bits. Boolean functions which satisfy the highest order SAC are always bent functions, also called maximally nonlinear functions, also called "perfect nonlinear" functions.

Bit independence criterion,

The bit independence criterion (BIC) states that output bits j and k should change independently when any single input bit i is inverted, for all i, j and k.

Optimal Asymmetric Encryption Padding

In cryptography, Optimal Asymmetric Encryption Padding (OAEP) is a padding scheme often used together with RSA encryption. OAEP was introduced by Bellare and Rogaway, and subsequently standardized in PKCS#1 v2 and RFC 2437.

The OAEP algorithm is a form of Feistel network which uses a pair of random oracles G and H to process the plaintext prior to asymmetric encryption. When combined with any secure trapdoor one-way permutation f, this processing is proved in the random oracle model to result in a combined scheme which is semantically secure under chosen plaintext attack (IND-CPA). When implemented with certain trapdoor permutations (e.g., RSA), OAEP is also proved secure against chosen ciphertext attack. OAEP can be used to build an all-or-nothing transform.

OAEP satisfies the following two goals:

1. Add an element of randomness which can be used to convert a deterministic encryption scheme (e.g., traditional RSA) into a probabilistic scheme.

2. Prevent partial decryption of ciphertexts (or other information leakage) by ensuring that an adversary cannot recover any portion of the plaintext without being able to invert the trapdoor one-way permutation f.

The original version of OAEP (Bellare/Rogaway, 1994) showed a form of "plaintext awareness" (which they claimed implies security against chosen ciphertext attack) in the random oracle model when OAEP is used with any trapdoor permutation. Subsequent results contradicted this claim, showing that OAEP was only IND-CCA1 secure. However, the original scheme was proved in the random oracle model to be IND-CCA2 secure when OAEP is used with the RSA permutation using standard encryption exponents, as in the case of RSA-OAEP. An improved scheme (called OAEP+) that works with any trapdoor one-way permutation was offered by Victor Shoup to solve this problem. More recent work has shown that in the standard model (that is, when hash functions are not modeled as random oracles) it is impossible to prove the IND-CCA2 security of RSA-OAEP under the assumed hardness of the RSA problem.

Diagram of OAEP

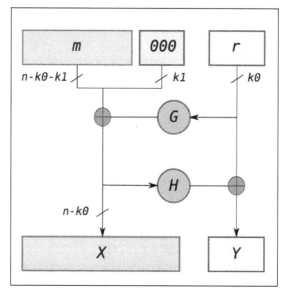

OAEP Diagram.

In the diagram,

- n is the number of bits in the RSA modulus.

- k_0 and k_1 are integers fixed by the protocol.

- m is the plaintext message, an $(n - k_0 - k_1)$-bit string.

- G and H are typically some cryptographic hash functions fixed by the protocol.

- $\oplus$ is an xor operation.

To encode,

1. messages are padded with k_1 zeros to be $n - k_0$ bits in length.

2. r is a randomly generated k_0-bit string.

3. G expands the k_0 bits of r to $n - k_0$ bits.

4. $X = m\text{oo..o} \oplus G(r)$.

5. H reduces the $n - k_0$ bits of X to k_0 bits.

6. $Y = r \oplus H(X)$.

7. The output is $X \,||\, Y$ where X is shown in the diagram as the leftmost block and Y as the rightmost block.

To decode,

1. recover the random string as $r = Y \oplus H(X)$

2. recover the message as $m\text{oo..o} = X \oplus G(r)$

The "all-or-nothing" security is from the fact that to recover m, you must recover the entire X and the entire Y; X is required to recover r from Y, and r is required to recover m from X. Since any changed bit of a cryptographic hash completely changes the result, the entire X, and the entire Y must both be completely recovered.

Message Authentication Code

In cryptography, a message authentication code (MAC) is a short piece of information used to authenticate a message—in other words, to confirm that the message came from the stated sender (its authenticity) and has not been changed in transit (its integrity).

A MAC algorithm, sometimes called a keyed (cryptographic) hash function (which is somewhat misleading, since a cryptographic hash function is only one of the possible ways to generate a MAC), accepts as input a secret key and an arbitrary-length message to be authenticated, and outputs a MAC (sometimes known as a *tag*). The MAC value protects both a message's data integrity as well as its authenticity, by allowing verifiers (who also possess the secret key) to detect any changes to the message content.

Definitions

Informally, message authentication code consists of three algorithms:

- A key generation algorithm selects a key from the key space uniformly at random.

- A signing algorithm efficiently returns a tag given the key and the message.

- A verifying algorithm efficiently verifies the authenticity of the message given the key and the tag. That is, return *accepted* when the message and tag are not tampered with or forged, and otherwise return *rejected*.

For a secure unforgeable message authentication code, it should be computationally infeasible to compute a valid tag of the given message without knowledge of the key, even if for the worst case, we assume the adversary can forge the tag of any message except the given one.

Formally, A Message Authentication Code (MAC) is a triple of efficient algorithms (G, S, V) satisfying:

- G (key-generator) gives the key k on input 1^n, where n is the security parameter.

- S (Signing) outputs a tag t on the key k and the input string x.

- V (Verifying) outputs *accepted* or *rejected* on inputs: the key k, the string x and the tag t. S and V must satisfy.

  $\Pr[\, k \leftarrow G(1^n), V(\, k, x, S(k, x)\,) = accepted\,] = 1.$

A MAC is unforgeable if for every efficient adversary A

$$Pr\left[k \leftarrow G(1^n),\ (x,t) \leftarrow A^{S(k,\cdot)}(1^n), x \notin Query\left(A^{S(k,\cdot)},\ 1^n\right), V(k,x,t) = accepted\right] < negl(n),$$

where $A^{S(k,\cdot)}$ denotes that A has access to the oracle $S(k, \cdot)$, and Query($A^{S(k,\cdot)}$, 1^n) denotes the set of the queries on S made by A, which knows n. Clearly we require that any adversary cannot directly query the string x on S, since otherwise she can easily obtain a valid tag.

Security

While MAC functions are similar to cryptographic hash functions, they possess different security requirements. To be considered secure, a MAC function must resist existential forgery under chosen-plaintext attacks. This means that even if an attacker has access to an oracle which possesses the secret key and generates MACs for messages of the attacker's choosing, the attacker cannot guess the MAC for other messages (which were not used to query the oracle) without performing infeasible amounts of computation.

MACs differ from digital signatures as MAC values are both generated and verified using the same secret key. This implies that the sender and receiver of a message must agree on the same key before initiating communications, as is the case with symmetric encryption. For the same reason, MACs do not provide the property of non-repudiation offered by signatures specifically in the case of a network-wide shared secret key: any user who can verify a MAC is also capable of generating MACs for other messages. In contrast, a digital signature is generated using the private key of a key pair, which is public-key cryptography. Since this private key is only accessible to its holder, a digital signature proves that a document was signed by none other than that holder. Thus, digital signatures do offer non-repudiation. However, non-repudiation can be provided by systems that securely bind key usage information to the MAC key; the same key is in the possession of two people, but one has a copy of the key that can be used for MAC generation while the other has a copy of the key in a hardware security module that only permits MAC verification. This is commonly done in the finance industry.

Message Integrity Codes

The term message integrity code (MIC) is frequently substituted for the term MAC, especially in communications, where the acronym MAC traditionally stands for Media Access Control address. However, some authors use MIC to refer to a message digest, which is different from a MAC -- a message digest does not use secret keys. This lack of security means that any message digest intended for use gauging message integrity should be encrypted or otherwise be protected against tampering. Message digest algorithms are created such that a given message will always produce the same message digest assuming the same algorithm is used to generate both. Conversely, MAC algorithms are designed to produce matching MACs only if the same message, secret key and initialization vector are input to the same algorithm. Message digests do not use secret keys and, when taken on their own, are therefore a much less reliable gauge of message integrity than MACs. Because MACs use secret keys, they do not necessarily need to be encrypted to provide the same level of assurance.

RFC 4949 recommends avoiding the term "message integrity code" (MIC), and instead using "checksum", "error detection code", "hash", "keyed hash", "Message Authentication Code", or "protected checksum".

Implementation

MAC algorithms can be constructed from other cryptographic primitives, such as cryptographic hash functions (as in the case of HMAC) or from block cipher algorithms (OMAC, CBC-MAC and PMAC). However many of the fastest MAC algorithms such as UMAC and VMAC are constructed based on universal hashing.

Additionally, the MAC algorithm can deliberately combine two or more cryptographic primitives, so as to maintain protection even if one of them is later found to be vulnerable. For instance, in Transport Layer Security (TLS), the input data is split in halves that are each processed with a different hashing primitive (MD5 and SHA-1) then XORed together to output the MAC.

Standards

Various standards exist that define MAC algorithms. These include:

- FIPS PUB 113 *Computer Data Authentication*, withdrawn in 2002, defines an algorithm based on DES

- FIPS PUB 198-1 *The Keyed-Hash Message Authentication Code (HMAC)*

- ISO/IEC 9797-1 *Mechanisms using a block cipher*

- ISO/IEC 9797-2 *Mechanisms using a dedicated hash-function*

ISO/IEC 9797-1 and -2 define generic models and algorithms that can be used with any block cipher or hash function, and a variety of different parameters. These models and parameters allow more specific algorithms to be defined by nominating the parameters. For example, the FIPS PUB

113 algorithm is functionally equivalent to ISO/IEC 9797-1 MAC algorithm 1 with padding method 1 and a block cipher algorithm of DES.

An Example of Message Authentication Code Algorithm

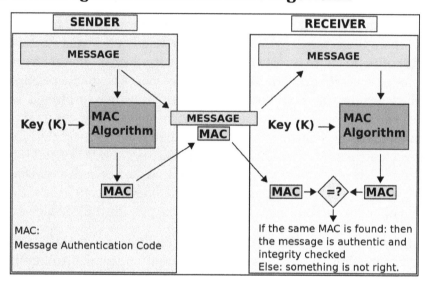

In this example, the sender of a message runs it through a MAC algorithm to produce a MAC data tag. The message and the MAC tag are then sent to the receiver. The receiver in turn runs the message portion of the transmission through the same MAC algorithm using the same key, producing a second MAC data tag. The receiver then compares the first MAC tag received in the transmission to the second generated MAC tag. If they are identical, the receiver can safely assume that the integrity of the message was not compromised, and the message was not altered or tampered with during transmission.

However, to allow the receiver to be able to detect replay attacks, the message itself must contain data that assures that this same message can only be sent once (e.g. time stamp, sequence number or use of a one-time MAC). Otherwise an attacker could — without even understanding its content — record this message and play it back at a later time, producing the same result as the original sender.

One-time MAC

Universal hashing and in particular pairwise independent hash functions provide a message authentication code as long as the key is used at most once (or less than k-times for k-wise independent hash functions. This can be seen as of the one-time pad for authentication.

The simplest such pairwise independent hash function is defined by the random key $key = (a,b)$, and the MAC tag for a message m is computed as $tag = (am + b) \bmod p$, where p is prime.

Secure Channel

In cryptography, a secure channel is a way of transferring data that is resistant to overhearing and tampering. A confidential channel is a way of transferring data that is resistant to overhearing (i.e., reading the content), but not necessarily resistant to tampering. An authentic channel is a way of transferring data that is resistant to tampering but not necessarily resistant to overhearing.

Secure Channels in the Real World

There are no perfectly secure channels in the real world. There are, at best, only ways to make insecure channels (e.g., couriers, homing pigeons, diplomatic bags, etc.) less insecure: padlocks (between courier wrists and a briefcase), loyalty tests, security investigations, and guns for courier personnel, diplomatic immunity for diplomatic bags, and so forth.

In 1976, two researchers proposed a key exchange technique (now named after them) — Diffie–Hellman key exchange (D-H). This protocol allows two parties to generate a key only known to them, under the assumption that a certain mathematical problem (e.g., the Diffie–Hellman problem in their proposal) is computationally infeasible (i.e., very very hard) to solve, and that the two parties have access to an authentic channel. In short, that an eavesdropper—conventionally termed 'Eve', who can listen to all messages exchanged by the two parties, but who can not modify the messages—will not learn the exchanged key. Such a key exchange was impossible with any previously known cryptographic schemes based on symmetric ciphers, because with these schemes it is necessary that the two parties exchange a secret key at some prior time, hence they require a confidential channel at that time which is just what we are attempting to build.

It is important to note that most cryptographic techniques are trivially breakable if keys are not exchanged securely or, if they actually were so exchanged, if those keys become known in some other way — burglary or extortion, for instance. An actually secure channel will not be required if an insecure channel can be used to securely exchange keys, and if burglary, bribery, or threat aren't used. The eternal problem has been and of course remains — even with modern key exchange protocols — how to know when an insecure channel worked securely (or alternatively, and perhaps more importantly, when it did not), and whether anyone has actually been bribed or threatened or simply lost a notebook (or a notebook computer) with key information in it. These are hard problems in the real world and no solutions are known — only expedients, jury rigs, and workarounds.

Future Possibilities

Researchers have proposed and demonstrated quantum cryptography in order to create a secure channel. If the current understanding of this subject of quantum physics is adequate, quantum cryptography facilitates the exchange of theoretically uneavesdroppable, non-interceptable, non-tamperable data. The mechanism is related to the uncertainty relation.

It is not clear whether the special conditions under which it can be made to work are practical in the real world of noise, dirt, and imperfection in which most everything is required to function. Thus far, actual implementation of the technique is exquisitely finicky and expensive, limiting it to very special purpose applications. It may also be vulnerable to attacks specific to particular implementations and imperfections in the optical components of which the quantum cryptographic equipment is built. While implementations of classical cryptographic algorithms have received worldwide scrutiny over the years, only a limited amount of public research has been done to assess security of the present-day implementations of quantum cryptosystems, mostly because they are not in widespread use as of 2014.

Modeling a Secure Channel

Security definitions for a secure channel try to model its properties independently from its concrete instantiation. A good understanding of these properties is needed before designing a secure channel, and before being able to assess its appropriateness of employment in a cryptographic protocol. This is a topic of provable security. A definition of a secure channel that remains secure, even when used in arbitrary cryptographic protocols is an important building block for universally composable cryptography.

A universally composable authenticated channel can be built using digital signatures and a public key infrastructure.

Universally composable confidential channels are known to exist under computational hardness assumptions based on hybrid encryption and a public key infrastructure.

References

- Google Chrome security representative statement, (2)HYPERLINK "https://twitter.com/justinschuh/status/364818561694302209" (3), Y Combinator (company). 6 Aug 2013. Retrieved 11, February 2020

- Simmons, Gustavus. "Authentication theory/coding theory". Advances in Cryptology: Proceedings of CRYPTO 84. Berlin: Springer. pp. 411–431. ISBN 0387156585

- "VMAC: Message Authentication Code using Universal Hashing". CFRG Working Group. CFRG Working Group. Retrieved 26, April 2020

Permissions

Index

A

Active Attack, 11

Advanced Encryption Standard, 9, 93, 118, 215

Asymmetric-key Algorithms, 8

Authentication, 5, 7-11, 18, 26-28, 44, 48-49, 54, 57-58, 81, 84, 95, 102, 118-119, 121, 130-131, 145, 164-165, 168-169, 173, 201-204, 219, 227-230, 232

Avalanche Effect, 218, 224-225

B

Base64 Encoding, 6-7

C

Cryptosystem, 12-13, 30, 81, 83, 88, 97, 99-100, 103, 105, 115-116, 139, 153, 161-162, 204-205, 220-222

D

Data Block, 9

Data Encryption Standard, 93

Data Integrity, 227

Data Obfuscation, 6

Decryption, 1, 6, 8, 27, 30, 33, 38, 41, 43, 49, 59, 80, 86, 88, 90, 93, 97-103, 109-110, 117-118, 123, 130, 132, 163, 183, 185-188, 192-193, 201, 203-204, 212, 218, 222, 226

Decryption Key, 39, 90, 97, 201, 204, 218

Dictionary Attacks, 16-17, 19, 27

Differential Power Analysis, 32-33, 160

Differential Power Analysis Attacks, 33, 160

Digital Fingerprint, 8

Digital Signature, 8-10, 14, 44, 54, 56, 102, 153, 156-157, 164-166, 168-178, 219, 228

Digital Signature Algorithms, 8-9, 170

Digital Signature Susceptibility, 14

Digital Signatures, 5, 7-10, 14, 54, 79, 83, 155, 159, 164, 166-172, 175, 177, 222, 228, 232

Discrete Logarithm, 10, 99-100, 102, 139-140, 148-149, 153, 155-156, 158, 161, 176, 179-180, 198

Dns Spoofing, 25

E

Elgamal Encryption, 101-102

Elliptic Curve Cryptography, 44, 102, 155-156, 160-161

Encryption, 1, 6, 12, 15, 17, 26, 28, 31, 36, 43, 47-52, 59, 67, 80, 83, 85, 89, 109, 115, 117, 123, 126, 130, 146, 155, 163, 168, 172, 182, 189, 194, 199, 210, 212, 215, 218, 228, 232

Encryption Scheme, 12, 18, 97, 102-103, 109-110, 155-156, 204-205, 212-213, 218, 226

Extended Euclidean Algorithm, 98

F

Feistel Cipher, 93, 186

Forward Secrecy, 95

G

Graphics Processing Unit, 17

H

Hash Function, 7-9, 14-15, 71, 73-74, 78, 104, 106, 108, 120-121, 140, 153, 166-167, 175, 177-178, 181, 224-225, 227, 229-230

Hybrid Key Distribution, 49

I

Information Security, 216

K

Key Confirmation, 10

Key Encryption, 1, 10, 43-44, 47-49, 51, 90-92, 95, 97-98, 110, 218-219, 222

Key Exchange, 26, 43-44, 93-95, 119, 156-157, 161-162, 175, 205, 231

Key Generation, 55, 94-95, 99, 101, 105-106, 109, 165, 173, 175, 181, 196, 204, 227

Known Plaintext Attack, 28-29

L

Lattice-based Cryptography, 111, 113, 115

Linear Cryptanalysis, 9, 216

M

Man-in-the-middle Attacks, 24, 26

Message Authentication Code, 219, 227-230, 232

Message Digest, 8, 73-76, 166, 177-178, 229

Message Integrity, 229

Modular Exponentiation, 34-35, 39

Montgomery Reduction, 40-41

Multi-party Computation, 189, 208-209, 211-212, 214, 216

Multivariate Cryptography, 102

N

Non Repudiation, 5

O
Optimal Asymmetric Encryption Padding, 225
Output Block, 175, 197

P
Packet Injection, 25
Passive Attacks, 11, 48
Personal Identification Number, 169
Plaintext, 1-3, 5-6, 8, 12-13, 21-22, 24, 28-31, 33, 43, 49-51, 79-81, 86-89, 91, 97-99, 101, 103-104, 110, 161, 163, 166, 183, 185, 190-191, 198, 204, 218, 220-221, 224-226, 228
Polyalphabetic Cipher, 87, 191
Power Analysis Attacks, 33, 36, 160
Power Consumption Attacks, 32, 35-36
Private Key, 8, 26, 38-39, 45, 47-49, 51-52, 55-58, 79-80, 90, 97-101, 103-105, 107, 109, 158, 162, 164-166, 169, 171, 173-180, 183, 186, 206, 222, 228
Proprietary Algorithms, 12
Public Algorithms, 12
Public Key Cryptosystems, 97, 103
Public Key Infrastructure, 92, 111, 171, 232
Public-key Authority, 44-47
Public-key Certificates, 44, 46
Public-key Cryptography, 44, 47, 96, 155, 186, 228
Publicly Available Directory, 44

R
Random Number Generator, 58-59, 142, 195, 199
Random String, 18, 51, 147, 154, 183, 227

Replay Attacks, 230
Rijndael, 9, 123-126, 223-224
Rsa Cryptosystem, 83, 97, 99, 205

S
Secret Sharing, 210, 213-214
Secure Communication, 26, 47, 57, 93, 211, 218
Secure Hash Algorithm, 8, 73
Session Hijacking, 25
Side-channel Attacks, 34, 39, 111, 160
Ssl Stripping, 25
Steganography, 121-123, 126, 131-132
Stream Ciphers, 93, 183, 186-188, 198, 216, 224
Substitution Cipher, 6, 50, 86, 92, 189-191
Substitution-permutation Network, 93
Symmetric Key Algorithms, 8, 183, 186
Synchronous Stream Cipher, 187-188

T
Tamper Detection, 26
Timing Attacks, 35-36, 38-39
Transport Layer Security, 229
Two-factor Authentication, 18, 27-28, 169

V
Virtual Machine Monitor, 38
Visual Cryptography, 123, 130-131, 133

9 781639 874446